EARTHBOUND DAVID BOWIE
AND THE MAN WHO
FELL TO EARTH
SUSAN COMPO

WITH LOVE TO HELEN AND GORDON ANDERSON

**EARTHBOUND
DAVID BOWIE AND *THE
MAN WHO FELL TO EARTH***

A Jawbone book
First edition 2017
Published in the
UK and the USA by
Jawbone Press
3.1D Union Court
20–22 Union Road
London SW4 6JP
England
www.jawbonepress.com

ISBN 978-1-911036-25-8

EDITOR Tom Seabrook
JACKET DESIGN Mark Case
PRINTED BY Everbest Printing Investment Ltd.

1 2 3 4 5 21 20 19 18 17

CONTENTS

FOREWORD
BY GRAEME CLIFFORD

I n May of 1975, Hank Aaron broke the career record for RBIs, Smokey Bear was retired from service, David Beckham was born, and a British film crew was landing in Albuquerque, New Mexico, to begin filming a sci-fi movie about a visitor from outer space starring David Bowie. It was the first (and only) time an entirely British crew had been given permission to do so, but because at the time New Mexico was a 'right to work' state, permission had been granted. The movie was to be directed by another Brit, Nicolas Roeg, a former master of the camera on *Lawrence Of Arabia*, *Fahrenheit 451*, *Petulia*, etc. He had previously directed (with Donald Cammell) the startling *Performance*, starring Mick Jagger, and *Walkabout*, a mesmerizing film shot in the Australian outback starring Jenny Agutter and Nic's little son Luke. This new film was based on a novel by Walter Tevis, whose first book, *The Hustler*, had already been made into an Oscar-winning movie starring Paul Newman. The stars were aligned!

The movie that was about to be shot was *THE MAN WHO FELL TO EARTH*.

Julie Christie had said to me, 'You should meet Nic Roeg' whilst we were shooting *McCabe & Mrs. Miller*, a gritty Robert Altman Pacific Northwest 'western' also starring Warren Beatty. We had been discussing film editing, and she told me she had just committed to star in *Don't Look Now*. Since I was already a fan of Nic's work, it didn't take me long to find myself on a plane to London as soon as *McCabe* had wrapped. Nic and I met one evening in a London pub, and as we stumbled outside after closing time, he mumbled, in his idiosyncratic way, 'Well, I suppose you've got the job.'

Thus began a lifelong friendship with a man who has had a profound effect on my career. After editing *Don't Look Now*, in which Donald Sutherland starred opposite Julie, we moved on to

The Man Who Fell To Earth (*TMWFTE*). Parking my massive rented Chevy Impala in the equally massive Hilton parking lot in midtown Albuquerque for the first time, I gazed up at the hotel encircled by a stunning cobalt blue sky. This was to be my home and 'office' for the next few months. Preproduction was already underway as Rodney Glenn and Melinda Rees, my assistants, and I supervised the setup of our editing equipment in a couple of rooms down the hall from the production offices. I was cutting on moviolas in those days, as I still preferred them to the then-current 'flatbeds.' I loved the feel of film running thru my fingers, turning them grey with the dirt and dust of its imbedded information. This personal tactile contact with your material has been lost in today's digital age, and I still miss it.

During Nic's busy preproduction schedule I would corner him as often as possible to discuss the script as it evolved. This was made easy because of the working relationship we already had from *Don't Look Now*. Getting inside Nic's head was my ultimate goal.

A crystal clear sunrise greeted the start of shooting at an abandoned coalmine near Los Lunas on June 2, 1975. It was the first scene of the movie, Newton's (David Bowie's) arrival on earth. David slid gingerly down a pink backlit mountain of coal shale, his face in shadow, features indistinct. An unidentified man in suit and tie observed his arrival. For me, this one wordless scene set up the mysteries and danger to follow.

And these mysteries and dangers were not lost on David. As shooting progressed and I spent more time with him, usually late at night, we wound up discussing the many allusions one could associate with *TMWFTE*, such as the fall of Icarus, Jesus (the savior), *Stranger In A Strange Land*, *The Wizard Of Oz* (his three helpers being Mary-Lou, Farnsworth, and Bryce) ... even Charles Bukowski was in the mix. But the similarities to Howard Hughes occupied most of our attention. Particularly his later disappearance from public view, as with Newton, and indeed with David's personal life and his search for solitude and privacy. He was a hugely talented, intelligent, imaginative yet unassuming man, and my time with him in the ether of New Mexico remains a personal treasure.

Back in the cutting rooms in London, my real work began. Whilst on location, I had fallen behind with my assembly because I had spent so much time on the set—valuable time for an editor to observe, discuss, and offer hopefully objective suggestions. Many shooting decisions are made based upon editing requirements. So whilst Nic went to Los Angeles to shoot the remaining scenes, I returned to London to complete the assembly.

When Nic arrived we looked at the assembly together to see what we had. Editing is a giant jigsaw puzzle. Scenes and dialogue can be rearranged, shortened, or completely eliminated. A limited amount of new dialogue can be incorporated without re-shooting. Working with Nic in the cutting room was an intellectual exercise. We would often discuss the merits of each decision long into the night, often spending hours on topics not related to the film at all. All-nighters were not infrequent. With Nic, what was going on behind each scene was as important as what you saw on the screen. This was what made my time with Nic so valuable to me. To explore the not so obvious, the true grammar of film.

TMWFTE is now a cult classic, admired by many. But when it was first screened in the US it was considered 'confusing,' 'obtuse,' 'hard to follow,' and too long. An attempt by the distributor to shorten it rendered it even more 'confusing,' 'obtuse,' and 'hard to follow.' Nevertheless, this shortened version opened in cinemas in

August of 1976. Fortunately, in Europe, the original version, which had premiered in March, remained intact. This original version was finally restored in the US and re-released in 2011.

Nic has always regarded the slavish adherence to 'plot' to be largely unnecessary. His focus has mostly leaned toward the exploration of inner feelings, visible emotion, and the (resultant) effect of 'plot' on the human psyche. In other words, to get inside his characters. He designs his visuals and edits his dialogue in an attempt to achieve this aim. Consequently, his movies require more attention and concentration on the part of the viewer. In fact, he regards the audience as a participant in the movie. As in life, one doesn't always understand what is happening or why at any particular point in time. So it is in Nic's movies. But if you allow yourself to be immersed in what is going on, rather than becoming frustrated by trying to figure it out right then, his movies become more accessible.

In this book, Susan Compo has done a marvelous job of laying bare the intricacies, disappointments, and triumphs Nic faced in bringing *TMWFTE* to the screen. Every movie has its tale, its cast of behind-the-scene characters, the liaisons, the fights, the backroom deals, and Susan seems to have found her way to all of them. She deftly exposes the movie within the movie without pulling any punches. Even though I was personally involved in production for almost a year, I found myself engrossed in story after story, detail after detail, that I had known nothing about or had just plain forgotten. Her exhaustive research and the sheer number of people she interviewed is impressive. There have been many books written about movies and celebrities, but this one stands out. You are about to be taken on a fascinating ride.

GRAEME CLIFFORD, *TMWFTE* FILM EDITOR, JULY 2017

A MASK WITH A PAST

PREFACE

I n early 1975, Mark Wardel was preparing to watch Alan Yentob's documentary *Cracked Actor*. 'I had just turned seventeen and was still living with my aunt and uncle in New Brighton,' he recalled. 'The program was a *big* deal for me as I was at the height of my Bowie obsession, and up until then there had been very little TV coverage of him in Britain. I was beyond excited at the prospect of an hour devoted to his coolest and most mysterious phase in the then impossibly far away myth-land of America, a phase I had been religiously following through tantalizing reports in the weekly music magazines.

'All week before the broadcast I had obsessed about the program and read and re-read the double-page *Radio Times* feature on it by Anthony Haden Guest. (I still have the cutting to this day.) I was stomach-churningly uncertain as to whether I would be able to watch it. There was only one TV set in the house and only one Bowie obsessive: me.'

The young Bowie aficionado caught a lucky break. 'The film went out on a Sunday evening and didn't clash with anyone else's regular viewing, and so after a lot of pleading, I was allowed sole possession of the lounge and (brand new!) colour TV for one of the most affecting hour's viewings of my life,' he said.

In particular, Wardel was intrigued by the mention of the existence of a life mask of the star. It began an early life's quest. 'I wanted to get hold of one since then,' he said.

Years later, Wardel, now a working artist, got his wish, and what he did with his acquisition is also compelling. 'A friend of mine who was a bigwig at EMI acquired a cast of the mask which he kindly let me borrow to make a mold from,' he recalled. 'The original was quite rough, with lots of blemishes and minor faults visible. Also, the cast didn't go far enough back to give much of the cheekbones, which were an incredibly important element of Bowie's sculptured look.

'I wanted to create an iconic version of the high-glamour 1970s Bowie, and so I smoothed and perfected the face to create a marble statue-like finish (while preserving the features) and built up the cheekbones at the side to complete the effect. I had also studied Bowie's many makeup looks of the period ... so it was natural for me as a painter to experiment with these myself as I now had, in effect, an endless supply of blank Bowie faces to work on.'

Wardel made 300 'Silver Duke' life masks for the 2013 London exhibition of David Bowie Is at the Victoria and Albert Museum. They were quickly snapped up. Then, in 2015, he received a message from someone within Bowie's organization on behalf of the star.

'When I was told that the Bowie office wanted my contact details, I was nervous that they might be about to tell me to stop making the masks, so I was very relieved that he actually wanted two for his official Bowie archive,' Wardel said. Even better, Bowie liked the masks, going so far as to say he thought they were gorgeous, and promptly purchased several more.

After Bowie passed in early 2016, demand for the masks 'did all go a bit crazy,' Wardel admitted. 'I really stepped back from it all after Bowie died as I'm appalled by the feeding frenzy of cashing in that is occurring and do not want to be seen as having anything to do with it. I still make a small number of masks for private clients and may mount an exhibition at some point ... but only when this overkill dust has settled.'

That the life mask may have originated during preproduction or filming of *The Man Who Fell To Earth* is important to Wardel. The film was released in Britain a year after the airing of *Cracked Actor*, and Wardel wasted no time in seeing it, although not at his friendly local movie house.

'I snuck into a notoriously seedy sex cinema in Liverpool to watch it,' he said. 'It seemed mainly to be showing only in such places, presumably to cash in on the fairly racy for the time sex scenes. I was once more transfixed not only by the cool, stylish, otherworldly brilliance of David Bowie but by the extraordinarily beautiful cinematography and stately pace and space of the film.'

While the work affects a wide swath of sensibilities, it particularly resonated with Wardel. 'In retrospect I realize that as an orphaned only child who had been shunted around rather a lot and was also just coming to terms with discovering I was gay, I subconsciously identified with the alienated personae projected by Bowie in much of his career, but especially within these two incredible films,' he said. 'For me, *The Man Who Fell To Earth* is a film as much about "masks," both literal and figurative, as anything else, and as such I see it as inextricably linked with what I'm doing with my Bowie masks.'[1]

SUSAN COMPO, MAY 2017

GENESIS
OF ALIEN
CHAPTER ONE

'I was raised—rather traumatically—in Kentucky,' author Walter Tevis told a CBS radio host in 1984.[1] The emphasis on pathos reflected as much on the location as anything familial or social. It's understandable: uprooting from a childhood spent in the Sunset Heights district of San Francisco (a city on its way to becoming synonymous for sophistication, raucous, enervating energy, ethnic diversity, and permissive attitudes) and Bay-adjacent Oakland for the rural, abject despondency of late Depression-era Kentucky is a surefire template for outsider identity. Little wonder the alien he created in his second novel radiated despair.

Tevis, who started writing when he was a boy ('verses for homemade greeting cards, poems about daddy and the like'[2]), made the cross-country trip by train on his own in 1939 after a yearlong stay in the Stanford Children's Convalescent Home south of the city. Far from Dickensian, the progressive Palo Alto institution was created to treat children with tuberculosis and rheumatic fever by advocating a regime of 'good nutrition, fresh air, and sunshine.'[3] Though the care was largely compassionate, Walter's first wife, Jamie Griggs Tevis, recalled him telling her about a horrific-sounding biweekly treatment involving a metal half-cylinder body cast. 'They [the doctors] strapped his hands to his sides so he wouldn't break the light bulbs in the box that raised his internal temperature to 107 degrees and caused him to have convulsions.'[4] Fortunately the treatment (hopefully exaggerated by a child's—and budding writer's—imagination) was abandoned.

While their son was hospitalized, his parents, Walter Stone Tevis and the former Anna Elizabeth Bacon, went east to Madison County, Kentucky, where they had both roots and a land grant. Part of their thinking was that a more bucolic, less fog-laden environment would

14

hasten a cure, but more significantly, their financial circumstances in California had taken a definite downturn. When their child was released he joined them, continuing a childhood narrative he'd describe as 'devastating.'[5]

Frail, rail-thin, and tentative, young Walter was unable to participate in traditional sports at Ashland School, but he rebounded surely enough to enlist in the US Navy in 1945, cannily adding a year to his actual age of seventeen. Stationed on board the USS Hamilton in Okinawa, he worked as a carpenter's mate, but he also 'played poker for seventeen months,' a gambling-related pastime that would inform his first novel. 'That was the background of my poolroom hustler,' Tevis said.[6]

It's likely the navy was also where Tevis indulged a familiarity with alcohol, and his rocky relationship with the bottle would temper his work and life for years to come. Recalling his first drink, he said, 'I was seventeen and working during Christmas at Western Auto in Lexington [Kentucky], putting together bicycles. After closing on Christmas Eve, the crew had a party and I had my first drink. It went to my toes and warmed me all the way down. I decided that was the way I wanted to feel as often as I could.'[7]

Discharged from the military in March 1946, Tevis returned to eastern Kentucky, with which he'd made peace, and graduated from Model High School in nearby Richmond. He matriculated to the University of Kentucky (UK) in Lexington with help from the GI Bill, which was a motivating factor in his having joined the navy in the first place. At UK he studied with Alfred Bertram ('A.B.') Guthrie, who'd recently written a western novel called *The Big Sky* featuring a restive Kentuckian en route to Montana via the Oregon Trail in the 1880s. (Guthrie was no slouch: his follow-up, *The Way*

West, won the 1950 Pulitzer Prize, and he went on to write the screenplay for the 1953 elegiac western film *Shane*.)

In 1949, Tevis received a bachelors of arts from UK and stayed on to earn a master's degree. Certain he wanted to write, he also continued a sideline obsession with pool, a game he had started playing in high school.

'Originally I wanted to be a poet,' Tevis said. 'I used to compose a daily sonnet on the way to the poolroom in Lexington.' He also finessed his pool playing at his high school friend Toby Kavanaugh's mansion, and began to refine the character of the table shark who'd dominate the novel he was formulating. No longer quite so awkward and uncertain, he 'learned to swear and developed my swagger in the poolroom.'[8]

After college, Tevis taught high school English in tiny Appalachian towns like Irvine, Hawesville, Carlisle, and Science Hill, and creative writing at Northern Kentucky Center (now Northern Kentucky University). He also began to publish short pieces of his own in *Esquire*, *Playboy*, *Redbook*, and *Cosmopolitan*. For the *Saturday Evening Post* he wrote a story called 'Cobweb' about a fairy who cursed. He managed to inspire and otherwise entertain his often-unruly young charges, who nicknamed their teacher Ichabod Crane after the schoolmaster terrorized by the Headless Horseman in Washington Irving's *The Legend Of Sleepy Hollow*.

Tevis met, fell in love with, and married fellow Carlisle High School teacher Jamie Griggs in 1957, and in 1959, Harper & Brothers published his first novel, *The Hustler* (expanded from a short story, 'The Best In The Country'), to great acclaim. It was quickly optioned by director Robert Rossen and made into a film starring Paul Newman and Jackie Gleason, ushering Fast Eddie Felson and Minnesota Fats into public consciousness. So affecting were the author's characterizations that for years to come several people insisted they were the inspiration for—or the actual embodiment of—Minnesota Fats, despite the author's protestations. 'I made up Minnesota Fats—name and all—as surely as Disney made up Donald Duck,' Tevis later said.[9]

The $25,000 windfall from the film option enabled Tevis to pursue his master of fine arts degree at the lofty, well-respected Iowa Writers' Workshop, located at the University of Iowa in Iowa City. While enrolled there, he gave an interview to the *Louisville Courier-Journal* that was notable in at least two ways. Firstly, he said to the reporter, 'I like it here but not as much as Kentucky,' indicating he'd come to embrace the place he once found anathema. Secondly and more tellingly, the title of the newspaper article was 'He's Writing A Second Novel.'[10]

'Every writer writes the same book over and over again,' Tevis later admitted. 'Disguising this is the trick.'[11] His sophomore turn was a sleight of hand that would initially confound any literary fans resistant to the then decidedly lowbrow category of science fiction, yet it defied the genre by displaying almost none of the trappings: space-age devices, little green men, aluminum. Rather, its tale of a visitor from outer space was, by its author's admission, 'a novel about falling into alcoholism.'[12] The lead character, Thomas Jerome Newton, was, Tevis said, an 'emotional self-portrait. I was writing to some extent out of my own estrangement and sense of alienation, and the growing fear that the only way I could deal with it was by staying drunk.'[13]

This second effort, tentatively titled *The Immigrant*, was something Tevis planned on writing during a year's sojourn in

Mexico. Despite *The Hustler*'s success, however, it would be rejected many times over by potential publishers.

San Miguel de Allende is located in the eastern Mexican state of Guanajuato. Known for its neoclassical, baroque beauty, it also hosted a flourishing arts community that was just becoming evident when the Tevises arrived. (Had they arrived but a few years later, they would have been there the same time as Beat icon and muse Neal Cassady, who'd eventually be found comatose outside of town on the railroad tracks after attending a birthday party. He died of exposure within hours.) The town's 6,000-foot altitude required some adjusting, but Walter had his own way of acclimatizing. 'Once I found out that a quart of gin was 80 cents, I stayed drunk for eight months,' he said.[14] That left only four months to transform *The Immigrant* into *The Man Who Fell To Earth*.

'All the good people in *The Man Who Fell To Earth* drink. My man from Mars becomes a hopeless alcoholic,' Tevis said, equating Mars with the book's Anthea, which his wife believed symbolized the lost California of her husband's youth.[15] It's a touching sentiment somewhat at odds with the book's dedication: '*To Jamie, who knows Anthea better than I.*'

No longer whiling away the hours at the Cuc, as the local watering hole La Cucaracha was known to the expat community, Tevis wrote on the dining room table, relying heavily on his own early life:

> The main idea in the book was, you know, here's this guy who comes from another planet and he's

tall and skinny, which I was. He can't walk very well. Everything seems heavy to him and there's this tremendous culture shock. And that was the way I felt when I first came here [Kentucky.]

My accent was strange, I was nearly crippled from having a rheumatic heart and rheumatic fever. That's what *The Man Who Fell To Earth* is all about. He can't take the gravity on earth …[16]

Once a publisher, Fawcett Paperback Originals, was eventually secured, Tevis's beleaguered but steadfast wife would at times retaliate by insinuating the book's second-class status—a science fiction book, of all things—was a result of his lack of commitment, as caused by his drinking.[17]

Unlike *The Hustler*, *The Man Who Fell To Earth* was not an instant success. It was well received but, because it was a paperback, under-reviewed, although it did eke out a notice in the *Los Angeles Times* dated April 28, 1963. 'There are some new weirdies in the science-fiction category,' William S. Murphy wrote. '*The Man Who Fell To Earth* (Gold Medal), 40 cents.'[18]

In time, however, the book sold some 300,000 copies: 'Not bad, but not that good by pocketbook standards,' its author admitted.[19] Yet there was some consolation: the book was a runner up in 1963's Little Green Man citation (a precursor of sorts to the Hugo Award), losing out only to *Cat's Cradle* by Kurt Vonnegut, Jr.

Little Green Men aside, *The Man Who Fell To Earth* did not meld easily into the category of science fiction. There were no time machines, ray guns, or robots. 'I'm not in the least bit interested in the hardware of science fiction,' Tevis said. 'But the future of fantasy delights me. I see in it possibilities for psychological realism.'[20] This affinity began after he read, as a child, L. Frank Baum's *The Wonderful Wizard Of Oz*, another book largely overshadowed by its film version—and equally infused with significant, if subtle, political commentary.

Baum's tale of a capable innocent stranded in another world is a touchstone elaborated upon by critic Danny Peary. 'There is some validity to the seemingly wild notion that *The Wizard Of Oz* (1939) with its journey into a mysterious world, fantasy elements, and homesickness theme, has influenced the majority of pictures made since,' Peary writes, citing Oliver Farnsworth, Mary-Lou, and Nathan Bryce as the three characters the alien Thomas Newton enlists to try to help him build a spaceship with which to return to his home planet. This makes them the equivalent of the Scarecrow, the Tin Woodman, and the Cowardly Lion to Newton's Dorothy as they assist her in her desire to return to Kansas from Oz. 'Tragically, Newton can never go home: his friends aren't as comforting or resourceful as Dorothy's.'[21]

Religious parallels are also rife, which Tevis attributes to his bible-belt upbringing, during which he believed the New Testament to be historically accurate. 'Science fiction, as far as I'm concerned, is something of a religious medium. You can't make any logical or rational distinction between an angel and a visitor from another planet,' he said, adding that his visitor was also a kind of savior who was misunderstood and betrayed.[22]

The Man Who Fell To Earth is written in a hospitable, intimate style that almost comforts the reader into embracing its story. The epigraph from Hart Crane is not accidental: the poet's 1932 suicide by jumping off a ship into the Gulf of Mexico after a night of heavy drinking shadows both the story and its Icarus allusions. In Greek mythology, Icarus is the son of the ingenious builder Daedalus, who created the labyrinth. To escape Crete, Daedalus fashioned wings made of feathers and wax. When exuberant Icarus flies too near the sun, his wings melt before he falls into the sea where he drowns.

The book is a triptych: in 'Icarus Descends,' Thomas Jerome Newton arrives in an eastern Kentucky town on the edge of a coalfield, where he'd made landfall unobserved. Initially, he poses as an Englishman (but will also claim he's from Kentucky) and is described as tall, elfin, delicate, and shock-white haired, with eyes that 'are very strange.' For a being that will develop a predilection for alcohol—particularly ill advised for a guest from a dehydrated planet—he curiously can't hiccup. Of course, his alien constitution may have made up for these human side effects of alcohol.

Newton travels to New York City to join forces with patent attorney Oliver Farnsworth. Nathan Bryce is a college chemistry lecturer with whom the writing instructor Tevis identifies as he describes 'a disordered pile of student papers, horrible to contemplate,' that sends him out to a nearby bar with 'a jukebox like a diseased and frenetic heart.' Earlier, Bryce had contemplated Brueguel's *The Fall Of Icarus*, 'a painting he had once loved but now was merely used to.'

En route home from the bar, Bryce buys a roll of self-developing film manufactured by Newton's World Enterprises, and its charms and mysterious properties prompt him to seek out its inventor. Curiously, Bryce had encountered the film before, mistaking it for a packet of toy gun caps, which he tried to light after pouring alcohol over them. To his displeasure, they popped, but were odorless. 'He missed the smell of gunpowder—a fine, pungent smell.'

Newton travels to Louisville, Kentucky, and checks into the Brown Hotel, not far from the Seelbach Hotel, where Daisy married Tom Buchanan in *The Great Gatsby*. When Newton meets Betty Jo Mosher after having a funny turn in an office elevator, an ill-fated, unrequited romance is kindled on her part; Newton himself is indifferent and possibly oblivious. Instead, she serves as a kind of window to another socioeconomic strata 'of shabby, gin-and-used-furniture luxury in the cities, while the bulk of the country tanned its healthy cheeks by its suburban swimming pools … it seemed to Newton that Betty Jo, with her gin, her cats, and her used furniture, was getting the better part of the social arrangement.' Betty Jo goes to work as a maid for the cryptic, compelling entrepreneur.

By '1988: Rumplestiltskin,' Newton is living in an Appalachian valley beyond Harlan, Kentucky, and is desperately plotting his return to his native planet, Anthea, where his wife and children are in peril. Nathan Bryce meets Newton at his compound, and they bond over Bryce's whiskey and Newton's clear, water-like gin. Their fragile friendship and business alliance will be tested and then broken after Bryce pumps Betty Jo for information about her employer. Sloshed, she squeals, and Bryce takes a secret X-ray of Newton that reveals beyond a doubt he is not human.

During a long, talky denouement, Newton confesses to Bryce. 'It's hard to believe. To sit in this room and believe that I'm talking to a man from another planet,' Bryce says.

'Yes,' Newton replies. 'I've thought that myself. I'm talking to a man from another planet too, you know.'

It becomes evident that Newton will have to abandon hope, and his quest to return home. One of his servants, a Frenchman named Brinnarde, turns him in as an illegal alien. The CIA increases its involvement as he is imprisoned and assiduously examined. Tragically, X-rays to his eyes cause him to lose his sight.

'1990: Icarus Drowning' is the short final segment of the novel. Bryce, who now lives with Betty Jo, comes across a musical album of poems called *The Visitor* at a Walgreens Drug Store in Louisville. He recognizes it to be Newton's work and tracks him down to the East Village in New York City. They meet at a coffeehouse called the Key and Chain, where 'customers studiously dressed like bums.' Bryce approaches Newton, who greets him with warm chagrin. He tells his tale to Elbert, the barkeep, who refers to him using the hipster vernacular 'Dad.' Then, Newton effortlessly signs a check to Bryce for a million dollars, saying he learned to handwrite by watching the film *A Letter To Three Wives* while still living on Anthea.

Finally, the bartender says to Bryce, in reference to Newton, 'I'm afraid that fellow needs help.'

The Man Who Fell To Earth is a kind of passion play, laden with allusions to mythic Icarus. But it's as if it isn't water the man has plunged into but alcohol. For all its alienation, thwarted vision, sociopolitical commentary, and heartbreaking homesickness, it's the most gin-soaked text this side of Charles Bukowski. By the end, Newton is a hungry ghost, almost drowned.

Readers were reticent, reviews were sparse, but once *The Man Who Fell To Earth* was released, its film rights were continuously optioned. First past the post was bandleader, clarinetist, and unlikely lothario Artie Shaw, who likely snapped it up on the strength of the fully realized film version of *The Hustler*. Shaw's Artixo Productions' acquisition was noted in *Film Daily* on March

3, 1966, with news that Shaw himself was writing a script based on the Fawcett Paperback Original.

Shaw had written a novel in 1956, *The Trouble With Cinderella: An Outline Of Identity*, but it might not have proved a promising precursor to screenwriting. As Shaw's biographer, Tom Nolan, put it, 'The work was a memoir, a harangue, a sociological expose, a philosophical argument, a confession, a defense, a work of entertainment, a self-indulgent ramble.'[23] In other words, it was a mess.

Shaw created Artixo (so named when he learned that Arteixo, Spain, was pronounced 'Artee Show') after he turned his back on his career during the Big Band era. In the mid-1960s he noted that his still-touring contemporaries 'aren't selling music any more, they're selling nostalgia to middle-aged people who want to relive their youth.'[24] His many marriages—to screen sirens Lana Turner, Ava Gardner, and the feisty Evelyn Keyes (Shaw's eighth wife), among others—weren't enough to keep the dynamo occupied, so, after a friend took him to a screening of Bryan Forbes's disturbing and effective *Séance On A Wet Afternoon*, he decided to go into the film business.

'The movie was acclaimed in Britain but no American studio wanted to touch it,' Nolan writes.[25] But Shaw recognized its potential and imported and released it in the US, where it was well received. As a producer, he had a decent run: he bought the French thriller *Enough Rope*, based on the novel by the author Patricia Highsmith, but by the time the Italian *Oh, Those Swedish Girls* was on the menu, Artixo Productions' film division had run its course.

Whether Shaw ever made a start on *The Man Who Fell To Earth* is unlikely, as was its next home of record. Christopher Dewey and

James Friedland started Cannon Films in 1967. They made their way importing Swedish soft porn, but by 1970 opted for more serious fare. Their film *Joe*, written by Norman Wexler (who received an Academy Award nomination for his script) was a tale of junkie hippies versus Establishment/working man starring Peter Boyle and featuring the debut of a young actress named Susan Sarandon. Made for $106,000, it garnered some $19 million in box-office receipts, respectable reviews, and a whole lot of attention.

By 1971, Cannon was offering fare like *Crucible Of Horror* (*The Corpse* in the UK) and the dire *Who Killed Mary What's Er Name*. Into this fold came *The Man Who Fell To Earth*. On March 27, A.H. Weiler reported in the *New York Times* that Cannon had optioned the Tevis novel, with a screenplay forthcoming from Richard Wheelwright. It was, Weiler opined, the story of 'a gentle man looking for a peaceful place.' He couldn't help himself from adding, 'Wonder if he's come to the right place?'[26] Mary Murphy in the *Los Angeles Times* also reported the Cannon purchase along with that of another property, *Night Of The Witch*.[27]

Richard Wheelwright took a well-worn road toward becoming a working writer. A native of Covington, Kentucky, a city south of Cincinnati, Ohio, Wheelwright, like Tevis before him, made his way up to the University of Iowa and its Writers' Workshop, where he received a master of fine arts in 1960. It's likely he crossed paths with Tevis in Iowa, either as a student or as he transitioned into teaching there. Wheelwright soon wrote a novel called *Jump* and its subsequent screenplay adaptation (also known as *Fury On Wheels*) about a Southern stock-car racer. It was certainly textbook Cannon fodder, but also unusual subject matter at the time for literary fare.

In 1972, Wheelwright was awarded an Academy of Motion

Picture Arts and Sciences film writing fellowship, part of which he might have used to write the screenplay for *The Man Who Fell To Earth*. He stated that he was 'very interested in the math of probabilities … and the sciences,'[28] and the resultant script was by turns grounded, folksy, and even turgid. It's both true to the novel and prone to irrelevant characters and unnecessary pontifications.

Subtitled 'Steppingstone' after the space project's name, the script starts auspiciously enough. Newton appears in Blue Diamond, Kentucky, carrying a black attaché case as he enters the Jewel Box pawnshop. The proprietor is a wordy man named Maynard who suggests the suspicious yet enigmatic stranger pawn his ring rather than sell it. 'Everybody around these parts has fifteen-day jewelry to get by. Ever since the money went out of coal mining, the folks that stayed here live off the welfare and what odd jobs they can grub. Fifteen days of the month the jewelry's theirs. Rest of the time it's here.' He sends Newton away with $100 and a pawn ticket.

Newton's meeting with Farnsworth is faithful enough to the text, but when Nathan Bryce comes into the picture, things start to get momentarily weird. On the lawn in front of the girls' dorm at Pendley State University, the Golden Girl is practicing her routine of juggling meat axes. 'Her metallic gold fish-scale leotard gleaming in the sun,' she 'struts three steps forward and does a right shoulder arms with the two and a half foot meat axe. A hundred young men gathered on the lawn of Carrie Nation House applaud, yell, stomp and whistle.' She continues her performance to the accompaniment of a stereo tape player 'blasting *The Dawning Of Aquarius*,' while adding a second meat axe to the mix. She throws the blades skyward and then 'catches them waist high and continues whirling them without missing a strut. The crowd goes wild.'

Nathan Bryce observes a journalism student filming the action and is transfixed—not with the Golden Girl (whose name is Charity), but with the World Enterprises camera the energetic student wields. Then Charity disappears and is not heard from again. Perhaps she was from the future of the pierced and tattooed circuses common in the late twentieth and early twenty-first centuries.

Newton hires Monsieur Brinnarde, who is much like the novel's Brinnarde apart from having a neat sideline in falconry. He meets Betty Jo, who is very countrified and unsophisticated and professes a taste for the popular but bland country music of Lynn Anderson. She makes a brief play for Newton but quickly fades into the role of a besotted and soused caregiver. When she eventually takes up with Bryce, it is after they bond over a shared fondness for apple butter.

Meanwhile, Newton isn't doing much apart from drinking and ruminating about his plans to go home. Tipsy one night, he reverts to his native tongue, which sounds eerily Maya: '*Nivaran to monutan/Dama tlan dama, dladan: iko, galata: gathuran, diva nido/ go nigatulan.*'

When Newton confesses to being an alien, Bryce barely reacts, and it's equally uneventful when Newton is arrested, medically examined, and finally released. As well as Oliver Farnsworth, a television newsman is there to meet the freed but now sightless man. Newton tells the reporter he is abandoning his space project. An underwhelmed unit manager cuts in. 'Wrap it up and get out of here. Nothing happened. It wasn't worth the trip.' Wheelwright does, however, provide a poignant, subtle ending. 'The technician turns the monitor off. The picture diminishes into a glimmering white dot on the dark screen—like a dying star flickering out somewhere deep in space.'[29]

Overall, Wheelwright's take is curiously dispassionate, and with its distinct lack of action and empathy it would not have made for good viewing. What Walter Tevis thought of the screenplay is not known.

The film company Cannon was subsequently sold to self-proclaimed 'Go-Go Boys' Menahem Golan and Yoram Globus, whose exploits are riotously covered in Mark Hartley's 2014 documentary *Electric Boogaloo*. Newton likely made a lucky escape. 'It would have been a Flash Gordon movie,' laughed Howard Rubin, Hollywood agent turned New Mexico Film Commissioner. 'Those guys [Golan-Globus], they had a five-year run in Hollywood. If you had to call on Golan-Globus, you were not a happy agent. Their reputation was terrible.'[30]

In London, it was the turn of David Cammell, who'd been an integral part of Nicolas Roeg's singular *Performance* (co-directed by David's brother, Donald), to option the momentarily resting property. David Cammell was the signatory to the option, recalled Si Litvinoff, the film's original producer. 'Nic claimed that he was a front. I do not know the truth of it, since Nic often marginalized people in order to support his claims.'[31]

The story captivated Roeg, although he admitted he found it not much more than 'a great shell.'[32] He assigned Paul Mayersberg (*Siddhartha*) to write the screenplay. A former film critic, Mayersberg had previously written a book, *Hollywood: A Haunted House,* plus two projects for Rocg that had failed to materialize.

Mayersberg was quick to recognize Tevis's affinity for the Icarus myth, L. Frank Baum's Oz, and Fitzgerald's *The Great Gatsby*, among other references. 'Tevis is a man drawn to symbols,' he later noted.[33]

He also relished the science fiction milieu that played against type, and the sensibility Tevis had demonstrated in *The Hustler*: 'being the best is superior to winning.'[34]

Writing about the film for *Sight & Sound* magazine in 1975, Mayersberg quoted a blurb for the edition of the book he had:

> Thomas Jerome Newton. He walked into the Kentucky town with papers in his pocket that proved his identity, marked him as no different from the men and women around him. ... There was one important difference, however: despite his human name, he was not human. He was a refugee from a world far distant in space, a world ravaged by the ultimate war ... a world that was dying. He came to Earth to seek salvation for his people ... but he was met with only bitterness and mistrust. For he was different: he wasn't human![35]

Mayersberg ditched the sales hyperbole and instead viewed it both as a mystery and a love story, or a combination thereof. '*The Man Who Fell To Earth* is much more about the mystery of love than the mystery of the universe,' he wrote. He drew Tevis's ire for saying the book was 'obscure,' before backtracking with, 'When I say that the book is obscure, I don't mean that it has gone totally unremarked for the past twelve years. I mean that very few people have read it, although quite a lot had heard of it.' Cold comfort for Tevis, who would smart from this comment for the rest of his life.

'The fact that the book had not reached the screen before struck me as surprising,' Mayersberg continued. 'The novel seemed to have most of the necessary ingredients on the basic level for an exciting and, above all, unusual film.' He thought the task ahead—writing the screenplay—would prove fairly straightforward. But that changed with the first draft. 'Slowly I began to see why the book had not been filmed before. In an odd way, it was too much of a good thing.'

Nathan Bryce, the Chemistry professor was, for Mayersberg, 'perhaps the easiest character to transcribe to film terms ... this character turned out to be the hardest from the point of view of the writing, both structurally and in the dialogue, to get right.' He tried to move him away from a traditional 'detective' role, a person facing 'too many questions without answers, too many clues, too many puzzled looks.

'In the book, for example, Bryce begins to doubt Newton almost at the outset ... he set out in a way to trap a quarry. We substituted the idea of Newton as a query, rather than a quarry,' Mayersberg wrote. This meant the men were destined to become friends. 'As in some of Graham Greene's writing, surprising friendships between men take on the suspenseful movement of detective yarns. The friendship between Dr. Bryce and Newton becomes dangerous because, as we all know, friendship is the most profound form of detection.'[36]

Mayersberg opted to delete any overt political references, including one to the President of the United States, but he reserved the right to comment. 'It is impossible to tell an interesting story about the United States today without referring to a social and political context,' he said. This meant inventing a shadowy character who recognized the threat to the status quo posed by Newton's World Enterprises.

Lastly, the novel's substantial timespan was addressed with a view to Roeg's fascination with film as a time machine. Characters—apart from Newton—would age, and some would even die, but there would be no other indication of or reference to time.

This construct would not be easy to pull off. During editing, Roeg and film editor Graeme Clifford shuddered as Bryce said, 'I can't believe I've been here three months already.' 'I can't believe that got by,' Roeg confessed to Jarvis Cocker in 2013.[37] Similarly, a reference in an early version of Mayersberg's screenplay read, 'NEWTON has changed. He is older.'[38] That line was quickly nixed before filming began.

Once David Bowie was secured for the role of Newton—the first person to be cast, despite Candy Clark's insistence that it was she—Mayersberg set about the script in earnest, retaining Kentucky as its setting. He also opted to include some Bowie songs, as well as Elton John's 'Rocket Man,' presumably for commercial value if not precise relevance. 'Rocket Man,' he posited, would play in the final scene as well as soon after Newton has revealed his true self to Mary-Lou.

> WE DISSOLVE TO: a dazzling, star-filled sky. A small silver vehicle comes out of the stars slowly toward us. It seems to flash itself like a star. We hear Elton John's song, 'Rocket Man.' 'She packed my bags last night.'

It was suggested that Bowie's music be featured twice.

> Mary-Lou's cat comes into the room as the music machine produces the David Bowie number 'Space Oddity.' Using his remote control device … Newton turns on a dozen TV sets after another. There is no

sound except Bowie's music. The images of the state of America, the world, private detectives, etc. coupled with Bowie's music suddenly seem utterly ridiculous.

The second time would be when the mysterious, watching stranger reappears near the conclusion.

> The MAN is outlined against the light. He is the MAN from the Kentucky coalfields. We hear a familiar pop song faintly: Bowie's 'Changes.'[39]

'[Mayersberg] might have put that in there for obvious reasons, but it was never seriously acted upon,' said Graeme Clifford. 'When you write a script, you write it to sell a product or an idea. When you shoot a script, you shoot a script to make a movie, so the two scripts are not necessarily the same thing. One's a selling tool.'[40]

The script as written is largely the one that would be shot, save for a few instances. It opens with Newton going into the Jewel Box, but in keeping with the novel, the owner is a man. Oliver Farnsworth's assistant is a Japanese houseboy named Trevor, not a maid, as in the novel. Reacting to Newton's alien appearance, Mary-Lou vomits rather than pees. Newton's actual voice is described as squeaky, and his eventual album, *The Visitor*, will consist of squeaking sounds. In both novel and screenplay, we are left in no doubt as to the fate of Newton's family on Anthea, but the sound is different.

> As the WOMAN'S fingers rest on the forehead of the CHILD, the WOMAN starts to emit the same squeaking noises we heard from Newton when he

remembered how he fell to Earth. The CHILD is dead.[41]

The film's final scene in the script is put succinctly (and poetically): 'The Stars.'[42]

As a courtesy, Walter Tevis was sent a copy of what would become the shooting script, which was still set in Kentucky. He somewhat self-effacingly responded to Nic Roeg.

> *Note*: This is an excellent script. Consequently some of the suggestions that follow will seem trivial. For that I apologise; I felt it better to say these things, however slight some of them are, in the hope that a few of them might be useful.[43]

He immediately goes to bat for Nathan Bryce and his choice of reading material.

> *Masterpieces In Paint And Poetry* has, for me, the ring of *kulturbolshevimus* [sic], like *Great Moments From The Great Symphonies*. Couldn't it be given a simpler title, like *Poems About Paintings*, or something, so as not to imply that Bryce lacks culture?

Tevis opts for a faster film speed for Newton's product, and then gently corrects the perceived geography and customs.

> The Kentucky Mountains are never 'snow-capped' as far as I know. (At this point I might mention

that I am aware that Kentucky is probably not identifiable from within the movie. If you want it to be, I don't think it would be a violation of actuality to have that sign on Page one read: HANEYVILLE, KENTUCKY Pop. 7300 since many Kentucky town signs do in fact read that way.)

Gaining confidence, Tevis writes:

> After train passes, camera moves slowly up to night sky, star-filled ... the star should be fuzzy, white, blurred—a genuine telescope photograph, perhaps, from Mt. Palomar Observatory [in California]. There should be nothing jazzed-up about this; it should look like inscrutable 'astronomy.'

Tevis insists Newton not shake hands with Bryce ('Might break his hand bones') and disdains having the latter wear a digital watch. 'I conceive of him having distaste for the futuristic,' Tevis writes. Ever the scholar, he corrects the key Latin phrase to read 'per *ardua* ad astra' and states:

> Americans don't generally say 'Pity.' Or maybe Peters isn't an American? And again, he might say it anyway, although, 'It's a shame' or 'Too bad' would be more like him. I'd have Peters' last word be 'Shit.' For the incongruity. And we could use a small laugh at this point.

Tevis's suggestion that Mary-Lou not say Newton's wife on Anthea is 'no bloody good' but rather 'I'll be she's no damn good,' was, like the majority of his comments, ignored.

Adamant that his work avoid contemporary references he found particularly heinous, Tevis adds, 'I wouldn't intercut to those aerial shots of Central America. The *Chariots Of The Gods* implications are, to me, deadly since I find that a meretricious book.' Biblical allusions are another story.

> A slack-jawed youth from room service asked me yesterday what the movie was about. I said, 'It's about a man from another planet who comes to Earth peacefully and things go badly for him.' That's all I said. And the young man said, 'That's kind of like Jesus Christ, isn't it?' I became slack-jawed and said, 'Yes.'

He was unhappy about the 'gratuitous' violence that met Farnsworth.

> Though I risk being put in Coventry for this, and banned from theaters for life, I must say that I don't like that gun firing alternately. Too arty. But maybe you're good enough, Nic, to get away with *anything*.
>
> If you do it, and I like it, I'll send you a bottle of Kentucky whiskey. If you do it and later regret it, will you send me a bottle of Scotch?

Tevis concludes by asking that Bryce not say to Mary-Lou, 'When we have the moon, it's too much to ask for the stars.' 'Sounds sententious,' he says, before informing Roeg that 'Americans say Santa Claus and never Father Christmas.' Newton's penultimate (or even last) line, he believes, should be, 'You know, I never got a chance to see the oceans. Not up close.'

Yet for all his notes' camaraderie and seeming bonhomie, the sober Tevis of the future would reflect back on a screenplay he found confusing and regret not having the chance to work on it. 'I could have done a better job with my left hand,' he later said.[44] Elsewhere, he added, 'The screenplay was written by a guy with no screen credits who had written a snotty article [in *Sight & Sound*] in which he said that it [the novel] was an obscure science fiction novel that nobody ever heard of. Hell, it sold half a million in paperback long before they made the movie.'[45]

ON ROXBURY DRIVE

CHAPTER TWO

Throughout early 1975's preproduction stages and beyond, 622 N. Roxbury Drive in Beverly Hills would become a nerve center for the film. The eleven-room dwelling was built in 1926 and remodeled in 1962 as a Hollywood interpretation of an English stately home. The house itself had Hollywood pedigree: it was owned by Harry 'Coco' Brown, an aspiring screenwriter and son of producer Harry Joe Brown, who made western movies with Randolph Scott and famed director Budd Boetticher. The younger Brown had been at Stanford University with Howard Rubin, who was instrumental in obtaining the 5,000-square-foot, five-bedroom residence in which Roeg and company moved in and set up shop.

Though others have stated that David Bowie—who lived on nearby Doheny Drive—was the first to be cast, Candy Clark, who played Mary-Lou, claims otherwise. 'I was the first person hired on the movie,' Clark told me. 'I was just handed the part by Nic Roeg.'[1] At that time, Clark, a native of Norman, Oklahoma, was riding shotgun on the strength of her Academy Award–nominated performance in George Lucas's 1973 film *American Graffiti*, a film Roeg much admired. Prior to that, she'd left Texas for New York City, where she worked as a secretary. She met Jack Nicholson at a party, and the actor gave her phone number to casting agent Fred Roos, who in turn recommended her for a part in John Huston's *Fat City*. During the making of that film, she dated co-star Jeff Bridges.

As stunning as she was captivating, Clark was also compelling enough to command the attentions of the charismatic preacher Marjoe Gortner, whom she married in 1978, and the incomparable ballet star Mikhail Baryshnikov. Indeed, hers was a romantic track record to rival that of Artie Shaw. After briefly dating Si Litvinoff, she began seeing Nicolas Roeg, whom she'd met on a double date with

Litvinoff and another young woman. Ensconced in that relationship, she accompanied the director to an interview.

'I was waiting for him [Roeg] while he was doing an interview,' she recalled. 'We were both of us at this hotel and he had a meeting—he told me to wait outside in the lobby. He said, Here's the script if you want to read it while you're waiting. Obviously he must have been in that meeting for a while, so I read the whole thing. I said, This is a fantastic story, you've got to do this, and he said, Do you want the part? It was that simple and that quick.'[2]

Musician John Phillips, who would later become involved with the film's soundtrack, told another story. His paramour of the time, South African songbird Geneviève Waïte, lived in the flat in which *Performance* was filmed, and had also been courted by Roeg. Waïte, Phillips maintained, was first in line for the part, until an argument between Roeg and Phillips led to blows in New York City's Reno Sweeney nightclub and quite possibly jeopardized Waïte's chances to play Mary-Lou.[3]

Clark remained adamant that the part was always hers. 'Geneviève? Never.'[4]

David Bowie, who'd been scouting around for a film role after pursuing the rights to George Orwell's novel *1984* as well as Robert Heinlein's *Stranger In A Strange Land*, would find gold dust in the character of Thomas Jerome Newton. 'Certain subjects had an obvious pull for Bowie,' Ian Penman wrote of the part in 2017. 'Loss of innocence; self willed fall through excess and addiction; media overload; English artfulness and reserve, and the landscape of American spectacle and get-it-now emptiness.'[5]

As Bowie distanced himself from his best-known musical creation, Ziggy Stardust, he took on a new persona that flirted with 1940s noir—a curiously good fit for the mysterious man from Anthea and certainly for a would-be movie star. While Paramount Studios campaigned for Robert Redford to play the part of Newton, Roeg had considered Peter O'Toole and then Michael Crichton (who met the towering height requirement), both of whom his producer Litvinoff felt lukewarm about. Mick Jagger, who'd starred in Roeg's *Performance*, was bandied about, too, but quickly dismissed by the director as 'too strong.'[6] At one point, Roeg also considered a doctor he met at a party, who, at a height of six foot eight inches, was 'physically unusually satisfying to look at—so he was startling.'[7]

Roeg claimed he came across Bowie while watching the affecting BBC TV documentary *Cracked Actor* by Alan Yentob, although casting agent Maggie Abbott is also credited with bringing the musician to Roeg's attention. 'Maggie was significant,' said Litvinoff. 'As Bowie's agent, she suggested him and got *Cracked Actor* for us to see, despite Nic's claim of accidentally seeing it on TV, and worked with us to get him.'[8]

Candy Clark had another take as to who first thought of Bowie for the part. 'Arlene Sellers. She's the one that suggested Bowie.'[9]

No one disagreed on one aspect of the lead-up to casting, however: that Bowie kept Roeg waiting for hours in the rock star's New York apartment before finally arriving to discuss the role. 'I was always going to do it,' the tardy star said upon arrival.[10]

It was a smart and somewhat lateral move for a performer who had long wanted to return to film, having appeared in dramatic roles on the big (and small) screen before, in an episode of British television's *Theatre 625* entitled 'The Pistol Shot' in 1968, and a two-second snippet in the 1969 theatrical release *The Virgin Soldiers*. He'd also done a short called *The Image* in 1967, an advertisement for Lyons Ice Cream directed by Ridley Scott in 1969, and played Pierrot in *Looking Glass Murders* by Lindsay Kemp's mime troupe Turquoise in July of 1970.

While the opportunity to work with a director who was coming off the critical and cult successes of *Performance* and *Don't Look Now* was not insignificant, Bowie also had his distinctive eyes wide open. 'I knew from the beginning when I was offered this thing that I wasn't making a *Tommy* or something,' Bowie told United Press International's Bruce Meyer in 1976. 'But I also knew that because [Roeg] was making it, if I really wanted to do serious films, in ten years' time I could look back and say I was very proud to have been in that film. ... I suppose I should have a box office smash. If I do too many box office failures, I'll only be used by those quaint, unknown directors, which is lovely, but it's not going to help me. You've got to be practical these days.'[11]

The practicality was, regardless of what was going on in his admittedly troubled personal life, Bowie equaled perfect casting. 'It wasn't just the spaceman connection,' Paul Mayersberg later told Paolo Hewitt. 'It was because of the lone melancholic figure that Bowie represented, with an uneasy ecstasy in his voice.'[12]

'I can't think of another actor in the world that was right for that role,' said Anthony (Tony) Richmond, the film's cinematographer. 'He was like a spaced-out spaceman. Bowie was definitely out-there.'[13]

He was out-there for sure. Rock critic Lisa Robinson recalled at the time seeing a 'cadaverous' Bowie sitting with guitarist Jimmy Page, 'in the dark on a sofa in a corner suite at New York's Plaza Hotel ... watching the same fifteen minutes of *Lucifer Rising* over and over again, snorting line after line of cocaine.'[14]

Early on, the film's costume designer, May Routh, made the short drive east from the Roxbury location to 637 N. Doheny Drive to meet with Bowie. She found him in the smallish, dimly lit two-bedroom rented house with an exaggeratedly outsized front door frame, seated on a dark loveseat with his wife Angie. On the coffee table was the requisite 'big pile of coke.'[15]

'David was convinced that Aleister Crowley's and William Burroughs's idea that drugs could be one's conduit to art and clarity would work for him,' the former Mary Angela Barnett, known as Angie, told me.[16] She and Bowie were married in Bromley, southeast of London, in 1970, but by the mid-70s their marriage was on stony ground. 'During this time in Los Angeles, David was becoming less and less communicative,' she said. 'I could feel him pulling away from me.'

Bowie would make no secret of his drug addiction, referencing it in his work and in time varying the degree of his use from a $200 a day to 20 grams a day habit.[17]

The drug that was synonymous with the era had a long history. In *Writing On Drugs*, social scholar Sadie Plant looks at, among other addictive substances, the alkaloid that is derived from the green leaves of the coca bush native to the altitudes of Bolivia and Peru. Sometimes known as Mama Coca, a mythical beauty who lay buried beneath the first coca bush, the drug made its way to Europe in the mid-1800s and became popular especially when added to wines and elixirs in the 1880s. At that time, Plant notes, 'Mama Coca's legendary fine looks and long tresses were woven into the Art Nouveau swirls of advertisements for an endless stream of products.'[18]

'Jules Verne, rushing around the world in only eighty days, declared that "the wonderful tonic wine" was capable of "prolonging life" and Blériot made the first flight across the English Channel with a bottle of Mariani [cocaine-laced wine] in his pocket,' Plant adds. Bartholdi, who designed the Statue of Liberty, was likewise enthralled. 'It is very probable that had I taken it twenty years ago, the Statue of Liberty would have attained the height of several hundred metres,' he raved.[19]

Robert Louis Stevenson wrote *The Strange Case Of Doctor Jekyll And Mister Hyde* over six days during a cocaine binge. 'That an invalid in my husband's condition of health should have been able to perform the manual labor alone of putting 60,000 words on paper in six days seems almost incredible,' his wife, Fanny, attested.[20]

By the advent of World War I, both England and the USA had introduced legislation to control drugs. 'The kick Cole Porter got from cocaine would quietly be replaced by champagne, and drugs dropped out of public sight and into the culture's new unconscious mind,' Plant writes.

Cocaine re-emerged, fully formed, in the excesses of the 1970s. And it wasn't just errant rock stars that were held in the drug's thrall. Country music giant George Jones was in so deep he'd sometimes perform as one of his alter egos, Dee-Doodle The Duck, and quack his way through his repertoire and anecdotes. And in no way was its use limited to artists: by the early 1980s, cocaine's presence was almost ubiquitous in New York and Los Angeles, on TV dramas, in films, and on the surfaces of hard plastic CD cases and silvery mirrors.

That cocaine was part of Bowie's life did not deter his casting in the slightest. He promised his director it wouldn't be an issue, and Roeg, for his part, was unperturbed.

Preproduction continued on Roxbury, but it wasn't all work. 'It was a party scene at times,' Routh said. She recalled one morning when 'a hapless friend of a PA [production assistant] borrowed a basket to carry up toast and orange juice to a man she'd picked up.' The man in question turned out to be Daniel Ellsberg, famous for having leaked the Pentagon Papers (about the Vietnam War) in 1971, and no friend of the US government. 'Here we are trying to get Green Cards and Daniel Ellsberg is in the house!' Routh exclaimed.[21]

For Bowie, changes were afoot as he hired powerhouse attorney Michael Lippman to replace Maggie Abbott as his agent. Lippman savored his reputation for being tough, saying, 'I created this persona that people respected and slightly feared ... I got what I wanted.'[22] He cited music impresario Clive Davis as a mentor and role model. 'I never saw a man that would work that hard and long every day. He inspired me to put in the time.'[23] That study helped Lippman secure his new client a $75,000 appearance fee, plus another $75,000 to write the soundtrack for *The Man Who Fell To Earth*.[24] It would signal the start of acrimonious shifts to follow.

ZIA STARDUST

CHAPTER THREE

New Mexico has been a popular film location since the industry's infancy. In 1898, when the state was still a territory, Thomas Edison filmed *Indian Day School*, an awe-inducing fifty-five-second actuality, as documentaries were then called, a slice-of-life look at a school day on Isleta Pueblo in Bernalillo County. A few years later, the legend goes that silent film star Mary Pickford and her director D.W. Griffith became intrigued by the high desert scenery outside the Victorian train town of Las Vegas (New Mexico) as they travelled by rail from New York to California. They returned to Albuquerque in 1911 to make *A Pueblo Legend*, a two-reeler directed by Mack Sennett in which Pickford, soon to be America's Sweetheart, played a Hopi maiden. 'The Isleta Pueblo offered some of the finest scenic opportunities ever put into a picture,' Griffith raved.[1]

The state's diverse and breathtaking landscape—from the Hi-Lo Country expanses to poignant and picturesque pueblos, the dramatic and shadowy Sangre de Cristo Mountains, stark white sand dunes, Billy The Kid western lore in then-lawless Lincoln County, picturesque Santa Fe (the nation's oldest capitol city) and hardscrabble existences in extreme conditions on and off tribal lands, the state known as the Land of Enchantment made for a striking backdrop.

Hollywood became a frequent visitor, and the New Mexico Film Commission was formed around the time Kirk Douglas made *Ace In The Hole* in 1950. Under the helm of people like Ken Marthey (himself a cinematographer and artist) and Jeanne Swain, the commission did a competent if modest job of making the film industry welcome.

Enter Howard Rubin in early 1972. The California native and disillusioned Hollywood player—whose roles in the industry included 'motion picture packaging, personal managing, agenting'[2]—threw off the mantel of the film business and went to live a quiet life on a ranch in El Rito, New Mexico.

Or so he thought.

Rubin, described in a *Santa Fe New Mexican* profile in 1975 as wearing 'green pants, a colorful patchwork shirt and crepe sole shoes,' had been a fraternity brother at Stanford with Richard Zanuck, son of Golden Age movie producer Darryl. After graduating in the 1950s, the two young men went travelling in Europe and contemplated their futures.

'I was telling him how I really didn't know what I wanted to do,' Rubin said. 'He said, Well, you ought to get busy and do something. I said, That's easy for you to say: you're the son of a famous producer. Someday you'll run a studio.'

When Zanuck retorted with the suggestion that Rubin become an agent, Rubin took the advice and ran with it. He opened and operated his own small agency before joining William Morris and then MCA.

'MCA was put out of business by Bobby Kennedy through an anti-trust suit,' Rubin explained. 'Our boss, Lew Wasserman, had to decide to get out of the movie business or stay in. Lew's son and I started a company called IMA. My partner went to Europe and signed Steven Boyd, and I signed a lot of the young people that MCA had.

'It didn't work out for us. I formed my own little tiny company and took Ryan O'Neal, Susan St. James, twenty-to-thirty young clients, and started on my own.'[3] Eventually Rubin became O'Neal's personal manager.

Tiring of Hollywood in the early 1970s, Rubin retreated to New

Mexico. But the quiet life of a rancher didn't entirely stick, and soon he was restless. 'I asked my lawyer, an ex-MCA lawyer who lived here, Who's running for office?' Rubin said. 'I always liked Democrat politics in LA. He told me about an underdog Hispanic guy who was running for governor, and I organized the Hollywood portion of his campaign.' The underdog, Gary Apodaca, won.

After that, Rubin clearly had the governor's ear. 'I told him what I thought about the movie commission, which was really just an extension of the Albuquerque Chamber of Commerce,' he explained. 'One film commission guy was Snakey Campbell, so named because he rounded up rattlesnakes. That's what the film commission was like. A lot of these guys, it wasn't like they understood that it was a movie business. It wasn't about your town, it was about making a movie in town. How cheap can we buy the rooms in the hotel?'

Apodaca got it. 'You know so much about the film business, why don't you take over the film commission?' he asked Rubin, who agreed with one caveat: 'Only if I have to report only to you and get to use your plane whenever I need it.'

A deal was struck, and Rubin was appointed to head the film commission, at that time rather verbosely known as the New Mexico Motion Picture Industries Commission, in February 1975, at a salary of $16,044 per year. The commission itself would have a budget of $110,000, Fred Buckles of the *Roswell Daily Record* reported. (Buckles seemed to have a thing for salaries: he usually ended his column with a rundown of the highest paid local officials.)[4]

The first day on the job, Rubin told his three co-workers, 'You don't know me, I don't know you. The governor's asked me to make some changes. That's what I'm going to do. Let's give each other a few months and see how we mesh.'

The mesh was more like mush. 'Turns out … no,' he recalled. 'They're government employees, and I come from Hollywood and I am a businessman. I thought I could run this commission like a business, and the governor agreed with me. The governor, he's the star of the state.'[5]

Along with the newly laid-off commission employees, there were others who weren't entirely thrilled with the appointment of Rubin. At a press club function held in the rooftop garden of Albuquerque's Four Seasons Motor Inn (surely one of the few motels to have such an upscale feature), Rubin was beginning his address when an interloper wearing a blue jumpsuit and a scarf around his head said 'pardon me' before hitting Rubin in the face with a lemon meringue pie and then rushing out. 'I used to be an agent for Soupy Sales,' a startled Rubin said while wiping frothy egg white from his face, 'and that's the only connection I can make.'[6] (Sales was a popular slapstick comedian with a staple of pies-in-the-face. He was also the father of two young sons, Hunt and Tony, who would later join Bowie in the band Tin Machine.)

Comedy gags aside, Rubin soon dug in his crepe-soled heels, and within a few months, several new projects were slated to be filmed in New Mexico. One was a television documentary about the atomic bomb to be filmed at Los Alamos, Alamogordo, and White Sands Missile Range; another was *Missouri Breaks*, which would star Jack Nicholson and Marlon Brando. With the latter, try as he might, Rubin could not manage to keep the entire production in the state. While New Mexico could offer 'several life zones: desert, forest, plains, high mountains—everything except ocean or subtropical,' it was no match for Big Sky Country. 'Right now they're up in Montana,' Rubin told the *Santa Fe New Mexican*, about the cast and crew of *Missouri Breaks*. 'Unfortunately I couldn't recreate Montana for them.'[7]

Three other films were set to be filmed locally: *Welcome To Xanadu*, starring Linda Blair of *The Exorcist* fame; a Richard Pryor project called *Adios Amigos*; and, as Fred Buckles reported in his *Roswell Daily Record*, 'Lion International's *The Man Who Fell To Earth* with locations in Roswell, Los Lunas, Artesia, Albuquerque, Alamogordo, Santa Fe, and Los Alamos.'[8]

Rubin had known Roeg long before he enticed him to come and film in New Mexico. 'I met Nic when I was at La Scala in Beverly Hills, which was kind of my restaurant where I took clients. The owner was a friend, he was a waiter before he was an owner—that kind of restaurant,' Rubin said. 'It wasn't near what it became,' he added, about the soon-to-be very tony eatery. 'Nic was there with I don't know who, but I was in one booth and Nic was over here and we were close. They had both been imbibing and the conversation got higher and higher and I finally had to say something.

'That was my introduction to Nic Roeg,' Rubin continued. 'Then we met properly. We were going to do a movie at MGM, a remake of *The Postman Always Rings Twice*. Nic was tied to it for a while; Ryan [O'Neal] was going to be in it. Jim Aubrey, who came from CBS to MGM for an hour … they thought it was going to save the studio. There were a lot of saviors for the studio.'

Rubin had met Roeg's colleague Si Litvinoff even earlier, when Litvinoff made a film written and directed by Rubin's client Gerry O'Hara. 'He made a movie called *All The Right Noises*,' Rubin explained. 'It didn't do very well but it had a hot actor at the time, Tom Bell. Si was looking for European distribution, so I sold it to Zanuck at Fox. It did better there.' Chances are, knowing Litvinoff would have eventually led him to Roeg. 'Once you know one British person in Hollywood, you know them all,' Rubin said.

Litvinoff told Rubin about Tevis's novel, and Rubin was enthused. 'Si had a great, great story mind. He's the best story analyst I've ever come across in finding material.' Rubin then began talking up New Mexico as a location, and soon Roeg's intended art director, Brian Eatwell, and Eatwell's girlfriend, costume designer May Routh, were being given a tour of New Mexico in Governor Gary Apodaca's plane.

According to associate producer John Peverall, who had another job working in the London offices of the Columbia Broadcasting System (CBS), *The Man Who Fell To Earth* was originally set to be shot in California.[9] The shift in location was equal parts persuasion and practicality. 'One big problem with filming [in Southern California] is that it's become crowded,' Rubin told the *New Mexican*. 'You can hardly go anywhere without seeing telephone wires … here I can take you out of town five minutes and give you a 180 or maybe even a 360 without anything in it.'

There were other contributing factors. 'Mobility of equipment is one reason,' he continued. 'But more important than mobility are the demands of the audience who know when something's been shot on a back lot.'

At the urging of Fred Banker, the film commission's Hollywood liaison, Eatwell and Routh were headed east, to the heart of the southwest. Eatwell had worked with Roeg on *Walkabout* and during the early days of *Don't Look Now*. He would have continued with the latter project, too, were it not for a change in location. 'When they moved to Venice, the Italians wouldn't let them bring an English art director,' Routh said.[10]

Routh, who was born in India, studied design at St. Martin's College of Art, where she met Brian Duffy, who'd become a well-regarded photographer. 'We ate, slept, and dreamed fashion,' she said.[11] She worked as a model and then for the advertising agency J. Walter Thompson, where she created drawings for Ponds beauty products.

Soon Duffy and his flatmate, Len Deighton, started their own film company. Their first project was *Oh, What A Lovely War*, and Routh, who was in a love affair that had gone south, went in that direction to work in Italy as an assistant on the film.[12] There she met and fell in love with Eatwell, who'd been working on *Godspell*. Her career continued in a parallel non-secular vibe when she assisted Yvonne Blake in doing 'modern hippie-type clothes' for *Jesus Christ Superstar*. There was a synchronicity and serendipity to she and Eatwell being a couple, Routh believed, because production and costume design are interdependent.

Eatwell and Routh had by now left London for Los Angeles, but were 'practically starving' by the time *The Man Who Fell To Earth* came along. 'Nic wanted Brian and he was lumbered with me. Brian was very involved, he would go to meetings, but until the money came in place, there was nothing we could do,' Routh recalled. 'When it was green-lit, we all went out to dinner at Scandia. Candy Clark was there, Si, Brian and I … I could hardly say anything as I couldn't believe we'd been saved.'

In Santa Fe, Eatwell and Routh were met by Ken Marthey of the film commission. 'He took us all over,' Routh continued. 'We came back and then told Nic and Si Litvinoff.'

'We were so fortunate New Mexico fell into our laps,' Eatwell said.[13]

Roeg would be best pleased. 'It was almost uncanny, as though the script had been written after a reconnaissance,' he would say.[14] Having never visited the state, he was stunned by what he found. 'It didn't fit into, necessarily, the general world picture of the United States landscape,' he said. 'Every foreigner has their picture of the United States and it doesn't ... well, hardly ever, envisage New Mexico.'[15]

While the state was the perfect fit for the film—'We need a strange landscape, like the surface of another planet,' Peverall had said[16]—vistas and salesmanship were not the only factors in the decision. New Mexico was lucrative, first and foremost, because it was, and had always been, a 'right to work' state. That laid the groundwork for an almost entirely British crew to be able to work on the project without violating any laws. This was complemented by the United Kingdom's Eady Plan (as the Eady Pool was known), a scheme that refunded a distribution gross to profitable movies made by British personnel. 'We had at my determination a mostly UK crew to take advantage of the Eady Plan,' Litvinoff said, adding that New Mexico's work setup was likewise 'significant.'[17]

A crew familiar with each other working in an alien environment: that, in itself, was significant. As Peverall announced, the movie would be the first British film to be made in New Mexico. It would also be able to take advantage of relatively lax regulations and roll out a tight-knit crew of some 'forty-five men from England,' as the *Albuquerque Journal* put it: friends and colleagues who would be, if they decided to stay, aliens in a strange land.

The state would hold one other big surprise for the filmmakers. Though the film was shot at a time when the small town of Roswell was a sleepy backwater and not a touristy UFO hub, they'd nonetheless soon learn that New Mexico's environs had a higher rate of extraterrestrial sightings than anywhere else on the planet.

John Peverall came to New Mexico in January 1975, expecting the state to resemble its eponymous neighbor to the south. 'But it's not like that at all,' he said. 'There's a softness here—a kindness.'[18] The locale can foster the misconception of being in another country. Rumor has it that, for years, many Americans believed they needed a passport to visit the nation's forty-seventh state. Indeed, searching the state on the internet brings up the prompt, 'Is New Mexico in the US?' And then there's the matter of Santa Fe, a city often described as the most foreign of US cities. (New Orleans may beg to differ.)

New Mexico has been occupied for centuries by Ancestral Pueblans (a designation that's come to replace the Navajo-coined *Anasazi*, which translates to 'Enemy Ancestors'). Spanish explorers, searching for the City of Gold, claimed the region for Spain, which held the territory until 1821, apart from a brief Pueblo revolt between 1680 and 1693. Mexico's independence from Spain in 1821 led to the creation of New Mexico, and the region was Mexican land until 1848, when the US took over.

New Mexico's population is largely Spanish-American (Hispano), Native American, Anglo, and Mexican, and its varied history a tourism director's dream. With sites and subjects including Chaco Canyon, Los Alamos, Billy The Kid and the Lincoln County Wars, the often-derelict Route 66, the Carlsbad Caverns, and 13,000-foot mountain peaks, the state is glorious and complicated. In the early twentieth century, the railroad brought artists and tourists alike, many of whom, like Georgia O'Keeffe and Alfred Stieglitz, settled near Taos (later, and briefly, a hippie haven centered around counterculture movie star Dennis Hopper).

During World War II, the Los Alamos Ranch School (previous boarders include William S. Burroughs and Gore Vidal, neither of whom liked it very much) was requisitioned to develop Robert Oppenheimer's Manhattan Project and a test explosion of the resultant atomic bomb would occur at White Sands' Trinity Site in 1945.

In addition to its radioactive legacy, the state is well known for what happened in the small community of Roswell on or about June 14, 1947, when a large, disc-shaped object plummeted down on a ranch just outside town. A rancher found odd metal pieces on his property and took the debris to the county sheriff. The military was quick to act—the New Mexico Military Institute had been based nearby since 1881—stashing the materials away and closing the site. The official word was that it was a weather balloon, an explanation later updated as a balloon equipped with microphones that was part of a Cold War preemptive exercise.

Still, the mysterious event turned into an urban legend, propped up by numerous books and documentaries touting conspiracy theories involving UFOs and aliens. The Roswell UFO Incident became a cottage industry for the town that had until then billed itself as the Dairy Capital of the Southwest. The mostly conservative, largely military city was reluctant at first to embrace UFO affiliations, but the greenbacks generated by little green men (so ubiquitous that one now appears on the official seal of the city) were impossible to ignore.

UFOs, aliens, and Roswell are synonymous. The city boasts the International UFO Museum (with its refreshingly modest admission fee of five dollars), the Area 51 Museum inside the Alien Zone cafe, streetlights with glowing alien visages, an annual UFO convention with a handy 5k/10k alien-themed run, and a spaceship-shaped McDonalds, just for starters. Its Wal-Mart Supercenter, the very essence of affordable conformity, was decorated with UFOs and an alien, until, in 2013, they mysteriously disappeared. A call to the store in 2017 to verify this found the wary employees certain they were being pranked. However, the redoubtable RoadsideAmerica.com has a photo to verify that the bland big-box store once boasted a bit of extraterrestrial flair. Its verdict post-removal? 'No longer merits tourist attention.'

Kitsch and tourism aside, New Mexico does have a plethora of UFO sightings; for the cast and crew about to descend on the state in the summer of 1975, the coincidence would be a happy accident—a filmic symmetry.

In May 1975, influential *Los Angeles Times* writer Mary Murphy (whose beat was the film and television industry) made a high-profile note of the impending movie but concentrated mainly on its star. 'British rock star David Bowie has dreamed of becoming a movie star for a long time,' she wrote, adding that he'd play 'a creature from outer space, "which is how he sees himself," says an unidentified friend.'[19] His connection with acting was intrinsic. 'I feel like an actor when I'm on stage, rather than a rock artist,' Bowie had told *Rolling Stone*, as early as 1972.[20]

The trade publication *Box Office* acknowledged the forthcoming film, too, describing it as 'a mysterious American love story spawning a quarter century.'[21] Bowie, notoriously phobic about air travel, arrived from Los Angeles with his cohort Geoff MacCormack by Winnebago—'a giant shoebox on wheels,' MacCormack said, replete with bedroom, bathroom, shower, TV, a music system, and air conditioning.[22] Later, he would reunite with his friend, limousine driver, and bodyguard Tony Mascia (both Mascia and the limo would feature in the film). Bowie brought along a modest entourage, numerous books (as many as 400), a self-confessed prodigious coke habit, and its attenuate mindset.

He'd been living in Los Angeles, memorably insisting he'd seen a body fall from a rooftop next door to his Doheny Drive residence. 'A little trouble from the neighbors,' he'd worriedly shrugged. As part of his acting preparation, he'd watched *The Hustler* for insight into Walter Tevis's main characters.

Angela Bowie had her own forays into acting, and once auditioned for the role of Wonder Woman for a 1974 TV movie. She lost out—the fact that she didn't want to wear a bra might not have helped (although it'd come in handy for *Charlie's Angels* a couple of seasons hence). The part went instead to the cutesy, entirely wholesome, and suitably supported Cathy Lee Crosby.

Angie's considered opinion was that her husband would be ideal in the film. 'I thought it sounded like a perfect match: a sci-fi film about an alien after my "Light People" image of David and myself.'[23] She was not so sure about the director. 'David was very impressed with *Don't Look Now*, Roeg's previous film,' she said. 'I was not. I had seen *Far From The Madding Crowd*, which I thought was mediocre at best. After viewing *Don't Look Now* I knew that whoever the female actor was who worked with David in *The Man Who Fell To Earth* would be a party to Roeg's masturbatory directorial style.'

Her view was likely tempered by script meetings at the house, which she did her best to avoid. 'I made sure to be absent from the house a lot as David was not very good company at that time, secretive and driven, tight-jawed, and didn't enjoy my company at all,' she said. 'On two separate occasions Nicolas Roeg arrived at our home and ensconced himself with Candy Clark and David. When we were in Los Angeles at the Doheny house I walked into the living room after shopping and there was a state of disarray in the so-called script meeting. Corinne Schwab tried to sideline me from entering the living room, but of course that had no effect and I told them to find somewhere else to have their tête-à-tête script meetings.'

Clearly fuming, Angie continued to vent her displeasure. 'I told David that Nicolas Roeg was the same genre of filmmaker as Roman Polanski, except he wasn't that good. That did not go down well,' she said. 'Surprisingly enough I never had an issue with Candy Clark. I thought she was very professional. Candy was very polite and pleasant to me.'[24]

More than halfway across the country, in Chicago, a chartered plane ferrying the British crew arrived from Dublin. They'd celebrated and toasted their way over the Atlantic before landing in the Windy City. 'I'd loved to have seen that arrival in Chicago,' Howard Rubin laughed. 'I heard some people had a few drinks.'[25]

May Routh concurred. The passengers were 'all so drunk. The continuity girl, the police had to take her off.'[26] Susanna Merry was either particularly beyond repair or unlucky, as she was unlikely to be the only one feeling no pain.

The first local publication to make note of the film being made was the *Artesia Daily Press*, based in the small southeastern New Mexico farming and industrial town where much shooting would occur. The reporter noted 'the filming of a science fiction movie in New Mexico in June,' and mentioned that the Artesia Hotel, located at the northeast corner of First and Main Streets (101. N.

First Street), would be a focal point.[27] Brian Eatwell, his assistant Christopher Burke, and John Peverall had been in Artesia on April 22 to finalize details.

The nearby town of Roswell's press followed with an article entitled 'Film Set In Eddy,' which wordily described 'a science-fiction love story motion picture starring British pop singing star David Bowie.' Filming would last ten days, the report added, and would also take in White Sands and Albuquerque.[28]

Home base, however, would be Albuquerque, where the above-the-line stars would be staying at the former Plaza Hotel (in 1975 it was known as the Hilton) on Copper and 2nd Street, with the remaining cast and crew at the more modern (c. 1973) Hilton Midtown at 1901 University Boulevard NE, which featured, significantly, a large parking lot suitable for equipment and trucks.

The downtown Hilton had opened its doors on June 9, 1939, and quickly proved popular with politicians, tourists, and celebrities on location or otherwise requisitioned like James Stewart who frequented the hotel when he was stationed at Kirkland Air Force Base during World War II. Stewart became a fixture in the restaurant, ordering hamburgers and Scotch at the same time. Its décor was Southwestern Art Deco, featuring paneled wood, wagon wheel chandeliers, murals of oxen and horses carrying wagons, and, in the elevator, pictures of snoozing men wearing large sombreros.

By the 1960s, the hotel tried to keep with the times, installing an Astroturf-carpeted rooftop bar and the 'space age' Blue Parrot restaurant, but by 1974, new president E.H. Gene Goatley was trying to bring back its earlier incarnation, stating, 'We don't want the sterile, slick atmosphere of a brand new midtown hotel.'[29] In other words, the Hilton Midtown, which was precisely that. In addition to its ample parking lot, it also had a large pool. While those billeted downtown availed themselves of the western-themed bar and restaurant, the crew and others made the most of the pool and its nearby bungalows.

The atmosphere on and off set might have been fostered by what the urbane Buck Henry charmingly relayed as being 'a dinner party cast' but it was also clubhouse close, with a camaraderie between friends who'd recommended friends, as well as several couples: May Routh and Brian Eatwell, Nic Roeg and Candy Clark, Tony Richmond and Linda De Vetta, and Bowie and a variety of women. 'A lot of women came, a lot of women went,' Candy Clark (rumored to have been one of them) laughed.[30]

Henry, born to a silent film star mother and stockbroker father as Buck Henry Zuckerman in New York City, December 9, 1930, was one of the most accomplished and erudite of the cast. He was an established writer—with credits including the screenplays for *The Graduate* and *Catch-22*—and director as well as an actor. In the coming years, he would become a mainstay on *Saturday Night Live*, and in particular its enervating Samurai sketches. His casting as patents expert and attorney Oliver Farnsworth was suggested by Candy Clark.

Henry was keen to work with Roeg. 'Why should anyone not be in a Nic Roeg film?' he rhetorically asked.[31] He was also delighted to be able to blow a saliva bubble on screen—something he believed could only be allowed in a Roeg film, and the first such occurrence since Harpo Marx pulled off the act in a Marx Brothers romp. Lastly, he was eager to work in a location 'as exotic as New Mexico.'

Romantic involvements on a shoot create their own kind of weather, and it could be heavy and close as well as 70 degrees and sunny. 'They weren't exactly all harmonious relationships,' May Routh recalled. 'Tony and Linda argued a lot, had a lot of fights—mostly about Tony's drinking and hanging around with Nic, all the boys drinking.'[32]

Routh and Eatwell forged a close relationship with stylist Martin Samuel and his wife Mary. 'We'd go out in the evening around nine to a French restaurant with four tables [likely Claude's Café],' she recalled. 'We became good friends there. People like Tony Richmond and Brian were old friends, drinking companions, hell-raisers. They lived in tents on *Walkabout*. Nic had a group of people around him that he trusted. He dealt with them and they were all GUYS. I was definitely not in that pecking order.'

Just as there was a divide between men and women, so was there a gap between upper-level cast and crew, and local talent. Alan Swain spent his first summer out of an Albuquerque high school wrangling extras for the film. He quickly learned where his sympathies lay.

'John Peverall told me, You're above the line and they're the line. Different classes of people,' he recalled. 'Of course I didn't understand any class stuff. The above-the-line guys stayed to themselves, and we made the choice that the below-the-line guys were more fun. They had these Cockney English guys who were stocky little tanks and liked to fight and drink. It was neat.'[33]

Swain's mother, Jeanne, had been a crucial part of New Mexico's fledgling film industry, working with Ruth Armstrong, who was a previous head of the Film Commission. 'My mom wrote the very first production services manual for the state of New Mexico,' Alan recalled. 'She started doing casting and was well loved by all the actors. I'd get jealous 'cos she had 200 kids.'[34]

For *The Man Who Fell To Earth*, Jeanne was casting extras along with her son, working out of an office in the downtown Hilton. Jean Jordan, writing in the *New Mexico Independent,* detailed the process.

> If you've got a yen to make it big in flicks, you just might saunter over to the Albuquerque Hilton Inn and listen for a British accent. *The Man Who Fell To Earth* starring rock star David Bowie ... is ostensibly about an alien from outer space who come to earth for a spell. Andy why is it being filmed in New Mexico? Because—and take it for whatever it is worth—'the Land of Enchantment looks so much like the mysterious desolate planet Bowie just left' [Editor's Note: in real life or the movie?] Oh well. I guess the British regard any uninhabited area larger than two square feet as mysterious and desolate ... . Extras for the science-fiction film are being handled by Albuquerque's Jeanne Swain. Going wages are $18 for the day ... . Speaking parts, and there aren't a tremendous number but some, begin at a minimum rate of $172.50 per day. Not bad.[35]

Jordan also set her gaze on *Welcome To Xanadu* (later renamed *Sweet Hostage*), which was being filmed in Taos, starring Linda Blair. 'Those of you with cinematic yearnings might polish your squash blossom necklaces, put on your stained cowboy hats and loll around the entrance [of the Taos Holiday Inn],' she suggested.

One local didn't have to stand around anywhere. Lillybell Crawford was cast early for *The Man Who Fell To Earth,* and she was positively adorned in squash-blossom necklaces and turquoise and native jewelry. She appeared as the attendant in the film's antiques shop, where Newton exchanges a ring for cash. The almost spellbinding Crawford was born in the Oklahoma Territory on February 12, 1902, and during the Depression she oversaw Roosevelt's Works Project Administration's Navajo Weavers. She was also the founder of the Volunteer Services Program at what was then known as Bernalillo County–Indian Hospital (later University of New Mexico Hospital/Bernalillo County Medical Center).

Crawford's appearance as the shop owner was not her acting debut—she'd appeared in *My Name Is Nobody* with Henry Fonda and *The Man And The City* with Anthony Quinn—but it was memorable and full of gravitas. She appraises Newton through her cat's-eye glasses with a mixture of skepticism and wonderment and he responds with equal captivation.

Their scene at the Jewel Box (actually an abandoned barber shop) was shot between June 2 and 5 in Los Lunas on Main Street in what the front-page story of the Belen *News Bulletin* referred to as the Jewel Box–Trini's Bar complex. Chagrined that no photographs of Bowie would be allowed to be taken, lest their cameras be smashed by 'a real big guy' (likely Mascia), the reporters turned to one of the film's publicists (possibly Steve Jaffe). 'He just wants a normal life,' the spokesperson insisted, adding, 'I know David loves New Mexico. It has all the elements we wanted.'

The tight security, the spokesperson insisted, was because 'the producers don't want a mass of rock followers to interrupt Bowie. … There's really no extras involved. We have cast all the parts.' The article mentioned Lillybell Crawford as an Albuquerque woman cast as the owner of the Jewel Box. 'Wearing reams of turquoise jewelry around her neck, she sold Bowie a ring [sic] during filming.'

In another scene,' the story continued, 'Bowie lay on a bench in front of the jewelry store.'[36] In fact, that was a particularly standout moment, as the film's hair stylist Martin Samuel attested. 'That was right at the beginning of shooting in the first couple of days. The [hair] was just gorgeous. I thought, Oh my god, it's amazing, the way it was hanging back in the morning light, the sun on it. I was just blown away. The color was just gorgeous, and it worked well with the blond front.'[37] Indeed, the colors gleam like the attractive state flag, echoing the way its yellow backdrop edges around the straight lines of a red Zia sun.

Samuel had come to New Mexico at the behest of makeup head Linda De Vetta. The London native gravitated toward hairdressing early in life, starting out at a local salon before moving to a higher-profile one in upscale Mayfair, and then helping launch Crimpers, the country's first unisex salon, on Baker Street. Hair styling was coming into its own in the 1960s. Top stylists like Vidal Sassoon were celebrities in their own right, and they were also sought after to do hair for television commercials.

With clients like Alan Parker and Ridley and Tony Scott, working in film was a natural progression for Samuel, who also did styling for commercials prior to moving on. One such film was *Stardust*, starring David Essex, the follow-up to 1973's *That'll Be The Day*, which featured Essex and Ringo Starr. London-born Essex was an actor as well as a singer, but as Tony Richmond, who also worked on the 1974 film, insisted, 'David Essex and David Bowie had nothing in common.'[38]

Samuel, who had since relocated to Los Angeles, was set to do the period musical *Bugsy Malone*, populated largely by children portraying gangsters and their molls, but no dates had been fixed. So when he got a call from De Vetta, already in New Mexico, 'Obviously, I jumped at it, because it was a fabulous thing. I read the script and in the normal fashion, I discussed with Nic the needs,' Samuel said. 'I had a conversation with David—his was the look that we discussed first—and he told me he wanted this particular [hair] color to bring with because it wasn't obtainable in the US. We tested it out when I got there—his hair was mostly all blond then. We had about a week and got the look together. And he loved it and Nic loved it and it worked. It was Newton.'[39]

Samuel proved indispensible. 'I was always on set with David,' he said. 'I never left him.' But he would start the day with Clark. 'I would have hours with Candy before David even came to set. Her time was much more intense to get ready. Her stuff was very complicated.' Samuel emphasized that Roeg was particularly focused on his leading lady. 'He was very intense and he really wanted me to come up with some good stuff for her, all these different looks and periods … right the way through to her getting older and fatter. And her as the alien as well.'

According to Clark, the makeup sessions 'took five hours a day. I worked it out that I spent ninety-six and a half hours just sitting in a makeup chair.'[40]

Clark's travails aside, the little town of Los Lunas would take a while to recover from the spectacle of the film's star, whose 'bright red hair and unisexual look seemed to irritate some watchers,' the *News Bulletin* noted. 'Police holding back traffic along Main Street didn't understand all the fuss over the odd-appearing Bowie. If the film relates to the singer as performer, then it can only be considered "freaky."'[41]

In early June, Walter Tevis was back in touch, offering script suggestions and including a cover letter to British Lion Films that began with a formal 'Sirs':

> The enclosed suggestions are offered voluntarily by me and may of course be ignored. If they are used, however, I would expect to be remunerated in the following fashion:
>
> A small credit on the screen (not in any way to replace my contracted-for author's credit) as 'Story Consultant' or some such, as you see fit.
>
> And either of the following:
>
> 1. An expense account for driving with my wife from Athens, Ohio, to Albuquerque and back, together with our expenses for four or five days while we visit the set. Probably in July. Or to London in August.
>
> or 2. $1,500 (fifteen hundred dollars).
>
> Okay?[42]

Tevis's somewhat plaintive and deceptively modest missive must have been met with a swift reply, because days later he was photographed on set near Los Lunas, 'enjoying a cold drink [a Budweiser] in the hot New Mexico sun,' as the local *Valencia County News* reported.[43] Filming had commenced on Monday, June 2, with a clear sunrise over Madrid right after Newton's landing.

Madrid, a former mining town at the time still owned by the Albuquerque and Cerrillos Coal Company who gave the production full permission, captivated or at least gained the attention of May Routh and film critic George Perry, who had joined the set on assignment for London's *Sunday Times* with photographer Brian Duffy. Routh recalled, 'The very first scene was Madrid. There were little coal miner cottages … a strange black hill and all the shapes that it made.'[44] Perry remembered the location somewhat more ominously. It had, he said a sign that read, 'Welcome to Madrid—Keep Out.'[45] So much for the welcome wagon.

'Driving miles across nothing,' is how Perry described the town. 'Draft dodgers with large dogs lived there. Then it was only bikers. Even the FBI wouldn't go near the place.'[46]

'We came here in 1973,' local gallery owner Eric Johnson explained to me. 'Madrid was a ghost city, much too large to call a ghost town. Bikers would have been deliberately trying to frighten them [cast and crew]. The gangs from California, especially the Hells Angels, had more of a sort of legal authority over the town than the sheriff did. They would have made certain that the movie people knew who was boss.'

With a population of at best, three hundred, the ghost city would have noticed the film being made. 'The filming almost completely turned the town upside down,' Johnson said. 'Everybody ended up making room for them one place or another. Everybody was involved. We owned an International Harvester Garage in the downtown part of Madrid and they used it to store almost all their stuff and when they left, we inherited lumber, tools, chairs.

'Nobody supported or opposed the idea of doing a movie here,' he continued. 'We tried to be neighborly.' In terms of their being minimally intrusive, however, Johnson felt the filmmakers 'were richer rather than they were orderly.'

Cast and crew were spotted around the town, but the residents did not immediately clock them as British. 'I don't think anybody was aware they were English,' Johnson said. 'We knew there were English people involved but we thought of it as a Hollywood film. Some people knew who Bowie was but we didn't have much of a sense of it. We knew he was the star of the movie.'

The major players made the daily trip to Madrid from Santa Fe, but two or three groups 'just kind of camped in Madrid for a while,' Johnson said. 'Madrid didn't even have indoor plumbing at that point.'

What the area did have was a major industry in growing marijuana, and Johnson said this led to some tensions. 'Anybody with a camera was highly suspect: *Who's going to look at this?*' Johnson noted. But if anything, he added, 'the filming was an amusement for the tourists,' some of whom would have seen movie people in the Mineshaft Tavern, where they drank and, with caution, ate. 'They probably ordered hamburgers and fries,' Johnson said. 'New Mexican food is extremely spicy, and a bowl of chili in New Mexico is not a bowl of chili beans. A bowl of chili in New Mexico is a condiment.' And a near-lethal one at that.

The Mineshaft has a relatively nondescript exterior, but the interior is a historical landmark. Notably, it once had a white stripe running down the middle of the bar, designating the county line. 'That county line meant that the bad guys and the good guys—the bad guys and the sheriff—could have a drink together,' Johnson recalled. 'They just sat on different sides of the line because the sheriff had no jurisdiction on the other side of the line and the bad guys had no reason to shoot him.'

The most memorable feature of the Madrid shoot—apart from the decaying miners' shacks with alternating red and green roofs, so painted because of the town's designation as Christmas City—was the Breaker Building on the city's south side. The building, which isn't a part of the mine, is where the coal was broken down into usable sizes before being loaded onto railroad cars. Roeg wanted to film inside the dilapidated edifice, but the mining company told the crew that it would only be possible if they took out two million dollars in insurance for safety reasons. The filmmakers demurred but they got a trade-off.

It seems the mining company was also unhappy about Newton coming down the coal hill. 'The company didn't want him to do the scene where he climbs down the gob pile [comprised of pieces of coal too small to sell off] toward the breaker,' Johnson said. 'The tailings are trailing behind him as he comes down the hill. It wasn't stable and the company was afraid that if anybody went up there, it would cause some sort of avalanche and people could get hurt. But they compromised: they got that scene but they couldn't get inside the building.' It still didn't rest easy with the locals. 'We were all worried about it,' Johnson insisted, thinking an avalanche would certainly impact the breaker structure. 'We thought the whole building might have collapsed and slid right into town.'[47] So Bowie as Newton's palpable apprehension on his precarious descent came with a precedent.

After Madrid, filming then moved down to Los Lunas, where cast and crew would remain for the next three days, creating commotion and causing curiosity. 'The main thing a film company causes when it comes to Los Lunas is excitement,' another local newspaper story noted. 'And when the star of the film is David Bowie, English rock singer of international fame, the excitement builds.'[48] Some of the crew ate lunch in the empty building next to the newspaper's offices 'on food prepared by caterers from Grants [NM].'

The catered meals would soon become the object of some concern. 'We went through two or three different show caterers,' Alan Swain recalled, 'because they [cast and crew] kept saying we put too much spices on the food, and to us it was already bland.' That was not surprising: red and green chilies are ubiquitous in New Mexican cuisine; to order both is to request 'Christmas.' 'Finally they got their own guy in,' Swain continued, 'so we spent a lot of time going out and getting hamburgers.'[49] Indeed, at one point Angie Bowie was pressed into service as a cook, serving meals out of a Winnebago that she'd drive each day to Fenton Lake.

Food aside, David Cammell told the paper how pleased he was with New Mexico. 'Cammell added in his British accent, "We found everything that was written in the script. We've had marvelous cooperation from everyone in New Mexico." That cooperation extended to the "orderliness" of those who came as spectators, but the report did not ignore the disappointment felt by many of the locals when they weren't allowed to photograph Bowie 'because of legal technicalities.'

Walter Tevis wrapped up his few days spent on location. 'I think he stood around and drank a lot of beer and hung out with the director's wife [sic],' his own wife later recalled.[50] He then returned to Ohio with a two-by-four board from the set autographed by Bowie for his daughter, and, more importantly, a strong impression of the man hired to play his Newton.

> When I first met Mr. Bowie on the first day of shooting (I call him Mister because of the dignity of the man. And because he's a gentleman.) I was stunned to see what I had years before imagined

become flesh—or something like flesh. It was creepy at first; dynamite after.

There's a fat man out there somewhere who calls himself Minnesota Fats after another character I made up (in my book *The Hustler*) and I've seen him do his act. But he never gave me the déjà vu of private imaginings that Mr. Bowie did. I suspect Bowie of being a great actor too. But let's wait till the movie comes out.[51]

Bowie later wrote to Tevis on a page with a photocopied thumb on it, 'as if someone was handing the letter to you,' Jamie Griggs Tevis remembered.[52]

Filming was slated to continue until August 2, with a Christmas release anticipated. Some seventy people would traverse much of the state. 'We shot all over the state,' cinematographer Tony Richmond recalled. 'The great thing about shooting in New Mexico, the topography changes very quickly. You can be in the desert and within fifteen, twenty miles a different sort of landscape. It's wonderful for shooting, wonderful. The skies are so beautiful.'[53]

On June 10, the *Hollywood Reporter* announced the addition of Rip Torn to the cast. The star of *The Cincinnati Kid, King Of Kings* (in which he played Judas), *You're A Big Boy Now*, and *Tropic Of Cancer* would, it said, play 'a Chicago professor obsessed by revolutionary petrochemical inventions of Bowie's company.'[54]

Elmore 'Rip' Torn was born February 6, 1931, in Temple, Texas, a hardscrabble prairie town in a state known for extremes and expanses. He went to Texas A&M, where he was, essentially, a frat boy before moving to New York to pursue acting, which he did in a big way, studying with Lee Strasberg at his Actors Studio. He had the acting chops, for sure, but it came with a temper—and a cantankerous nature to boot, which did not always sit well with Hollywood. 'First they said I was too young, then that I was too much trouble,' Torn recalled.[55] He had been in line for the role of George Hanson in *Easy Rider*, but a dust-up between Torn and Dennis Hopper put paid to that and the part went to Jack Nicholson.

For some of his Hollywood career and during the time he was married to actor Geraldine Page, Torn was represented by Howard Rubin. 'Rip is never easy,' Rubin said. 'I think on his tombstone it should say *Rest Easy*. I also represented Geraldine Page, and when the two of them got together, that was very bizarre. They had a love of acting, the two of them, that was pure.'

Rubin maintained Torn was less than happy with the role of Dr. Nathan Bryce, for which he received $3,500 a week or about $10,000 for the entire thirty-one-day shoot. 'I don't think he was thrilled,' Rubin added. 'I don't really think he embraced the character as much as he could have. I've seen everything he's done. He's a method actor, so he's deep into the character, and if it's not working for him, he's not easy to work with.

'Nic Roeg pretty much knew what he wanted, and it really was a director's film. Not a lot of room, on a tight schedule with not a lot of money, on location, no time for *what's this character about?*'[56]

Torn did put the requisite thought into his role. 'I learn about human nature from the characters I play,' he told the *Los Angeles Times*' Clarke Taylor. 'Bryce thought he was headed for freedom and financial security, but he would have been better off had he stayed in the classroom. At least there he was his own man. In the end, when he was down at the heel, it's too late to go back.'

Bowie was taken by Torn's mythic persona, finding him macho and erudite in an Ernest Hemingway/Norman Mailer mold. Torn was a close friend of the writer and fellow native Texan Terry Southern, who visited the set along with his fourteen-year-old son Nile.

Terry Southern, born in 1924, was a satirical writer and journalist whose work includes the screenplays to *Easy Rider* and *Dr. Strangelove* as well as the novels *The Magic Christian* and *Candy*. He also later taught screenwriting at both NYU and Columbia, right until his death in 1995.

'I think Southern, not Hunter Thompson, invented Gonzo Journalism,' the author W.K. 'Kip' Stratton told me in an email. 'He did so with an *Esquire* piece called "Baton Twirling At Ole Miss" years before Thompson tried something similar. I think his best work was his shorter pieces, especially nonfiction, and his screenplays. Dennis Hopper lied and lied viciously about Southern and his involvement with *Easy Rider*. In fact, Southern was essential to it even getting made.'[57]

Southern had also worked with Torn on *The Cincinnati Kid*. 'They cemented their relationship on *The Cincinnati Kid*, and he wrote some scenes specifically for him in that film,' Nile Southern recalled. 'There's a side to him where he likes to be out on his own in nature, fishing. He and my dad were such good friends that he'd come up with his family in a sort of little yellow school bus and stay on the farm in Canaan, Connecticut, where I grew up. Rip, my dad, and I would go hunting and fishing and I knew him as an outdoorsman despite all his great theatrical training and experience.'[58]

Oklahoman Candy Clark says she got along 'really well' with the Texan Torn despite the fact that they didn't have many scenes together. His was a contemplative view of acting: 'Talent is a responsibility. It isn't anything to get puffed up about,' he said, and to some degree his status as a Hollywood outsider may have had something to do with his politics at the time, during which he supported activist Angela Davis and the Black Panthers and was vehemently against the blockade of Cuba. 'I say I'm an American rebel, which means that I'm a constitutionalist and believe in the Bill of Rights,' he said.

He had another reason for his antagonistic treatment from the major studios. 'Abbie Hoffman [60s activist] once said that he didn't understand why I was so harassed. Well, I know how to shoot.' He continued, 'As long as a man does his work, why should his political or personal life matter? … There is a difference between someone getting knocked out of Hollywood and television and dying, and one who says, So what?'[59]

Someone who wasn't saying 'So what?' was producer Si Litvinoff, who was being edged out by Michael Deeley and Barry Spikings. They were all present in New Mexico when British Lion was acquired from J.H. Vavasseur Banking Group by Deeley & Spikings, a move noted on June 18 by *Variety*, which described the impending project as 'an event film with beaucoup violence,' adding that RCA had a stake in the picture.[60]

'Not true at all,' said Deeley, about RCA's interest. 'I wish they had.' He explained the maneuverings: 'Vavasseur were run by a famously wicked asset stripper called John Bentley. He had acquired Lion International, the studio company at Shepperton. British Lion was the number three because it didn't have any theaters and the other two did. That was spun off as Lion International and that's where … when I had shares in Lion International and swapped my shares, about 23 percent of the company for British Lion Films and then IIB came in as my banker. That's how they intermingled. Vavasseur were gone by then.'[61]

Not everyone was happy with a move that left Litvinoff marginalized, and indeed Litvinoff's antipathy did not fade over time. 'There is nothing other than denigration from me re: him [Deeley] after he and Barry agreed to finance *The Man Who Fell To Earth*,' Litvinoff asserted. The crew was also likely less than pleased when the man some of them referred to as 'Wheely Deeley' discontinued Litvinoff's practice of hosting an open bar at the end of each day's shoot. 'I could go way beyond what the crew called him,' Litvinoff added.[62]

It was a sentiment echoed by Rubin. 'Whatever Michael Deeley said to you, I would say that it was Si's film, Si's ideas that resonated through Nic. I mean, he hired Nic and Nic made that movie happen. Without Nic Roeg, you don't have anywhere near as good a movie. Si has a knack, an eye—always did. I used to think and still do, he really should have run a studio, because he has a grand view. But he was better doing independent movies.'[63]

Nile Southern also had a high opinion of Litvinoff. 'Si had been my father's attorney and agent for a period prior to *The Man Who Fell To Earth*, so they have a long history where Si was helping with business stuff. I knew Si and his wife, Toy; I kind of grew up knowing them. We had a German Shepherd that Si had arranged for us to get. It was a very special dog; I think it was related to Rin Tin Tin, the movie-acting dog.' Of course there were several Rin Tin Tins, so this was all the more likely.

'Si is more like a business guy who appreciates the arts, he loves a fine wine,' Southern continued. 'His communication style is more aggressive but always there's sort of love at the end. *Love, Si*.'[64]

Michael Deeley was born on August 6, 1932. After completing national service in Malaysia, he began working in film and television, editing and producing. He joined MCA International in the UK in the 1960s before partnering with Barry Spikings to form a variety of Great Western enterprises, among them Great Western Investments, which took over British Lion in 1973. That year, Lion released Roeg's *Don't Look Now* and Robin Hardy's seminal *The Wicker Man*, placing the company in an artistically interesting place that would also, at the time, bode well for *The Man Who Fell To Earth*.

'After *Don't Look Now*, Nic Roeg was very, very hot, well placed,' Deeley said. 'Trade will look at the last film the guy directed. Bowie was a star, had headlined one movie before [sic], and basically was a selling point.' Deeley was also happy with the location and its home base of Albuquerque. 'New Mexico was a right-to-work state, so there were no unions—no *forceful* unions,' Deeley said. 'It was a very relaxed place. I did that picture and then a year later, went back to do a much bigger picture with Sam Peckinpah [*Convoy*, 1978]. Nice thing about it was we stayed at the Hilton [Midtown] for fifteen dollars a night; went back a year later and it was sixteen dollars only. It's got a huge parking lot which is very good if you've got a hundred trucks.'

Rubin concurred about the union presence. '[The Teamsters] were not as strong as they are now. They were happy to have the work. What drivers we hired were mostly Indian people as I recall. They knew the territory. They were smart; they worked within the system.'[65]

'We had the one non-union generator in the country,' said Alan Swain. 'It was driven by this guy named Guy Badger. He would go to the craft service at lunch and then sleep in his truck.'

Swain was enjoying his time with the crew at the Hilton Midtown. 'There's a two-story in the back and we pretty much had the whole section to ourselves—production offices and housing—so that was a pretty rowdy part of the hotel. A pool, pretty wild times. Those guys liked to drink a lot and those were the days when the prop truck had beer on it.'[66]

It was about a mile from one Hilton to the other, and a giant letter *H*, which lit up in red at night, adorned the highest point of the older hotel, where the bigger stars were staying. The letter would serve as a beacon one night for Rip Torn.

'I had to go get him,' May Routh recalled. 'I went to the trailer, got in. He was lying in bed, his arm was out of bed, blood everywhere. It turned out he'd been out drinking with Nic, he'd been drinking with him until quite late and left there completely pissed. Walked directly, a straight line to the Big *H*, passed car lots, barbed wire fences, chain link fences … he'd lost half the sleeve of his shirt. He was going back that night to see if he could find it,' she laughed. 'It was a shirt his wife had given him, and he liked it.'[67]

Filming transitioned southeast with a move to Artesia, a modest agricultural and manufacturing community that official unit photographer David James called 'a half-horse town,' compared with his description of Albuquerque as both 'like a crossroads' and 'a one-to-two horse town.'[68] James, a photographer who'd transitioned into producing, was cajoled back to photography by Roeg. 'I thought it'd be a really cool idea to turn myself into a director and producer of commercials,' he said. 'I'd gotten a lot of magazine and fashion photography, a lot of calendars. I was actually producing in Blackburn, a three-and-a-half hour documentary for German television—when Nic Roeg called me.'

'What are you doing?' Roeg asked him.

'I'm producing a movie,' James replied. 'I'm a line producer.'

'David, don't be serious, you're a photographer. Come join me in New Mexico.'

James didn't have to think twice. 'I quit and left—because of Nic. I wanted to work with Bowie, of course, but I knew Nic from when he was a cameraman. I loved him. It was a golden opportunity.'[69]

James took a commercial flight to the USA and joined the action in New Mexico, shooting many black-and-white photographs and a handful of startling-in-their-color ones. The iconic stars-in-his-eyes photo of Bowie was taken on the balcony of an Artesia motel. He cited Bowie's 'haunted look,' which he said was enhanced by his habit of staying up for three days and then sleeping for three days in a row.

Significantly, Artesia had a handily abandoned, large and eponymous hotel, which, despite the pigeons roosting in its rafters, was ideal for filming. Years before, the hotel had been a luxury spot, and it was even a designated historic landmark, but it had since fallen into disrepair and was slated for demolition. As a result, a film crew was free to do whatever it liked with the interior and exterior.

Roeg said he liked Artesia because it corresponded to the more industrial part of the film's narrative. 'It had a wonderful old factory thing, the other side of the tracks, in a sense of the early 1920s, 30s look to it,' he said.[70] Stars camped in trailers or a modest motel May Routh described as 'a nice quiet room [with a] shower' on the city's Main Street.[71]

Linda De Vetta was not so charitable. 'We stayed in a ghastly motel,' she said, adding that she took a picture of second assistant director Michael Stevenson 'kicking a football on the pool deck of this grotty motel in the road.'[72]

David James took a different view. 'Artesia, I loved it,' he said. 'It's where I got my love of the sound of American trains going past. Our motel was on one side of the track, and we were shooting on the other side of the tracks and outlying areas.'[73]

They were expected to be there for eight days, beginning Monday, June 16. Despite the best efforts of Alan Swain, whom some referred to as 'Young Alan,' they were still in need of 120 extras; in particular forty-five women, forty men, and thirty-five children, for a church scene to be filmed that coming Friday.

The *Artesia Daily Press* repeated the call on June 17, asking this time for 'twenty more men, adults preferably, for Friday's filming of a sequence of *The Man Who Fell To Earth* which will be filmed at Artesia Presbyterian Church.'[74] They didn't need any more children, they said, but still sought 'a cross-section of ages, heights, and weights,' to be vetted by the casting director and paid eighteen dollars for their efforts, according to the Artesia Chamber of Commerce.

Friday dawned very warm, and throughout the day and into the night, the church was filled with actors, extras, floodlights, and equipment. 'That was a scene where Mary-Lou was very proud that she has got the church to sing an English song ["Jerusalem"],' Candy Clark said. 'She arranged that. That's how I felt about it. She got the preacher to do this. I bring him to church and now we're singing a British song. That's pride smiling. Oddly enough it turns out he doesn't even know the song. It gives the audience a hint that he's not really who he says he is. He's not really from England. Anyone from England would know the lyrics like most people [in the US] know "The Star-Spangled Banner."

'Mary-Lou doesn't notice that he doesn't know the song but anyone viewing, if they were following the story—which is not an easy story to follow—they would realize that he doesn't know his country's song. It's a clue. You'll see him lagging behind and trying to hear the lyrics and pretending that he knows the song,' she told me.[75]

Indeed, it is the one time Bowie sings in the film, his voice entirely distinct. The church's full choir performed, and local man Ben Cauble played the choir director as well as the minister saying a prayer. Cauble said of the proceedings, 'They put lights in the ceiling, but they took real good care of the church.' At one point, the congregation fed the crew a lunch—hopefully not too spicy— they'd made. Cauble was both struck and puzzled by the film's star, concluding, 'It probably didn't hurt him to be in a church.'[76]

On the morning of the filming, the *Artesia Daily Press* printed a picture of Ola Hudson looking exuberant in a *Man Who Fell To Earth* T-shirt designed by Candy Clark's brother, who was part of the crew, partaking in what she called 'a very happy-go-lucky set.'[77] His presence was noted by Chuck Mittlestadt in his local column, 'New Mexico Hollywood Reporter': 'Didja know that Candy Clark, femme star of *The Man Who Fell To Earth* currently shooting in New Mexico, has her kid brother on the payroll as a member of the production crew.'[78] Bowie's friend and sometime stand-in Geoff MacCormack also took stock of the crew of 'mostly Londoners' whose 'banter … reminded me of what I missed about London.'[79]

Less than an hour away from Artesia was Roswell, where filming would commence on Saturday, June 21. For Routh and Eatwell, it was a repeat visit. While at the motel in Artesia, Eatwell had carved 'some kind of Jesus head out of a piece of wood,' Routh explained, 'and, in doing so, he cut himself.'

After the cut had become inflamed, they quickly drove to the nearest hospital, a small cottage-style facility forty miles from Artesia in Roswell. There, Eatwell was given a potentially fatal penicillin shot. 'Nobody knew he was allergic. He practically died in the hospital there,' Routh said. 'Nobody knew. Everyone [at the hospital] was charming, though.'[80]

Extras were again an issue for the upcoming college scene, which would be filmed at the New Mexico Military Institute in Roswell. Alan Swain was tasked with finding five hundred people. 'We only got about two hundred and fifty,' he said. 'We didn't say anything, and there were more than enough people out there [at the institute]. I went up to the producer [Deeley] and I told him we saved $20,000, as we didn't need that many extras. He was all happy—*Marvelous!*'

An extra who didn't have to be recruited was Sabrina Guinness, who, as a coed, beguilingly picked up papers bothered by the wind and dropped by Torn's Professor Nathan Bryce. 'She was really beautiful,' Swain recalled. 'I had a crush on her for sure.'[81]

Guinness had come at the behest of Si Litvinoff, who entrusted her with looking after his two sons, of whom he had custody that summer.

The *Roswell Daily Record* used the occasion to write about Torn, who told them he was having trouble getting used to the New Mexico sun. 'I grew up in Longview and around Austin [Texas],' he told the paper, 'but I've been living in New York. There is a difference in intensity of light, you know.'

Torn conceded to have his photo taken and said, by way of apology, 'I hope I wasn't too grim. I have a grim look about me.' The scene in question, of Torn coming down the steps of the building and going to his car, 'lasted about twenty seconds [and] took about an hour to organize and film, as would the next take,' the reporter noted, before adding that filming wrapped early Saturday afternoon as cast and crew departed for Albuquerque.[82]

On a brief side trip, MacCormack, Bowie, and Bowie's assistant, Corinne (Coco) Schwab, borrowed a car and drove the short distance to Carlsbad Caverns, thirty miles of underground limestone caves that measured one thousand feet across. The attraction for Bowie, however, wasn't the curious cafe located inside the cave but rather what's known as its signature Bat Flight, when, at sunset, hundreds of thousands of Mexican free-tailed bats made their exit from the cave's mouth. On their drive back, MacCormack recalled, they'd perused an antiques fair, where Bowie bought a railroad pocket watch.

DUKE CITY

CHAPTER FOUR

George Perry was having a struggle securing interviews for his story for the *Sunday Times*. 'Getting ahold of Nic was a nightmare,' he said. 'If he wasn't behind doors with Candy, he was trying to sort out directorial problems. Hard to find time to talk about things in general. Very hard.'[1]

Roeg's affair with his leading lady did not go unnoticed—on location they rarely do—and might have been vexing for Bowie, who felt he was being somewhat edged out. 'At times it was very difficult for David with Candy, because of the way she was in a relationship with Nic,' Martin Samuel told Chris Duffy for his book, *Duffy/ Bowie: 5 Sessions*. 'I know he felt a bit pushed out sometimes. She was always trying to upstage him on camera, get into a shot, and it really drove David absolutely crazy. He had a rage about it afterwards to us.'[2]

Graeme Clifford saw it differently, however, from the point of view of Clark's character, and thought that any attempted upstaging was intentional as part of her enactment. 'Mary-Lou was drunk. She didn't listen when she was drinking.'[3]

Perry, a journalist, was a consummate observer, but even he didn't immediately grasp Roeg's rationale as to working with Bowie. 'What he did to him was not really tell him very much, even tell him what it was really all about,' he said. 'And this frustrated David terribly. He felt that he didn't know the character. Conversations with Nic would go off into a kind of opaqueness that made it hard to really understand.

'It was only later that one realized what he was doing: he was trying to throw him off course, deliberately disturbing his equilibrium because he wanted this notion of someone who had fled a planet that was being destroyed, appearing in a planet and having to cope ... and that really was David Bowie on the film site. Nic would be cackling wildly to himself over what he was getting. David would be playing a scene, being totally at sea—and delivering.'[4]

It wasn't just the actors who felt adrift at times, as Linda De Vetta attested. 'The hours we worked were really shocking,' she said. 'Because it was non-union, we would sometimes work twenty hours a day.'[5]

De Vetta had worked with Roeg before, starting with *Performance*. She grew up in Uxbridge, near Pinewood Studios (which, she insisted, held no sway over her chosen career). Her parents and school steered her toward art school, but she resisted. 'There was another girl at school who was exceptional [in art],' she said. 'I was just very good. I felt when I compared myself to this other girl, I wasn't good enough to do pure art.' Instead she landed upon a different idea. 'I wanted to do makeup not because I wanted to do films or television but because I wanted to paint on faces, so you're working on a contoured surface that joined up rather than painting on a flat one.

'In those days you couldn't go into ATV or BBC to train as a makeup artist until you were twenty-one because they didn't want silly little girls … but I actually got into ATV when I was twenty. I managed to get an interview and they gave me a test day to decide whether I wanted to do three months of training and then be an apprentice for the next two years to be trained as a makeup artist.

'You had to do a straight corrected makeup, an aging makeup and a character makeup,' she added. Confused by the latter instruction, she asked for clarification, and proceeded to paint a marmalade cat onto a face. 'To this day it's the best makeup I've ever done. I just winged it and strangely enough, did exactly what one does. It's actually logical.'

A catlike visage would reappear in De Vetta's future, and this time it would cause great difficulty. 'Strange, putting makeup on faces,' she sighed. 'You can get away with murder.'[6] Such Bowie-esque pronouncements give insight into why De Vetta, by most accounts other than her own, was the person closest to him on the film.

After working in television for five years, De Vetta took a chance and went freelance in film. She began working on *Performance* with makeup artist Paul Rabiger before he left to do a Bond film because it was more lucrative. Initially reticent to take over, she was then promised Rabiger's full salary—but only if she worked the entire film on her own. She did, instigating a pattern that would follow her throughout her sojourns with Roeg.

De Vetta travelled to meet her husband, Tony Richmond, who upon being hired to work on *The Man Who Fell To Earth* had gone off to Los Angeles three months in advance of his wife. She was familiar with Bowie's various personae and 'all the mad costumes and looks' but said it had no bearing on how she approached her upcoming assignment. 'As a makeup artist, the most important part of your job is to help the director move the story forward visually,' she said.

De Vetta came over to the USA on her own and not on the infamous Dublin-to-Chicago charter. But there was still turbulence ahead. 'When I got on the plane at Heathrow, the script was David as the alien had no eyebrows, no hair, I think no ears,' she recalled. 'It was very minimal. I got off the plane in LA, went straight to a meeting to find the alien now had no hair, no eyebrows, no nipples, no genitals, no fingernails, no toenails—and he had cat's eyes.'

Fortunately, wardrobe supervisor May Routh was 'savvy to

this information before I got there.' Routh cannily contacted Burman Studios in North Hollywood to help out. The eyes—full sclera lenses—would cause considerable hardship, ironically in Albuquerque, which De Vetta referred to as 'The City of Bausch & Lomb.' The contact lens manufacturers had recently invented soft lenses, which would have been extremely helpful in the scene where Newton puts his human eye lens back in. The scene was a late addition, leaving De Vetta to scramble to find a way to make it work seamlessly.

'We phone Bausch and Lomb and we say, If we give you a lens, would you make a [soft] lens?' she recalled. The makers refused because their new lenses hadn't been approved by the American Medical Association. De Vetta explained it was just for a film, but Bausch & Lomb wouldn't budge.

'Nic said, You do it, Linda,' De Vetta continued. 'Well, with what? So I made the lens out of cat plastic that is so highly toxic, I can't tell you. I painted it, covered it again, and said to Nic and Tony, You've got one take of this. It's the scene where he's standing in the close up mirror and he's putting it back in again. He's doing it in the mirror …

'David was really up for it, he was wonderful. Most actors would say, not a hope in hell. I told David it will sting your eyelid but your eye will be protected by the full sclera lens—no way can it affect your eye.'

One take turned into another and another until De Vetta stood in front of the camera and announced, 'I'm sorry Nic, that's it. You can't do any more.'

'I'm sure they used the first take as well,' she sighed.

Tom Burman of Tom Burman Studios recalled the scene. 'What

he did is put it [the lens] up to his eye and then he pulled it away. They just reversed the film so it looked like he went *pop* and put it right in.'[7]

'I think I cut the thing backwards,' Graeme Clifford said. 'It was visually easier, and I reverse-printed the film. Obviously it was a lot easier to take [the lenses] off than put it on ... so I just reversed it to make it look like it was going on more easily.'[8]

The aliens' cat's eyes were equally problematic. 'Those bloody cat's eyes,' De Vetta said. 'Nic wants the irises to go vertically. I thought, Right, okay. May had already art-worked a set of sclera lenses—they were lovely but they were too pretty, and Nic didn't like it. He said, Okay, this isn't really quite right—Linda, you do it. They had to be painted with acrylic paint and then had to be coated because acrylic paint is dry and the eyelid would stick to it.'

Another issue was that the lens, when pushed in, would rotate around and around. De Vetta solved this by putting two lead bars in the bottom to weigh them down.

The lenses were a challenge for the makeup artist but not the uncomplaining Bowie, despite the fact that as a child he'd had surgery on his eye with the dilated pupil—the result of a schoolyard scrap with his friend George Underwood. 'He'd had surgery on that eye and they'd sewn up the eyelid very tight,' De Vetta explained. 'It was easy to get the lens in the other eye, but it was a real struggle to get the lens in *that* eye.'

Bowie would later comment that the lenses were made further problematic by the fact that he was so dehydrated from both an errant lifestyle and the desert climate. One solution was to call in a Beverly Hills optician for the weeks they'd be using the lenses. 'That lasted two days because he was an alcoholic and was absolutely bloody legless by eleven in the morning,' De Vetta said. Bowie was having none of it. 'David then turns round to me and says, I don't want him. Linda, you do it.'

Roeg was not unsympathetic. 'The crew, they didn't get a lot of help,' he acknowledged.[9]

Buck Henry was having problems of his own with the eyewear; namely, his bottle-lens glasses, which gave the world a carnival appearance. Henry couldn't see out of them and had the lacerations and bruises on his legs to attest to it.

If the lenses were awkward for adults and accomplished performers, imagine what they were like for children and novice actors. Kevin Weber was a local Albuquerque kid just starting junior high school when he took on the part of Newton's Anthean son. He'd done some acting: standard fare like *Tom Sawyer* and *Snow White* at the local Music Theatre, and *Carousel* plus *Fiddler On The Roof* at the Civic Light Opera. But he'd also had a part as a barber's son in the feature film *My Name Is Nobody*, so he wasn't without professional experience.

Weber had answered a call for extras and was standing in for the boy hired as the alien son. 'When he became [unavailable], they asked me if I would like to do it, and I said sure,' Weber recalled. 'I looked younger than I was.' He was thirteen.

Weber remembered the contact lenses as being rather unwieldy. 'I couldn't see very well, but they were neat,' he said, adding that he enjoyed his time in makeup. His youth might have affected his initial impression of Bowie. 'I had no idea who Bowie was,' he said. 'He looked like a walking zombie.'[10]

By comparison, seventeen-year-old Alan Swain was floored. 'David Bowie was one of my idols, so it was kind of cool to work on the [film]. I was in that wondrous world of, *Oh my God, I'm working on a movie with David Bowie.*[11]

Swain also partook of watching the rushes at the Hilton. 'Some of the crew didn't care, they're just doing a job,' he recalled, but he knew there was 'a Moviola guy who travelled with us.'

'I was cutting on a Moviola,' Clifford said. 'Lots of editors at that time were cutting on flatbeds but I didn't like flatbeds. I found them slow and awkward. The Moviola was the motorcycle to the flatbed's school bus. However I used a flatbed to screen on—it was smoother than a Moviola and there was much less chance of ripping the film.

'In those days you'd watch the rushes on 35mm. I was editing in a hotel room in Albuquerque. You didn't move around—the editing equipment was very heavy and cumbersome.'

When filming transitioned to Santa Fe, the Moviola and flatbed stayed firmly planted in Albuquerque. 'For some reason the stuff went to Technicolor in England, and we'd get it back a few days later,' Tony Richmond said. 'We went and saw it. I can't think why they came from England—I don't know why they didn't come [from] here.'[12]

Albuquerque—nicknamed Duke City after the Duke of Albuquerque, Spain, which was slightly nicer than Candy Clark's name for it: Alba-Turkey—had already provided several locations. 'The new First Plaza with its gushing water fountain, the new First National Bank Building and several homes in the Four Hills area,' Howard Bryan of the *Albuquerque Tribune* noted.[13] The city also had a shop called Alan's Apparel For Men, located at 6713 Menaul Avenue NE, as Routh discovered. Perhaps the most unseasoned member of the crew—she charmingly didn't realize she needed doubles of each clothing item ('What was the point? It's going to be in the shot for one scene. Why would you want two? It's just a waste of money.') Routh freely admitted she was almost out of her depth. 'I had never worked on a film other than being an assistant. It was a real learning process for me.'

Still, Routh's wardrobe duties with Rip Torn once veered close to being a minder, and an ersatz one at that. 'There was a shop in Albuquerque called Alan's,' she said. 'They had Ralph Lauren, things that weren't *cowboy*.' That distinction was important, since Torn's role as Bryce, a college professor, called for suits and casual clothes. When Torn arrived at the shop for the first time, salesmen gathered around and soon proffered a bottle of champagne. Routh later complained to Torn that 'just because I'm a girl' she was not given the same treatment. When they went back, Torn 'stood rigid in the doorway.'

'Mr. Torn, Mr. Torn, what can we do for you today?' the salesmen asked.

'I'm not going to try on anything until you give May a bottle of champagne,' the actor insisted.

'I was mortified,' Routh recalled. 'They give me a bottle, it's ten in the morning and we're drinking champagne. I'm in charge of the car, and the star I'm supposed to be looking after, I'm getting him drunk.'

Routh asked Torn what he wanted to do right before they left the shop. 'I'd like to go to a fish-and-tackle shop,' the veteran fly fisherman responded, and upon receiving recommendations from the staff, he began talking shop about flies and tackle.

'So I left him there,' Routh concluded. When she got to the set, she was asked where Torn was. 'He's in a fish-and-tackle shop somewhere,' she replied. Later that night, Torn returned to the Hilton with trout, which the chef cooked and prepared for the crew. 'So it all worked out,' Routh surmised. 'He'd been out in the fresh air.' Torn would also cook trout with bacon and scallions al fresco for the cast and crew on at least one other occasion during the shoot.

Torn had much trepidation about an upcoming nude scene with a fetching young woman, played by model Linda Hutton, and again enlisted Routh's help. 'He had bought dumbbells that he announced I had to carry around in the back of my car. He wanted to build up his muscles and look good. But of course they stayed in the back of my car.'[14]

Of the local women cast as extras, one of them, Debbi Letteau, was competing with nine other young women to be Miss Albuquerque (a feeder for the Miss America beauty pageant). The contest, held at the Sheraton Old Town Inn on Friday, June 27, had among its judges Fred Williamson, John Peverall, and Brian Eatwell, taking time off from *The Man Who Fell To Earth* to judge contestants based on 'personality, poise, intelligence, talent as well as beauty of face and figure.'[15]

Letteau did not win, but she did make it into the film, as Alan Swain recalled. 'The people who were Rip Torn's family [in the bedside photograph] were my next-door neighbor and mom and a girl I went to high school with called Debbi Letteau. It's kind of a conservative town, so I think they got embarrassed to find themselves in a scene where [Torn is] making love with some young girl.'[16]

A young woman named Delana Michaels, who grew up in Ruidoso, New Mexico, had gotten her Screen Actors Guild card in 1973. Her agent sent her along to the *Man Who Fell* auditions, where she tested for the part of Rip Torn's secretary. 'It was very strange because I went in late in the afternoon and I thought, This isn't going to be anything,' Michaels said. 'I got there and they said, Oh there's one more. Come on in.'

After she went in and did the reading, assistant director Kip Gowans [with whom Michaels would develop a lasting friendship] told her she'd gotten the part as she was walking out the door.

'Really?' she replied.

'Yeah,' he said, adding, 'It's weird because the lady in front of you had gotten the part and we already told her that, but he [Roeg] liked you more.'

And which of her attributes or abilities clinched the part? 'This is so weird,' she laughed. 'The reason I got the part is, my fingernails were clean and polished. I thought, *whoa*.'

Michaels learned her lines quickly and shot her part. 'My scene was with Buck Henry but they ended up cutting it, so I didn't end up with any acting exposure for it,' she said. 'In the meantime, they had gotten to know me. I was about the same height as Candy Clark and fair-skinned, so they asked me to be a stand-in for her for the rest of the film.'

Michaels accepted and travelled around the state with cast and crew, including the film's star. She was relatively unfamiliar with Bowie's music, she said, and admitted to knowing next to nothing about him. 'The first night I met him we were out on location in a motel and I was rooming with the on-set nurse, Jill [known by some as Jill The Pill for her dispensary abilities rather than her disposition]. She was a very beautiful gal. We get this knock on the door and we open it and there's David Bowie standing there.'

'Can I just come in and hang out with you girls?' he asked.

'Well … sure,' came the reply.

'He was a super nice guy, very intelligent,' Michaels said. 'Just incredible looking. His skin was so beautiful, like porcelain. He was almost like a china doll. He's so perfect-looking he almost doesn't look real.'

Michaels was also completely unaware he was married. 'I thought he was trying to hit on the nurse, beautiful Jill,' she said. This would have been par for the course on the shoot. 'We would shoot in these old hotels,' she continued, 'and it was hotter than Hades down there [Artesia]. People would sort of disappear off the set and nobody knew where they were. Come to find out they were off with somebody upstairs fooling around—and that was going on A LOT.'

Filming continued at Albuquerque's abandoned Sunshine Building on Second and Central Streets, where one day Bowie began feeling unwell while sitting in the makeup chair. 'He was drinking orange juice,' Michaels recalled (other accounts say it was milk or cereal), 'and he noticed something foreign in the bottom of the glass of orange juice,' Michaels recalled. 'He started not feeling well so they immediately took him to the emergency room.'

Coco Schwab rushed Bowie to the hospital, leaving the entire cast remaining on set. 'Everybody's standing around going, Oh, no, what are we going to do now?' Michaels recalled. 'Finally the big mucky-mucks came over and kind of looked me over.'

'She'll do,' they said.

'What do you mean?' Michaels asked.

She was told that they needed to shoot the scene where Newton opens the bathroom door and reveals he is an alien. Next thing Michaels knew, 'they took my hands, because I was very fair-complexioned, and they cut off all my fingernails and they put this stuff on the end of my fingers so it looked like there was just a nub—there were no nails—and covered up my hands with makeup.' The crew gathered in the bathroom and shot behind Michaels' back. 'Those were my hands that opened the door. She [Mary-Lou] reacted to me and she had a really great scream. She screamed bloody murder, and she's so scared that she peed herself.'

Michaels hadn't seen the script so the extreme reaction might have thrown her. Fortunately, she'd been involved in the prep. 'I'd been out in the parking lot with the special effects guys and they're showing me how they're mixing up pear juice to make it look like urine,' she said.

Michaels loved the British crew but was bemused at times. 'Their terminology was so different—they called dailies "rushes" and would come in with a handful of something and say, Mind your back, boys, mind your back.' Roeg was even more of a challenge for her. 'He had this very dry, British sense of humor which I didn't get all the time,' she said.

Bowie had also fallen prey to Roeg's wry wit after having his feelings hurt when Roeg told him he didn't read enough. Bowie, true to form, was constantly with a book; at the time, he'd been reading Wilhelm Reich's disturbing essay *Listen Little Man*.

Clark, Michaels recalled, was 'nice to me on the set [and] kind of kooky, like her character. Buck was a little ... hmm ... he kind of stood off by himself.' She did form a bond with Rip Torn, however. 'We'd be hanging out on the bus at Fenton Lake waiting for the next shots to be set up. I was singing Bonnie Raitt songs and carrying on. He would tell me about fishing. He loved to fish and was happy being in New Mexico.'

Then there was Bowie. 'I would just sit there and gaze at him.

He had that beautiful face and then he smiles and his teeth are a little bit strange, so he looked totally different when he would crack that smile. I found him to be witty and laid-back like he was one of the gang.'[17]

Albuquerque was also a stand-in for the city of for New York, much like Candy Clark was, she claimed, for Bowie as he exits World Enterprises Headquarters in that city and gets into the limo. Clark was perhaps being disingenuous when she said, 'They needed a scene when Newton is coming through the revolving door and getting into a limousine. At this time he [Bowie] was very superstitious and he wouldn't fly. I found a little orange wig and I volunteered because I really wanted to go to New York! For an afternoon I had on his clothes, his hat, a wig, and they set up some barricades.

'Not a lot of people were watching but the few that were there were saying, whispering, There's David Bowie! I knew our jawline wasn't even close, so you can see I have my hand up to my chin when I walk out and get in the limo.'[18]

'Maybe she did double him,' Swain allowed. 'He had some substance things going on—but he was actually there a lot.'

A shift to Santa Fe coincided with the 4th of July holiday. Most of the cast stayed in bungalows at the historic Pueblo-style La Fonda Hotel on the city's plaza. One evening, guests in its lobby witnessed Bowie walking through in full alien makeup—a sight that probably stayed with them for some time. 'Grown men screamed,' he told celebrity interviewer Rex Reed.[19]

La Fonda opened in 1922, but there had been an inn at the location since 1609, in prime position literally the end of the trail west. Billy The Kid was rumored to have washed dishes there and played a rollicking piano in the bar. In 1925, it became part of the

  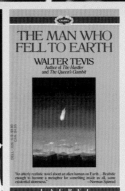 

TOP Jazz musician Artie Shaw, who acquired the film rights to Walter Tevis's novel *The Man Who Fell To Earth* in 1966. **BOTTOM ROW** A portrait of Tevis, plus three different editions of the book: the 1963 Gold Medal original, a 70s Laurel edition, and the Pan film tie-in version.

TOP ROW Cinematographer Tony Richmond and director Nicolas Roeg; David Bowie and his wife, Angie, at a Hollywood party, April 1975; an aerial view of filming at the First Presbyterian Church in Artesia, New Mexico. **BOTTOM ROW** A panoramic view of Artesia c.1913.

TOP ROW The Jemez Mountains, in whose shadows many of the film's outdoor scenes were shot; White Sands, which doubles as the alien Thomas Newton's home planet, Anthea. **BOTTOM ROW** The desert town of Los Lunas, New Mexico, c.1940; two more views of White Sands.

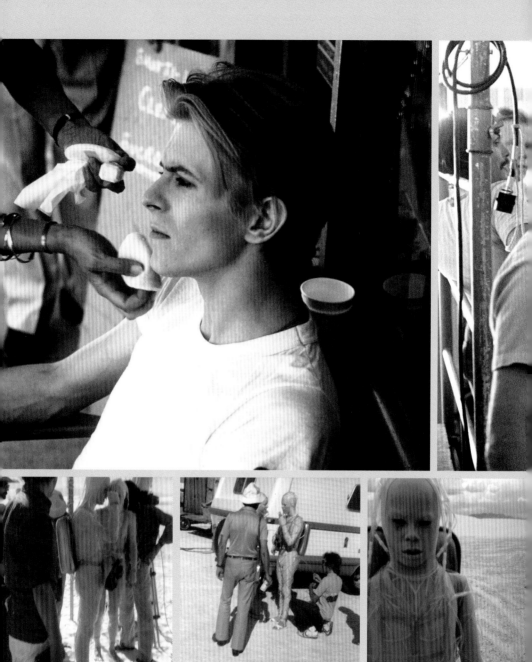

TOP ROW Bowie in the makeup chair; Nicolas Roeg (*left*) directs
Bowie (as Thomas Newton) and co-star Rip Torn (Nathan Bryce).
BOTTOM ROW A series of candid on-set photographs from the
collection of Kevin Weber, who plays Newton's son in the film.

TOP Nicolas Roeg (*left*), Tony Richmond (*center*), and Bowie on set.
BOTTOM ROW Two stills from the film, showing Bowie (Newton) and
Candy Clark (Mary-Lou) riding in a limo inspired by a scene from
Cracked Actor, and Newton preparing to undergo a series of tests.

storied Harvey House chain, which provided jobs for women (known as Harvey Girls) who wore trademark black-and-white outfits. La Fonda was 'informal yet elegant, relaxed, classy, often colorful,' writes Lesley Polling-Kempes in *The Harvey Girls*.[20] Bowie himself might have caused a scare at the hotel but he did not stay there, opting instead for an adobe home in the hills near town, accompanied by his assistant and gatekeeper Corinne Schwab.

Tensions were unusually high on that particular American Independence Day. The day before, the entire cast and crew had attended a lunch hosted by Michael Deeley at La Fonda, but that was a lull before the possible storm. Rumor had it that local bikers were incensed the British crew intended to work through the holiday, and the bikers planned to sabotage the shoot.

'Everyone was keyed up in case they heard the roar of motorbikes,' Perry said. 'It didn't happen.'

Instead, some took in the town's 4th of July parade, the highlight of which was a young boy perched atop a papier-mâché bull. Later that evening, in Albuquerque, David James, Bowie, and Roeg had a celebration of their own. 'Bowie and I and Nic celebrated my divorce from my first wife on the 4th of July, Independence Day.'[21] They toasted his newfound independence on a memorable, if next-day hazy, occasion.

On the 5th, however, there was more excitement. 'There was a shooting in the street when we were there, and I remember Duffy getting excited when he encountered a real-life police captain—just like something out of a movie,' Perry said.[22] The *Hollywood Reporter* was a bit less excitable. With a dateline of Los Alamos, where filming would progress, a reporter noted, 'Security protection has been reinforced and a one mile off-limits band has been established here around the rocket launching pad set of Nicolas Roeg's *The Man Who fell To Earth* in the wake of a nocturnal shootout last week at an earlier set outside Santa Fe.'

Santa Fe police were said to be searching for four people, including a driver, who overpowered security guard Louis Espinosa, handcuffing him to his car's steering wheel, taking his 9mm gun and 'breaking into the $300,000 adobe mansion housing expensive television equipment used in the picture.'

No one was present at the time of the attempted break-in. The quick-thinking guard honked his horn, garnering a neighbor's attention and then borrowed the neighbor's .22, with which he shot at but didn't strike the attempted thieves. 'The burglars fled without any loot, leaving in their wake bullet riddled doors and walls,' the report added.[23]

That episode led to day-and-night security being doubled at the Los Alamos location, with guards positioned around the ranch where Bowie was staying. There is, however, the possibility that it didn't happen. Steve Shroyer and John Lifflander, two reporters on assignment for *Creem* magazine, reported in their piece 'Spaced Out In The Desert' that an assistant working on the film told them about the alleged shooting, 'A guard got drunk on the set one night and started firing off his pistol. When everyone arrived he said he'd been attacked by a band of youths. He had to say something, he didn't want to get canned.'[24]

Love and murder were in the air—onstage, anyway—at sunset on July 8 when Bowie, Governor and Mrs. Apodaca, and the already legendary singer Odetta attended the Santa Fe Opera's outdoor performance of *Carmen* at its intimate hilltop setting. It's not known if the disparate personalities discussed the passionate piece.

The *Hollywood Reporter* kept its focus on the film's business side, noting that a deal was signed with Mayfair Productions for mobile location facilities.[25] Likely they were more above board than one creative individual Routh remembered. 'There was a guy called Mickey, and for some reason he'd managed to con British Lion into allowing a complete set of metal scaffolding. The film company paid for the rental of the scaffolding and paid for it to be sent back to England,' Routh said, although that's not exactly what happened. 'He actually kept it here [Los Angeles] and for the next ten years rented it out! He ran his office sitting in the Farmers Market [an industry meeting spot at Third and Fairfax Streets] by a pay phone! We had a lot of people who were very … enterprising.'[26]

On the 10th, *Variety* noted, 'National Film Finance Corporation took a piece of the British Lion feature.' It was a preview of financial maneuvers to come.

In mid-July, Angela Bowie swept into New Mexico to visit her virtually estranged husband with four-year-old Zowie in tow. She had few friends on site ('Angie was pretty strange,' said Perry[27]) but Alan Swain remembers her as 'interesting, almost like being Bowie. We never saw stuff like that out here too much.'

That she was with him in New Mexico at all was 'surprising,' Angie allowed, 'as he was doing everything in his power to try and alienate me and replace my counseling with drug dealers and … the assistant, Corinne Schwab.' Still, she went at the behest of her husband. 'To prove he was not out of control, he insisted that I come … and bring Zowie. We would witness his clarity.'[28]

Angie's time on location couldn't have been much fun for her.

'All I did was cook for David and Candy and Nic,' she recalled, 'and then endure the three- or four-hour drive every day to Lake Fenton. There was a snake in the house they had rented for us, so I was pretty cranky about Zowie's safety for the first few days.' She waited for such blatant safety issues to be resolved until 'snake was safely removed and empty pool covered up until I was satisfied that everything was safe for Marion [Skene, Zowie's nanny] and Zowie before I left!'[29]

Despite the awkward situation, she found her husband to be in good spirits. 'David was very happy on the set. He always enjoyed learning a new medium and jousting with the artistic free-for-all that resulted in making films or an album,' she told me. But that didn't mean she returned to Los Angeles on a positive note. 'I was so disgusted with Nic Roeg, David, and Corinne Schwab, who tried to act like some middle-school clique that I banished the state of New Mexico from my mind.'[30]

Zowie, still some ways off from being a preteen middle-schooler, was nonetheless 'a little mischievous,' according to George Perry, although he tempered that by adding, 'He was a really nice little boy, terrific. Children of rock stars are usually indulged. He wasn't.'[31]

'Zowie was very polite,' Swain said. 'He wasn't like we were: wild ruffians.'[32] The youngster was given a small movie camera by Roeg, possibly influencing the career choice of future director Duncan Jones on the spot.

Finally George Perry had a window for his interview with Roeg—but it came with a catch. Brian Duffy, the firebrand and loose cannon of a photographer renowned for his fashion shots and the exquisite cover of Bowie's album *Aladdin Sane*, decided he would come along on the interview and get a few photos.

While Duffy and Bowie got along famously ('They were both autodidacts from working class backgrounds,' Perry attested), Duffy had previously failed to endear himself to Candy Clark. After proposing a fashion shoot ('Candy beamed,' Perry said), Perry asked Duffy where he was going to get the clothes.

'Don't worry about it, I'll fix everything,' the photographer assured her.

'Ominous words,' Perry said. 'We go see Candy in the trailer, and he [Duffy] has a black bag that you would put in a trash can but it's full of clothes. Candy's smiling and happy, thinking she's going to be a great fashion star. Duffy tells her she looks great.'

'Okay, what am I going to wear?'

Duffy emptied the bag onto the floor and item after item of well-worn denim fell out: jeans, shorts, tops, all likely local thrift-store finds.

'What the hell is that?' Clark asked, affronted.

'This is your outfit.'

'I can't wear stuff like that.'

'You can, you will look wonderful.' Then, adding insult to her injury, Duffy added, 'What I want to get is the white trash look,' hitting an exposed nerve since that downhome look was precisely the image Clark wanted to shake off and move away from.

'She went into hysterics,' Perry said. 'She screamed and he beat a hasty retreat.'[33]

The interview with Roeg did not pan out much better.

'Nic and I are talking,' Perry recalled. 'Nic is doing most of the talking. He was a great talker, he expounds his ideas, some are quite outlandish. Duffy says, Here, you aren't going to let him get away with that, are you? That is bullshit!'

The director initially didn't flinch, holding firm that those were his views. But the calm demeanor didn't last for long. 'Duffy tells Nic how he should be directing the film. Within a minute or two, a furious argument erupts, and my interview is shot. The argument went on for several hours. At 2am in the bar at La Fonda, they were exchanging blows,' Perry sighed. 'It had got to that stage.'

David James had no such drama with his fellow photographer. He and Duffy 'talked shop and had a couple of drinks together,' James said. 'He was very cool. I liked him a lot.'[34]

Emotions, real and otherworldly, were also running high at the house where Bowie was staying. Angie had decamped and the snake had been removed, but there was still another problem. 'David got a fixation that the house had bad spirits,' Linda De Vetta said. 'He was very into that [the occult] although he didn't voice it that much.'

Bowie's dalliance with dark and/or unusual spiritual works at this time is in fact well documented. 'He managed to drag me up there with him one evening and wanted to do a circle of candlelight to exorcise the spirits,' De Vetta continued. 'I thought, How did I get roped into this? I guess because I was quite into astrology and he thought, Oh I've got one here.'

De Vetta said she didn't actually feel any malevolent presence. 'It's strange because I am someone who actually does feel things. There's a lot more going on than we know anything about. I went along with David because he wanted me to. He felt he exorcised it and got on with it.'[35]

Bowie had another strange request during filming when he said he wouldn't allow pig's blood to be used in a scene, prompting Tony Richmond to provide the human blood—the one and only time he did such a thing on set and in the name of art.

Filming also incorporated Fenton Lake, at 7,650 feet a high altitude body of water whose locale was so extreme that some remember oxygen being brought along. 'I imagine Bowie had oxygen,' Michael Deeley said, as well as 'people who were working hardest, carrying things, pushing dollies and stuff—they needed it.'[36]

Tony Richmond concurred. 'The driver that used to drive Nic Roeg and I to work, he had an oxygen tank in the back, and we'd have a whiff of oxygen in the morning.'[37]

Routh was more dismissive. 'People would be paying a lot of attention to themselves if they thought they needed oxygen,' she said, 'unless it was something you were taking to perk you up.'[38]

'You don't need oxygen at eight thousand feet,' Graeme Clifford said. 'I go skiing higher than that.'[39]

Oxygen aside, Deeley was surprised to find one establishment en route. 'There was a bar open on the way out,' he recalled. 'Imagine finding a bar open at that time of the morning.'[40]

Swain took it in his usual stride. 'There was a little bar called La Cueva up there by the lake, and we'd stop in on the way back home every night, buy a bunch of chips and whatever they had, a bunch of beer. When we were filming up at Fenton, we'd take two busloads of extras and crew to the mountains every day. We kind of ended up dividing into two groups of people—the ones who liked to drink and smoke and party in one bus, and the ones that didn't in the other bus.'[41]

Fenton Lake was used several times in the film. It was the house by the dock where Newton lived, and Bryce observed from the other side. It was also the body of water into which Newton's arriving capsule splashed down.

'The first explosion wasn't quite big enough,' Swain said, 'so they made a nice big explosion that looked good in the movie. The next day there were thousands of dead fish. The explosion killed all the fish in the lake. The whole summer the Youth Conservation Corps kids picked out the fish. The Fish Department wasn't too upset because they wanted to clean and drain the lake anyway, so that was their excuse to drain the lake and fill it back up.'

Rip Torn was in his element. 'He would disappear all the time, fishing,' Swain said. 'He was kind of a heavy drinker.' Such indulgence was likely in play when Torn (as Bryce) was driving the jet boat, headed for Newton's house. All of a sudden he called out, 'How do I stop this thing?' and proceeded to run into the dock. 'Nobody got hurt or anything but it was pretty funny,' Swain laughed.

Torn was not the only one fishing, however. 'We went fishing one time with David Bowie,' said Swain. 'Bowie wants to fish so we set him up a rig. He got bored kind of quick but he did do a little fishing.' Alas, he did not catch anything.

Swain also entertained the kids on a raft that was also serving as a platform. 'I took Zowie and Si Litvinoff's kid and some other bigwig's kid out there on that thing,' he recalled, 'and they yelled at me, You do realize if you drown the children you're going to not have a job.'[42]

Children on location were generally well looked after, but there was an incident when one of Litvinoff's children smashed his toe at the Hilton in Albuquerque. Howard Rubin went into overdrive. 'Si's a lawyer,' he said. 'So we had that little contretemps, Si and I. I said, you don't want to sue these guys.'[43] Litvinoff backed down.

Lifflander and Shroyer, the reporters from *Creem*, took note of, among other things, the fans and groupies who had followed their idol to New Mexico, and Swain saw these people in action, too. 'He had groupies—a group of three, two guys and a girl. They were really weird. The girl was giving blowjobs to get onto the set. One time I had my BB gun out there at Fenton and was shooting BBs at cans. Bowie came over and wanted to shoot BBs, so we let him shoot the gun for a while.

'He smoked cigarettes back then,' Swain recalled. 'He smoked a couple. As soon as he walked away, those guys scrambled over there and started grabbing all the cigarette butts and trying to pick the BBs off the ground. I said, How do you know that Bowie shot that one? It could have been one I shot. They followed the show around pretty much the whole time. They were from New York or something, total fanatics into Bowie.'

On departing Fenton Lake, the set was struck, the house torn down, the docks dismantled. 'I wish they'd kept that dock up here,' said Manny Sanchez, the park manager at Fenton Lake State Park. 'It would have been beautiful.'[44]

Los Alamos was the next stop. Rubin had high hopes for the location and one of its key features. 'I really wanted to see the Linear Accelerator, the one they shoot the light beams through,' he said. The Linear Accelerator, or LINAC, was installed in 1972, and is one of the nation's most powerful proton linear accelerators. Its eight hundred mega-electron volts send beam current to five major facilities that have scientific or defense mandates. It would surely have made for an interesting scene, but it was not to be.

'I did everything I could because they really wanted to film. I pulled a lot of strings, but they didn't get to,' Rubin said.[45] His influence and connections would be crucial when it came to acquiring permits to shoot at White Sands National Monument, where they were headed after a few final days in Albuquerque.

★

Joyce Haber, the doyenne of industry reporting for the *Los Angeles Times*, reported on July 24 that Bowie was interested in playing Frank Sinatra in a biopic. The influential Haber visited Bowie on set in New Mexico but was chagrined to be kept waiting for a long time. 'Bowie is pleasant, but the wait to get to him isn't. It can easily take eleven hours—and end up with only twenty-five minutes for a profile,' she wrote, adding that his publicist, Steve Jaffe, had told her, 'David is the happiest actor I have ever seen.'[46] Jaffe also gave the runaround to the two reporters from *Creem*.

On July 28, *Variety* noted that Constantin Films had picked up German and Austrian rights to the film, and on August 1 it acknowledged the signing of Bernie Casey, who'd play 'an ominous and enigmatic member of establishment power and authority.'[47] Casey, a native of West Virginia, was devoted equally to art and athleticism, eventually giving up a high-profile National Football League career to focus on acting. He was not, however, Roeg's first choice. His priority was 'a black man who could dive,' said Litvinoff. Two other actors under consideration, Lou Gossett Jr. and Roscoe Lee Brown, could not, but Casey dove effortlessly.

Casey's scenes have a kind of gravitas, and the swimming pool shot makes good use of southwestern light and color. Casey embraces Claudia Jennings (Litvinoff's girlfriend at the time) to great effect. Candy Clark put it well. 'I remember that scene with her hand and the long fingernails squeezing Casey's shoulders. The contrast of the two skin tones was very striking.'[48]

After that, filming recommenced in Albuquerque, with the second story of an abandoned building (formerly Washburn's Clothing and then the offices of the Albuquerque Department of Housing and

Development) at 122 Second Street and Gold Street SW becoming Newton's elaborate apartment-as-prison. A favorite waiter from the Hilton named Albert Nelson was cajoled into playing the servant who brought Newton his trolley of drinks—and his nervousness plus lack of screen experience forced several takes. 'He was terrified he couldn't say the lines,' Routh remembered.

Governor Jerry Apodaca visited the building with his wife Clara that day and gifted Roeg with one of five hundred 'Nueva Mexico' T-shirts Rubin had made. When it was later pointed out to the governor that 'Nueva' should have been 'Nuevo,' it signaled the beginning of the end for Rubin and his film commission, which was garnering an uneasy relationship with local actors' groups, the Chamber of Commerce, and now Apodaca. 'The misspelling of the name of the state caused even the governor to begin questioning Rubin's effectiveness,' the *Albuquerque Tribune* would report in a front-page story.[49]

Newton's apartment/prison was excessively decorated for a reason. 'It's a human zoo, rather like at the end of *2001* where they put a human who went to another planet in a sort of Dorchester fuck-all suite because that's what they thought they'd like,' Roeg told Dave Pirie and Chris Petit of *Time Out.* 'Newton's situation is the reverse: he's in his own zoo, surrounded by the most luxurious things.'[50]

Everyone was enlivened when rock'n'roll legend Fats Domino did a show at the Hilton Cabaret on August 5, especially Bowie and Geoff MacCormack. The childhood friends had bought 'Blueberry Hill,' Domino's signature tune, when they were both nine.

Scott McCoy reviewed the performance for the *Albuquerque Journal.* 'There are no frills in this show,' he wrote. 'No comedians selling underwear and warming up the audience. It's no fooling around. He's here to give the people what they came to hear.'[51]

Domino wasn't up for entertaining his fans after the show, however, no matter their level of fame or stature. 'We stumbled backstage with all the swagger and confidence of two guys who'd just polished off twenty-eight bottles of Budweiser,' MacCormack later wrote.[52] But Mr. Domino, it transpired, was not available for a private audience.

WHITE NOISE

CHAPTER FIVE

'**A**fter seeing the extraordinary landscape of the White Sands, it prompted me to think of this: strangers always see something that is unfamiliar, you know?' Nic Roeg later noted.[1] Action, artistry, and sheer physical ardor culminated during filming at White Sands National Monument and its adjacent Missile Site. The monument, 275 square miles of white gypsum dunes, some reaching heights of sixty feet, is the very definition of lunar white and alien landscape. 'It was just like we were on the moon,' Martin Samuel told me.[2]

Located fifteen miles southwest of the Air Force town of Alamogordo (actor Warren Oates, who likely passed through town around this time, affectionately called it 'Out of my Gordo'), the preserve's pristine dunes are created when rain and snowmelt combine to dissolve gypsum in nearby mountains, which then descends to the playa and dries and shapes in the desert conditions of wind and heat. The adjacent White Sands Missile Range is the site of the first manmade atomic explosion. On July 16, 1945, the blast sent up a rainbow-colored cloud and created a crater at its Trinity Missile Site location.

Logistics for White Sands were unwieldy. First, there were permits to get. Howard Rubin's ties to the governor were helpful, but still he admitted, 'White Sands was hard.' In addition to the exterior (Anthea) shots, there was the rocket launch, featuring an appearance by Apollo 13 astronaut Captain James Lovell (who, in real life, uttered the famous line, 'Houston, we have a problem,' when that spacecraft ran into serious difficulty. He later called the mission 'a successful failure.')

The scene in question required 250 extras, some of whom were airmen, and all of whom had to have top secret clearances to get on the base, as did the actors and crew. Then there was the weather. In August, daytime temperatures hovered around 104 degrees but would drop dramatically during evening shooting.

'The heat was hard on the UK cast and crew,' Litvinoff said. 'They were not used to heat.'[3]

'It was really hot and the British crew was dropping like flies,' Swain remembered. 'A lot of British guys got heat prostration and ended up in the hospital. Us locals had to carry the weight a little bit more.'[4]

Restrictions on vehicles meant items had to be brought in on a sled, and the homey monorail—Newton's transportation system on his home planet—malfunctioned and broke down a lot. The structure sat atop a truck that wouldn't start, and as a result it had to be pulled by a team of large horses. The train's look—like two soccer goals joined together and covered in sod spray-painted yellow— was something of a disappointment. Roeg, for one, was said to be enraged. Bowie, however, found it 'sweet.'[5]

Brian Eatwell's intention had been for it to look like an organic conveyance that suggested a culture on its last legs. 'Brian designed the other planet on the White Sands, with the train,' May Routh told me. White Sands took precautions to remain as pristine as possible. 'No automobiles were allowed, nothing trucked in that could affect the sand. Two horses were given, plus nine prisoners from the penitentiary!'[6]

'We were the first people to shoot at White Sands,' Tony Richmond said. In fact, they weren't: *King Solomon's Mines* had used the location, as had a handful of other films. But they were one of the few, and it was difficult. 'Everything you took in had to be brought in by horse on a sleigh. You couldn't use any vehicles. It was difficult because of the train, that transport thing, whatever you want to call it—it was weird. When that thing moved, it was pulled by horses. White Sands was wonderful to see.'[7]

It was captured magnificently on film thanks to Richmond, possibly benefiting from Roeg's experience as a DP on *Lawrence Of Arabia*. 'Tony had a good relationship with Nic,' Perry noted. '[It can be] hard when you have a director who's a good DP.'[8]

'Tony's not easy,' Howard Rubin added. 'He has his own ideas. Wonderful cinematographer: he was at the top of his game. To get [what he filmed] was not always easy; the sun was not always cooperating. I think one day they had hail.'[9]

Clear skies prevailed at White Sands, and Brian Duffy didn't miss the opportunity to take some exquisite photos. Geoff MacCormack recalled rising tensions as they waited in the hotel lobby while Bowie took his time getting ready for the shoot. All the while Duffy was losing the light. Still, the resultant pictures of the star are stunning. 'Bowie kept his body still,' his son Chris Duffy explained. 'Risky, really risky.'[10]

At White Sands, Bowie, Clark, Kevin Weber, and the young girl who played Newton and Mary-Lou's daughter all had to wear space costumes. These were designed by Routh but made by Tom Burman, a makeup artist based in North Hollywood. Special effects were in Burman's blood: his father, Ellis Burman Sr., did makeup for, among others, the 1941 film *The Wolf Man*.

'My background was that I worked on the very first *Planet Of The Apes* [1968] and the man who won the Academy Award for that, John Chambers, [he and I] started the very first makeup studio—the first independent makeup studio doing prosthetics,' the younger Burman said. 'The big secret was that we started not just to do motion pictures and television. We were working with the CIA to teach them how to make disguises.'[11] (Actor John Goodman played Chambers in the 2012 film *Argo*.)

Burman and his team were responsible for making (not designing) the cat's eyes, the spacesuits, and the appliances that enabled genitals, fingernails, ears, belly buttons, and toenails to disappear. 'I don't think anybody had ever done anything like that—that extensive in terms of body appliances before,' Burman said. He added that he'd done similar work once before on *A Man Called Horse*. 'This was kind of like an extension of that.'

Burman went to Albuquerque to take body casts and 'make appliances to cover whatever we wanted covered,' he said. 'Bowie was great.' Burman's assistants, Eddie Enriquez and Tom Herbert, observed as Burman set the makeup and prepared the suits, and the two men took over when Burman returned to his studio in Los Angeles to work on other projects.

The spacesuits—known as cooling suits—as realized by Burman were an elaborate creation. They were made from a kind of Lycra. 'The fabric was real sheer, a four-way stretch that had a kind of silvery … it was a shiny, almost pearlescent Lycra, very fine, almost like nylon stockings but a little heavier weave. It was a kind of silvery color, and your skin showed through it. We got it from International Silks & Woolens.'

The tubes on the backpack—a prototype hydration pack—were meant to highlight its cooling properties as the liquid ran through. However, getting the liquid to move involved creative strategies. 'What we did is we took one of those little home fire extinguishers and we emptied it,' Burman explained. 'We used an air compressor, put 160 pounds of air into it and bleeder valves. We put just enough liquid inside the tubing so we could run an air tube down to the bottom of it so it would blow little bubbles, little segments of water through the suit. And then by gravity it would fall back down.

'The only real challenge was to make sure the air pressure was up on each one of the tanks on their backs. Being small tanks, they would last probably about thirty minutes, then we'd recharge them for the next shot.'

Kevin Weber encountered some problems with the suit. 'My life support kept leaking and when I got wet, the cold desert night here was just that cold.' The clear plastic shoes the aliens wore also presented a challenge for the thirteen-year-old. 'The shoes were hard to walk [in] down the sand dune. I actually took the whole family down one take when I slipped—and down we went.'[12]

Weber talked to Esther Padilla from the *Albuquerque Journal* and spoke enthusiastically about his arrival in Alamogordo, where they were based during the White Sands sequences. 'After we had a fun plane ride, we were met at the airport and taken to the hotel. That night we dined with Lee Remick [girlfriend of assistant director Kip Gowans] and Rip Torn. Candy Clark and David Bowie were also there.'[13]

Because he was in the Screen Actors Guild, Kevin had to have a chaperone during filming. His father fulfilled that obligation. He gave Padilla a run-down of his son's day, starting with his 7:30am makeup call. 'There were four main makeup people, one for each child and each star. Each actor also had his own car to transport him to the set, and at the set, each actor was provided with his own air-conditioned dressing room,' the older Weber explained. 'After makeup, we'd go to the filming site and wait for Kevin's call. At the set the costume is sewn on, so Kevin kept his on all day.' Kevin's day ended at 10:30pm with another half-hour to have the makeup removed. 'It's very uncomfortable to take the makeup off,' he said.

Bowie had the relative luxury of being able to fall asleep at will (kind of a reverse narcolepsy). Famed LSD guru Augustus Owsley Stanley III (aka Bear) had perfected a similar ability when he learned self-hypnosis as a teenager during an interlude at a psychiatric hospital. 'If you do something with your mind, you can go to sleep in about a minute. I can sleep anywhere at any time,' he said.[14] Bowie, notoriously resistant to hypnosis, might well have learned to train his mind in a similar fashion and put it to good use during makeup calls.

'He's so marvelously controlled, David,' Samuel recalled. 'It was about a three-hour job and they would kind of wheel him in in the middle of the night, maybe 4:30 in the morning or something, and he would just stay asleep while they did his body, took out the fingernails and the breasts. I would prepare the hair to do the bald cap and then they'd wake him up. Linda would do his facial makeup.'[15]

Much easier was doing makeup for Torn. 'He was fine for me, easy for me, and also in those days I didn't put makeup on men unless it was a character or unless there was something that needed to be hidden or disguised,' De Vetta said. 'I liked the natural look. So many people,' she sighed, 'look with unseeing eyes.'

Although she had help from Burman's assistants when extensive makeup was called for (at White Sands; the scene where Newton reveals his true look to Mary-Lou), and Burman himself when the hefty, aged Mary-Lou needed foam rubber prosthetics as well as makeup, De Vetta was otherwise on her own.

'What changed in the script was this incredible time lapse where Buck [Farnsworth] had to age,' she told me. 'That wasn't in the original script. I said I really needed help, so an English makeup man, Neville Smallwood, came over to be my assistant and help me. While I was busy doing prosthetic makeup, Neville went up on the set. He'd done makeup on one of the actors and Nic hated it. They had a run-in, and Neville came back to the makeup room and said, That's it, I'm going. So I was ON MY OWN.'[16]

The situation wasn't a whole lot better for Routh, who wasn't thrilled with the cooling suits. 'I'd designed this outfit ... I'd never thought about how the liquid was going to get round. It had huge pumps in the back. I thought, They're so ugly! What am I going to do? They've ruined my name on the film!' she fretted. 'I was slightly taken aback by that. I could see where they'd glued the plastic piping together that when they started moving, the things were leaking but because the liquid was pale pink, it didn't show. But I was dying of a heart attack because of little things that were going wrong.'[17]

August 14 was a particularly memorable day for Kevin Weber. 'On August 14, I turned fourteen, and I died that day in the movie. Rip Torn, David, and I believe Candy Clark and her brother threw a small party for me when I got back to the hotel.'[18] While Weber wasn't the only kid to have a birthday during the shoot—De Vetta and Richmond's son George turned four in Albuquerque—Weber can still claim having had 'Happy Birthday' sung to him by David Bowie when he turned all of fourteen.

Many remember being impressed or even starstruck when they met astronaut Jim Lovell. 'Even Bowie feels strange meeting James Lovell,' Roeg recalled.[19] Martin Samuel took pictures of his young son with the astronaut, and May Routh wasted no time getting an autograph. 'Brian was horrified,' she said, recalling him saying, 'What are you doing asking someone for their autograph? That's not the kind of done thing.'[20] She took no notice.

The otherwise unflappable De Vetta was equally smitten, for a time. 'We were stuck way on the horizon in White Sands,' she said. 'I could see them [Lovell and others] walking toward and Tony ends up in fits of laughter with me. [He said,] I've never seen you starstruck in my entire life. I was starstruck over James Lovell. He signed a couple hundred-dollar bills.

'Starstruck as I was,' she added, 'we then had dinner with him [in Alamogordo], and he was one of the most boring men in the world. I couldn't wait to get away.'[21]

Candy Clark, meanwhile, spoke to the local Alamogordo paper about a man she found far from boring, and who had become her favorite director. Roeg, she said, 'makes shooting interesting and has great ideas.' The reporter, Jimmie Kay Dale, described Clark as 'vivacious' and the role she was playing as 'a girl whose days are numbered in the most mysterious love affair of the century.'[22]

While they were still at White Sands, Nile Southern made a road trip with his father, Terry, leaving Los Angeles's Chateau Marmont Hotel at the invitation of Rip Torn. Southern had been working on an adaptation of his novel *Blue Movie*. 'I think he wanted a break, it was time to get out of town,' Nile Southern said. Terry also thought it'd be a great opportunity for his son to get in some time behind the wheel, despite Nile, at fourteen, not yet being eligible for a learner's permit. They headed out in 'a rental car, some kind of Ford. My dad favored Mustangs so maybe it was a Mustang, but I doubt if it was anything too top notch. He didn't have an expense account that I know of.'

The road itself didn't present a big challenge for the teenager. 'Because it was so flat and straight, those roads were great to drive,' he said. A teenager, he was only somewhat aware of Bowie's work but, in an unusual twist, already a fan of Brian Eno.

Terry Southern didn't miss the chance to show his son the many offbeat roadside curiosities along the way. 'I'd never been out into the desert west,' Nile recalled, '[and] there's the roadside attractions of snakes and weird things. My father, being from Texas, was sort of used to those kinds of things so he made sure we stopped and looked into the snake pits.'

One incident stayed with the young man. 'We were going up into a more mountainous area and there was a motorcycle driver who'd had an accident that was really grisly, his foot was dangling, severed. I thought, Bad things can happen out here in the desert.'[23]

Bad things, surely, but magical ones as well, as a story he later wrote illustrated.

RED HEAD ON WHITE SAND—MY FIRST (AND ONLY) ENCOUNTER WITH DAVID BOWIE
By Nile Southern

We took a road trip from LA to New Mexico—to visit Rip Torn on set. Terry knew Nic, and I had seen it casually summarized in the *Hollywood Reporter*'s 'Films In Production' listing—so cool to see Nic Roeg, David Bowie, and New Mexico mentioned in the same breath. I think Terry was asked, probably by Si [Litvinoff], to cover the shooting for a magazine story—but no story materialized, and we really just ended up taking this road trip so I could learn to drive. We were to show up at the Alamogordo Missile Range—350 miles of white sand. I had my Super-8 camera, and was constantly filming stuff. We met up with Rip alongside some creek about fifty miles from the location—he had set up his own little day camp getaway there—and treated us to glorious freshly grilled fish, beer, and probably a little pot—though I was too young to partake.

When we arrived at the missile range, there were checkpoints and eerie displays of warplanes, rockets, bombs, and missiles—very surreal. Most bizarre were the limitless cascading hills of white sand—and the idea that somewhere, behind a dune, we would find the massive film crew. I was in love with moviemaking, and when we finally found the set, I was very impressed by how many cameras Nic had in play, the generator trucks, lights blazing—all against the white-out backdrop of white sand and blue sky. They were shooting the scenes set on the water-depleted 'home' planet—the barren wasteland the White Sands Missile Range represented—and the pitiful state of the alien's withering family. In one shot, Candy Clark, in full reflective gold skin suit and cat-eye contact lenses holds her dying child, and in another, shot from a long distance away, she stands holding a curved Plexiglas—as she sends a distress signal. I filmed a lot of the crew, Nic, and actors preparing the scenes—which, because of the intense heat and reflected light everywhere, required giant umbrellas at the various camera stations. Walkie-talkies were used to good advantage, and most of the women crewmembers were dressed in shorts and cowboy hats to deal with the heat. A few scenes involved the bizarre-looking space vehicle—a massive, Tootsie Roll–like orange/yellow vehicle made of papier-mâché—that actually moved along a sturdy track of eye-beams. As the light was fading, the space vehicle got stuck in the sand, and the crew worked feverishly to get it out. Finally, by sunset, a cowboy wrangler utilized a team of horses to pull the vehicle along and get it back on track. Everyone's spirits were lifted at that moment—and the spacecraft's headlamp—making it look like a kind of Cyclops beast, turned on.

In the early evening, we settled into the motel, where the production was staying. There was a night scene to be shot later, and Nic suggested my dad and I visit David Bowie's room, and 'try to get him to eat something!'

Bowie was stunning, sitting shirtless on the bed, grinning ear to ear under his black Stetson hat. As I recall, the beige blanket was pulled up to his waist, and he seemed to relish holding forth from this position—a combination glamorous cowboy, bad boy and Alien. There was a massive square of waxed paper on the bed—and on it, a small mountain of cocaine. No wonder Nic was concerned (and not there)—I later heard that Bowie was under strict orders not to indulge. There weren't many of us in the room, and probably my dad (and everyone) held back on tooting in front of me. As I looked around, I noticed Candy looking radiant, sexy, and continuously smiling—her hair wet and dark, skin moist in a white terrycloth bathrobe—her knees pulled up to her chin. She, too, was enjoying her role as freshly ravished giggler—and I guess sitting on the carpeted floor outside the bathroom was less obvious than sitting down in that state on David's bed.

My father casually said we were going to order room service, and asked David if he wanted anything. 'No thanks, Terry, I just ate Candy!' came Bowie's classic reply. Candy blushed and smiled, drawing her knees up even more. We were all floored and laughing— David had a way of disarming while also frolicking in the beauty and excitement of juicy life. For Terry, who wrote the novel *Candy*, the double-entendre was no doubt all the more perfect.

That night, we all met at another location, which was the press conference outside the space launch pad—where Alien Thomas Newton is whisked into a limo, amid press frenzy. The spaceship is in the background and there were well over one hundred people there, between the crew, actors and extras. The atmosphere was very much like Fellini's *8½*—and there was a similar vibe of excitement and mystery. Nic took my dad and I up to the top of the launch scaffolding. It was very high up—like being on a Ferris wheel looking over a teeming fair. With the movie lights, technicians, crowd, trailers and generators, the atmosphere was exhilarating. Nic looked like a little boy at the height of his own fun. He took me aside and said, 'Isn't this great?!? This is what moviemaking is all about—it's like childhood—like making magic!'

Nic impulsively asked Terry to appear among the journalists for the final shot. Terry had a knack for being in the right place at the right time—so, I think Nic picked up on that, and thought it'd be great (and sort of funnily true) to have Terry clued-into the significance of Newton's arrival. During the shot, one of the press members turns to Terry, who seems to be with the entourage.

'Terry Southern! Terry Southern! What do you make of all this?'

'Well, it's unprecedented,' Terry says. And indeed it was.

★

As shooting in New Mexico gathered to a close, many reflected on a consummate occurrence when a giant cumulus cloud appeared outside of Los Lunas. 'We were convoying and all of a sudden the camera truck, director, DPs, and everybody pulled over to the side of the road and pulled out the cameras and shot the cloud,' Alan Swain said. 'It was really cool—kind of looked like a UFO. That was a lucky thing to get that kind of iconic shot in the show.'[24]

'A great cloud just hung there all day,' Richmond added. 'Stunning.'[25]

As goodbyes were said, the producers gave Alan Swain some money and told him to go to school and continue to study. Instead, he went into the movie business. Kevin Weber made plans to come west and visit Tom Herbert at Burman Studios and check out behind-the-scenes Hollywood. David Bowie decamped to his hilltop Los Angeles dwelling at 1349 Stone Canyon Road to work on the film's soundtrack—retaining Samuel as his hair stylist—and similarly the majority of the remaining cast and crew had gigs lined up already, too.

Some filming had been done in Los Angeles: Gil Turner's liquor store and Tower Records, both on the Sunset Strip; Newton's in-his-cups coda at MacArthur Park; and an empty swimming pool where the outer space love scene was filmed. ('They were jumping up and down,' Routh explained.[26])

'When we had to shoot scenes in LA, the liquor store, the Kabuki bar … I couldn't bring any crew,' Richmond said. 'It was rather wonderful.'[27]

Los Angeles and London shored up shooting, but the movie owes a big debt to the Land of Enchantment that played a dramatic, versatile, and entirely captivating role at a very good price.

BEING GENIUSES TOGETHER
CHAPTER SIX

For a director in the enviable position of having three artistically acclaimed films—*Performance, Walkabout,* and *Don't Look Now*—in his portmanteau, to be kept waiting for several hours in February New York City might have been both a trial and an affront. But Roeg expressed no anger or irritation about having to cool his heels for a meeting in David Bowie's apartment while the singer finished making music.

'He kept recording when I arrived and kept calling to say that he wouldn't be long,' Roeg later said. 'I kept waiting.'[1]

Writer Ed Kelleher thought that, after an hour, Bowie figured he'd blown it and continued to delay his return. When the recalcitrant star arrived five hours late, he and Roeg talked until the early hours. 'Don't worry, I'm going to do it,' Bowie said about the film offer.[2]

Geoff MacCormack said *Walkabout* and *Don't Look Now* 'simplified David's decision to work with Roeg,' and although the cagey star feigned ignorance of Roeg's work, he was clearly familiar with *Performance*.[3] Bowie later said of the meeting, 'It didn't take me long to realize the man was a genius.'[4]

What Bowie thought of the script is a mystery. Author Vivien Claire writes in her 1977 book about the star, 'Bowie liked the character but not the script.'[5] However, he told Rex Reed he hadn't read the script, instead making decisions guided by blind faith and instinct. 'I have total confidence,' he said. 'Is that awful?'[6]

Bowie often distanced himself from the label 'rock star,' and while he may have created several iconic characters, he didn't apply that somewhat limiting term to his own persona. 'Who wants a career in rock'n'roll?' he chided Rex Reed.[7]

Born David Robert Jones in Brixton, South London, on January 8, 1947, he soon moved to Bromley, a significantly more suburban southern suburb. Entranced by music, he parlayed his talents into a riveting career that was both single-minded and askance, as if he were always searching for a better fit. By 1974, he'd gone through several permutations and personae and was casting about for a film role into which he could spread his sometimes soaring, sometimes fledgling wings. One plan was to turn George Orwell's *1984* into a film, but Orwell's widow was not interested. So, when Roeg came calling, Bowie was understandably intrigued.

Nicolas Roeg was born in London on August 15, 1928. A career in film was always on the cards and, after completing his national service he rose through the ranks from tea boy to clapper to assistant director. Interestingly, his film work began in earnest in 1947, the same year Bowie was born. While working at Marylebone Studios, he fell under the spell of Marcel Carne's *Les Enfants Du Paradis*, 'with its inextricable melding of performers' lives with the somewhat more real events on stage,' as Roeg biographer Joseph Lanza put it, before pointing out, 'It will later become one of the many inspirations behind *The Man Who Fell To Earth*.'[8]

Leaving a prestigious and secure position as a sought-after cameraman, Roeg opted for directing, working closely with David Cammell. Roeg was sitting pretty in '75, following *Performance*, *Walkabout*, and *Don't Look Now. Time Out* decried:

> On the strength of these three, Roeg can claim to be Britain's most visually sophisticated filmmaker. For a man who started at the bottom of the ladder as a humble assistant operator on MGM's British products in the fifties (like *Ivanhoe*) it is a remarkable achievement. Roeg's shift from cameraman to

director … seemed an odd career twist at the time, but with the benefit of hindsight it is possible to detect his virtuoso colour style behind the films he photographed for directors as major as Truffaut (*Fahrenheit 451*), Corman (*Masque Of The Red Death*), and Lester (*Petulia*).[9]

Roger Corman, the self-styled King of the B's (due to his vast low-budget output), might be pleased to find himself in such rarefied directorial company. He had chosen Roeg to work on the well-regarded *Masque* because, he said, 'His work on a film had won a cinematography award at a major European festival.'[10] Corman chronicler Beverly Gray, a former member of his creative circle, said she knew he had 'great respect' for Roeg and was particularly fond of the film they did together. Corman wasn't alone in his admiration for the rising star. 'We had one of the great cameramen in England,' *Masque* star and horror legend Vincent Price later said.[11]

Among Roeg's other photographic triumphs were David Lean's *Lawrence Of Arabia* (1962) and, after he was let go from Lean's *Doctor Zhivago*, *Far From The Madding Crowd* (1967). On *Lawrence*, Roeg quickly learned that Lean only very reluctantly let second-unit directors shoot anything, since he thought 'a second-unit director really wants to make his own film.'[12] In a disagreement over how to shoot *Zhivago*'s love scenes—Lean wanted stark, cold, and colorless, while Roeg opined for beauty and warmth—he was replaced by Freddie Young.

'I enjoyed being part of the film that was being made,' Roeg said, but he felt that when it came to dealing with Lean, 'I was on the wrong planet.'

'I predict that you will be a good director someday,' Lean told Roeg, 'but I'm afraid you can't photograph this film.'

'Lean's prediction that Roeg would become a good director came true,' Lean's biographer, Gene Phillips, concluded.[13]

Roeg moved on to directing but as Diana Lisignoli, writing in 1983's *Magill's Cinema Annual*, put it, 'Beginning with his debut on the eccentric *Performance* (1970), he has yet to escape from the designation of "visual stylist" to achieve the coherence of vision that would enable him to become a major auteur.'[14]

George Perry maintained that Roeg's relative lack of stature in film circles had to do with his country of birth. 'Nic is one of the great unfulfilled geniuses of British cinema,' he said. 'The word "British" is the problem. If he'd been a French director, he'd probably be [more highly lauded].'[15] May Routh touched upon a similar mindset when she said, 'Being English, it's quite difficult to talk about your own work unless you're criticizing it.'[16]

It wasn't just the film elite who made Roeg's path a difficult one. He was, as Justin H. Smith writes in *Withnail And Us: Films And Film Cults In British Cinema*, 'too avant-garde for the tastes and pockets of Hollywood financiers.'[17] Still, he secured financing for *The Man Who Fell To Earth* on the strengths of previous works and, without a doubt, the marquee attention and appeal of the lead actor he'd hired.

Among the various reasons Roeg provided for choosing the film was that the main character put him in mind of a friend who had been in the Egyptian army. After King Farouk was overthrown, the friend had to leave his family and his country and come to America, where he eventually lost touch with his wife and children and began seeing another woman. His wife eventually resumed contact with her husband and wanted the family to come join him in the States.

'At this point he had to make this decision,' Roeg recalled. 'The night before his family arrived in America, he left the woman and the pain he went through was incredible. Mr. Newton reminds me of that special person who got away and left someone behind.'[18] Bowie would say he was affected by the 'very sad, tender love story,' about 'man in his pure form brought down by corruption around him.'[19]

Roeg's casting of Mr. Newton was facilitated by agent Maggie Abbott, and she does not mince words about this. 'There is only one truth here,' Abbott says. 'David was not only a client of our agency Creative Management Associates, where I'd been at the London office for some time, but I also spent a lot of personal time with him, Angie, and Zowie, often at their house, went to all his shows, and knew him extremely well.' In her 1993 book *Backstage Passes*, Angie Bowie states that she herself pleaded Bowie's case to Abbott.

Abbott insisted she had not seen Alan Yentob's documentary about Bowie, *Cracked Actor*. 'Actually, though I knew about the doc, I still hadn't seen it until I got hold of the tape and showed it to Nic and Si Litvinoff after a lunch where I suggested David for the role.'[20]

On the strengths of the documentary, Roeg pursued Bowie for the part. *Cracked Actor* was filmed in and around Los Angeles and Philadelphia in September 1974 by BBC producer Alan Yentob for the *Omnibus* television program. In one segment, Bowie, emaciated and with the pallor of the milk he's drinking straight from a waxy carton, lambasts the City of the Angels, sings along to the radio, and generally pontificates as he rides along in the same limousine that would feature in *The Man Who Fell To Earth*.

Though he's often referred to as being incoherent and out of it throughout the fifty-four-minute film, journalist and cultural critic Simon Reynolds offered a different take. 'Legend maintains that *Cracked Actor* is the portrait of a rock star in meltdown. Yet his conversation in *Cracked Actor* is not fractured: it's lucid, articulate, razor sharp.'[21]

Bowie was said to be 'in total awe' of Roeg, who took a considerable casting risk.[22] One executive voiced his concern over Bowie's lack of experience by saying 'It's a very complex part, and we're worried about his acting.'[23] But Roeg shrugged this off. Inevitably asked to compare Bowie to Mick Jagger, he replied, 'David has a much deeper essence than Mick,' adding, 'David and Mick have something in common: they're both ruthlessly honest with themselves. Both are separate and individual people of our time. Their act is their acting.'[24]

Of Bowie, he added, 'Someone in his position is open to flattery all the time, but David is very, very astute. He is spontaneous as an actor, with exceptional body control. I think he has a beautiful face, very much of our society. He projects the image of being frail and vulnerable but he has a very strong constitution—he used to play football a lot—although he never seems to sleep.'[25] (Erratic sleep patterns aside, Bowie did play some football, aged ten, while attending Burnt Ash Primary School in south London.)

'A lot of rock stars think they can just transfer their art or personality to film,' Roeg added. 'David is an exception to the rule. He is a performer. His whole magnetism comes out in acting.'[26]

'I think there is mutual admiration,' Si Litvinoff later said of Bowie and Roeg. 'They are both extraordinarily well-read, inquisitive, and sophisticated with unique, original and provocative avant-garde taste.'[27]

'The casting of David was natural because they needed someone who looked as though they came from somewhere else and he fulfilled that beautifully,' George Perry noted.[28] Tom Milne, in *Sight & Sound*, would sum up the appropriate casting when he wrote, 'One point on which critics are unanimous is in finding David Bowie entirely convincing as a visitor from another planet.'[29]

Bowie pretty much kept to himself on location. 'Bowie seemed like he was there and not there,' said Howard Rubin, 'but I think that's David Bowie.'[30] Bowie also told Tom Burman, 'I'm not from this planet.'

'I knew that,' the canny special effects man replied.[31]

Bowie likely had a strategy or two. 'Even though I'm certain that our small crew of Englishers seemed a bit alien in the midst of the New Mexico cacti culture, the cowboy-heavy near fights ... that I avoided, the sweltering border bars helped mold me into the kind of useful alien Nic could do something with,' he later said.[32]

'His actual social behavior was extraordinary,' Roeg recalled. 'He hardly mixed with anyone at all.'[33]

According to Alan Swain, 'Bowie, he kind of kept in that character. He snorted a lot of coke and drank, and we just felt like maybe he was a method actor.'[34] When he did spend time with people, it was Geoff MacCormack, Coco Schwab, or his driver, Tony Mascia.

Mascia, an unreconstructed tough guy, was born in the Bronx, New York City, in 1933. 'I'm like his father,' he once said of his relationship to his employer, though they were only fourteen years apart. Mascia turned down the opportunity to work for Rod Stewart for more money in favor of working for Bowie. 'David's a cool kid to work for,' he added. 'A brilliant guy, the painting, the writing. He's a very generous kid, very shy, but with me he can be himself.'[35] It was a strong friendship. When Mascia later got married, Bowie served as his best man.

Swain was also a fan of the burly bodyguard. 'We got more time with Tony Mascia,' he said. 'He was a real neat guy, a New Yorker. He told us some funny stuff and liked hanging around with the local guys.'[36]

Corinne Schwab's remit was strictly Bowie. In 1973, she'd answered an ad in London's *Evening Standard* for a Girl Friday at Bowie's Mainman offices, and her unwavering loyalty kept her by his side for the remainder of Bowie's life. She was unyielding in her protection of him, and largely credited for helping him eventually kick drugs. But she wasn't easy. Rumor had it she was related to the Schwab family of the Los Angeles landmark drug store, but her pedigree likely rested solely on her own squared shoulders.

Similar determination was needed when working for Roeg. 'It was just so different working on a Nic Roeg film because he bent all the rules of a working practice,' De Vetta said. 'You worked until you dropped. I had only just met Tony when I worked on *Performance*. We were shooting in Lowndes Square, and [it was announced] if you don't want to do any more, you can go home. I came home at midnight and Tony was furious. *You don't do that, Linda.* We'd already done sixteen hours. That's the way Nic worked, and he wanted to go on until there was no one left on the set, day in, day out. You just worked endlessly.

'There was also a day where we worked day-night-day, and after we worked the day and the night, I thought, Well, this isn't so bad. By the afternoon, I couldn't even walk in a straight line. I was absolutely all over the place.'[37]

Graeme Clifford knew the risks but he wanted the chance to

work with Roeg again. 'I'd pursued Nic to do *Don't Look Now*. Basically I flew myself to London and got the job to edit [it]. That in turn led to *The Man Who Fell To Earth*. It was just sight unseen. I didn't give a rat's ass about the script. I just wanted to work with Nic. Nic is as much interested in the grammar of filmmaking as the actual directing.'[38]

Clifford was someone who did spend time with Bowie. 'Toward the second half of the movie he and I got a little closer, so I would hang out with him occasionally in his hotel. I remember he was always in a different hotel from where I was because I was with the crew. David was never in the hotel I was in, put it that way.'

Making a film was an eye-opener for Bowie, who had an immediate wake-up call. 'I'd never known about getting up so early,' he said.[39] He felt strongly that the film was his real life; offstage, his shadow. 'Nic just said, Be yourself. I think he realized that I had some serious problems at the time and just thought, He's perfect. Just put him in, change his clothes, and let him walk through it,' Bowie said. 'Some days my face would ache through not being able to use it and having to be absolutely expressionless. It was three months of being totally *the iceman cometh*.'[40] To Rex Reed, he said, 'To me [the film is] a love story. I don't feel like a creature from outer space. I feel very romantic.'[41]

Roeg viewed Bowie's performance even more charitably. 'There is a difficult line between who is an actor and who is not. Bowie has a totally uninfluenced originality—uninfluenced by previous roles, or by fear. That's the great hallmark of his originality, and I think that's the quality I saw in Mr. Newton, too,' he said. 'You in the audience think perhaps he's from outer space. I don't think that's definite. Perhaps he's from inner space. All we see is what's in his mind.'[42]

Roeg also believed the film to be a love story with a science fiction undercurrent, 'not rooted in technology but in the possibility of things,' and the resultant film is peculiarly human.[43] 'Roeg has more in common with [author] Graham Greene than his fellow directors,' the writer Lee Hill concludes. 'Like Greene, he has the heart of an adventurer but the eye of a moralist.'[44]

'The family walking across the plains, that entices me,' Roeg said of the White Sands scenes. 'It had a certain believable, personal quality to it.'[45] Roeg used two cameras during filming. 'It's so very precise,' he said. 'Doing a scene over using a different camera angle, you know exactly what you're getting each time.'[46]

'I never again worked on a movie that felt as imbued with such a sense of magic and foreboding as Nic's sci-fi classic,' Bowie later said. The star, who'd also begun writing a semi-autobiography entitled *The Return Of The Thin White Duke* while on location, was also affirmed that he really did have film in his blood. He told Anthony O'Grady in the *NME* that he'd completed a film script about a Howard Hughes–type character, and Joyce Haber repeated her news item about his plans to star in a film about Frank Sinatra, which probably made Sinatra devotee Tony Mascia beam with pride. 'His friends say that David can duplicate Sinatra's incredible phrasing, which is some feat, since no other popular singer has been able to do that, although many have tried,' Haber noted, adding that Bowie 'now spends more time writing screenplays than lyrics.' She concluded that *The Return Of The Thin White Duke* was set to be published at Christmas, 'by his own company—natch.'[47]

Bowie was an avowed Sinatra fan, telling Haber he was 'outwardly the epitome of the American Dream. He's succeeded in the way all Americans dream is possible. And the subsidiary aspects of Frank are

141

so fascinating. By that, I mean his supposed connections with the underground. The American Dream has not held up, but Sinatra captured the essence of it.'

Asked to name a representative of the British Dream, Bowie replied, 'King Arthur, maybe. We have exactly the same stars, same birthday, and we look alike.'[48] Musician and arranger Paul Buckmaster, who would work with Bowie on the potential soundtrack for *The Man Who Fell To Earth*, was also aware of the star's predilection for the fictional king. 'He was always very interested in the Arthurian legend,' Buckmaster told author Chris Campion. 'He was reading … a man called T.H. White, *The Once And Future King*.'[49]

On August 23, 1975, Mary Murphy in the *Los Angeles Times* reported that Bowie had formed his own film production company, Bewley Brothers, and that his first project would be a film version of *The Rise And Fall Of Ziggy Stardust And The Spiders From Mars*, with Bowie in the lead. His second project also had an outer-space connection. In *Young Americans*, he would write about 'the first non-American astronaut to join the US space probe.'[50]

By fall, the paper was heralding Bowie as the premiere choice for the role of Rudolph Valentino in an upcoming Ken Russell movie, while Roeg was talking up his soon-to-be-released feature to *Films & Filming*, describing it as 'a mysterious American love story not too far ahead of its time.'[51]

But as budding writer and filmmaker Nile Southern recounted, Roeg's talent was imbued by his absolute love for his work. Nile's father, Terry, had known Roeg from the scene surrounding Andy Warhol in London in the mid-1960s. 'He told me that everyone knew everyone in that scene of The Rolling Stones and the art world that converged in 1966 or so,' Southern said.

'I was pretty young and I wasn't included in some of the things going on there,' he said of his visit to the New Mexico set in 1975. 'I do remember that night being very magic, that feeling in the film *8½* where the movie that they're making has to do with the launching of a rocket ship and it's exciting and the press is there.

'Nic's version of that was so lively and he was like a child at the circus with this expression and he was really having a great time that night and also celebrating it: This is what making movies is all about, it's like magic.

'My dad was thrilled because my dad thought that he was charting out this life for me. He was frustrated in not being able to direct himself, for not choosing that path. He thought, My son will be the youngest film director. I was only fourteen; I had my movie camera. What a great introduction to movie making, with Nic Roeg doing this incredible night shot and being as enthusiastic as he was.'[52]

THIN ALABASTER
CLOTHESHORSE
CHAPTER SEVEN

F or a movie Roeg described as just ahead of the contemporary curve, the same could be said of its fashion. This is especially unique considering its science fiction elements, a touchstone that sent many designers and costumers into a space junk stratosphere. But not this time. *The Man Who Fell To Earth* is surely one of the most surprisingly fashionable films of any genre since cinema's golden age.

Writer Andy Webster referred to Bowie in the film as a 'thin alabaster clotheshorse,' while the star himself facetiously and self-deprecatingly commented that his acting preparation was 'akin to putting a hat on.'[1] The fedora he sported certainly provided a nod to Hollywood's heyday. The film's sense of style has much to do with Bowie's originality—his director had called him 'an absolute deflector of whatever's fashionable' but also May Routh and Ola Hudson.[2]

Bowie's wife Angela also inarguably influenced his fashion sense. She added a dose of Old Hollywood glamour she'd appropriated for herself, and he ran with it, moving away from the glitz and the outré but elegant garb toward tailored, understated suits. Of course, there's fashion and there's fashion: Angie maintained her husband's fervor for clothes extended beyond bespoke. 'David was drawn to costume designers as sex partners,' she said with her usual candor. 'Natasha Korniloff with the Lindsay Kemp theater company; Ola Hudson, the Los Angeles–based designer … made many outfits for him after Freddie [Burretti, a previous and very significant designer for the star] had told David in no uncertain terms that he was not interested in having an affair with him,' she alleged.[3]

Ola Hudson was a talented, up-and-coming designer who'd lived in Europe prior to returning to her home town of Los Angeles, where she shared a shop called Skitzo with another designer. The store was located just off Santa Monica Boulevard and around the corner from the famed Troubadour club. She described her portion of the shop as 'all pop art black-and-white squares,' while the other woman's section was the polar opposite, 'romantic flowers and whatever. At that point I was just creating dresses I could sell. I had been very influenced by my time in Europe. It was all about English fashion.'[4]

An article in the *Los Angeles Times* entitled 'All Together: An Artistic Environment For A Talented Family' described Hudson at the time as 'an innovative young fashion designer' and noted that she was married to musician Tony Hudson.[5] One of her sons, Saul, would become something of a musician as well, changing his name to Slash before eventually joining a band called Guns n' Roses.

Ola began working for—and sometimes dating—David Bowie, and for the film Bowie asked her to copy the 'narrow single-breasted suit … in slub silk' she'd previously designed for him.[6] There would be three suits in total, two black and one blue. 'He had one suit of his own that he liked very much and he suggested her to copy that,' Routh said. 'She did that in LA, with fittings here.' Routh was much taken with Hudson's striking appearance. 'I'd never seen anyone black with a polished head. I was like some idiot child, walking around astonished. The whole thing was a revelation to me. I can't explain how naïve I was.'[7]

Candy Clark recalled Hudson as 'a very nice woman' and 'a very talented friend of David Bowie's. She made him some nice suits.'[8] Bowie wore the suits over a succession of Viyella long-sleeved shirts sent over directly from the Harrods' children's department.

Clark's clothes in the film were considerably more off-the-peg, suiting her vaguely floozy, certainly small-town-girl look. Nothing had been set aside for her wardrobe in advance, and the hokey look took some getting used to for Routh. 'I had been a fashion illustrator and I covered Paris fashions, [went] to the various collections. I came from that kind of background. So people like Candy Clark, I'd never met. She turned up and said she had a great idea of what to wear in her opening.' Routh was alarmed. 'I thought, Oh my god, that's the most hideous thing I've ever seen. What do you mean, you're going to wear that in the film?'[9]

Routh soon got into the spirit, even ordering a yellow dress with rickrack trim straight out of a J.C. Penney catalogue. The crisscross floral-printed fabric shoes with a corrugated sole that Mary-Lou wore were even more down-market, coming from Woolworth's. Her heart-on-her-sleeve (and all over) dress subtly suggested emotional and romantic vulnerability.

Other items were cleverly contemporary and fashionable: Bowie's plastic jelly shoes were originally meant to suggest cloth hospital booties and later replaced by the real thing. The jellies resurfaced when Newton as detainee wore them with clam digger trousers. The duffel coat—featuring one of the best uses of the now-ubiquitous hoodie—was requested by Roeg because of its universality. However, the one used in the film caught Routh's eye in a Beverly Hills sportswear shop largely because of its loden green color—she had previously only seen camel-hued ones in Britain.

Mary-Lou wears her own camel-colored hooded coat when she cuts a lonely swath as she leaves the hotel to head for home. The Pierre Cardin bathrobes worn by Newton and Mary-Lou, with their logo a vaguely fetal swirl, were intended to suggest the cozy closeness of His and Her wear. Mary-Lou later clings to his bathrobe in a scene reminiscent of Fitzgerald's spellbound Daisy caressing Gatsby's shirts.

The spongy spacesuit with the balled nose, suggesting the carnival midway's plastic inflatable bouncy clown head from which a drunk belches and beckons early in the film, used material improvised from the lining of a camera case. It was initially bulbous in the nether regions, but Bowie had helpful suggestions as to how to cut and tailor the outfit, which was held together with glue.

On the film Routh was also exposed to industry backstabbing for the first time when a wardrobe supervisor brought over from England made it his mission to get her fired. 'I thought everybody was committed to getting the thing [film] off the ground. He wasn't. He wanted to get rid of me. I wasn't aware, I was very protected by Brian and Si.' Later, Routh discovered the supervisor 'drunk and asleep, locked in a honey wagon. So he was flown back to England. I was taken aback—I hadn't realized there were other sides to the industry. It wasn't everybody charging ahead.'[10]

Routh briefly returned to Los Angeles, and when she was in Western Costume Company, she fortuitously ran into a friend. 'A man called Ron Beck was standing in front of me,' she marveled, and quickly recruited him for the film. 'He came and it was such a relief. The department worked then. It really made a big difference when he came along.'

While she was at Western Costume, Routh put in a request for clothing for the mountain family who appear as a time-slip apparition in an unscripted scene Roeg had thought up. She was extremely happy with what they sent. 'I took things out of the box and I was very pleased, because they put in things for little babies, and a bowler hat.'

It turned out Routh wasn't the only one who liked the outfits. 'They found people to be the extras—people like mountain men, who were not actors. I know that they stole some of the clothing, including the hat, and we had to pay for that.'

Kevin Weber doesn't know what happened to the difficult-to-walk-in Perspex shoes worn on the alien planet; nor does Tom Burman. It's possible they met the same fate as much of the rest of the wardrobe: at the end of filming, the items were donated to the Albuquerque Goodwill.

Bowie's fedora, which he wore in his cups during the closing scene, had a more touching legacy. The hat originally belonged to Claudia Jennings, and shortly after filming he gifted it to a girlfriend in Berlin who was undergoing chemotherapy.

Another fedora, this one black, was also a gift, to the musician Moby, who upon misplacing it after a night of indulgence became so despondent that he did the only thing he felt reasonable: he got sober.

If any doubts remained about Bowie's status as a fashion plate, these were put to rest in April 1976 when a collection of teenagers put together by conservative, upscale clothing retailer Bullocks asked their Teen Board in West Covina, California, to name their fashion idols. Clark Gable, the King of Hollywood who'd been dead for over a decade, won, with honorable mentions for Henry Winkler, Robert Redford ... and David Bowie.[11]

But special credit and accolades must be reserved for Hudson. Paul Gorman, bespoke fashion arbiter, author, and chronicler of British culture, provides the following assessment.

★

MWFTE: OLA HUDSON
By Paul Gorman

The contribution of the accomplished British costume designer Ola Hudson to David Bowie's visual identity and also to his career must not be underestimated.

By creating a formal yet otherworldly collection of garments for *The Man Who Fell To Earth*, Hudson—who died in 2009—ensured that Thomas Jerome Newton's appearance chimed perfectly with his character. In doing so, Hudson's costume designs provided a bridge between Bowie's late glam phase (as displayed on the 1974 US *Diamond Dogs* tour) and the formal, crisply tailored look of the Thin White Duke for the live dates promoting *Station To Station* two years later.

For the seventy-three-date *Diamond Dogs* tour—which was split into two sections, the latter part rejecting the stagecraft of the former by adopting the format of a soul revue—Bowie's stage-wear was designed by a member of his inner circle, the young British tailor Freddie Burretti.

Spending downtime in Puerto Rican and African-American clubs, Burretti and Bowie had absorbed the style of the emerging disco scene, in particular the short hair, forties zoot peg pants, braces and long key-chains. These were all elements of Bowie's onstage transformation from Ziggy Stardust when the dates kicked off that summer and were followed by the so-called 'Philly Dogs' shows, which showcased the so-called 'plastic soul' interpretations of the sounds of black Philadelphia feeding into the next studio album, *Young Americans*.

But by the time Bowie, his wife, and their son relocated to Los

Angeles in early 1975, the performer had made the break with manager Tony de Fries and cut ties to many in the Mainman circle, including Burretti (who would later work for Valentino and died in Paris in 2001).

In LA, Bowie began a relationship with the costume designer Ola Hudson, mother of guitarist Slash (born Saul Hudson). This soon developed into a full fashion collaboration, which reflected the changes Bowie was intent on making to his personal appearance.

Hudson was married to the illustrator and graphic designer Anthony Hudson, who had transplanted his family—including young Saul and his brother Albion—from London to the West Coast in search of work in the early 70s. He produced album sleeves for the likes of Neil Young and Joni Mitchell, and Ola modeled, notably in an advert for Dewar's whisky, which conveyed her striking beauty and wild afro hairstyle to great effect.

A professional costume designer, Hudson also worked with several musicians—including The Pointer Sisters, Ringo Starr, Diana Ross, and John Lennon—on their stage-wear and as a stylist.

'My mum started working with David professionally at first,' said Slash later. 'I'm pretty sure that's how it started. Then it turned into some sort of mysterious romance that went on for a while after that. He was around for a while.'

So close was Hudson to Bowie that she accompanied him and the actor and her friend Dean Stockwell on a visit to Iggy Pop during his spell in UCLA's Neuropsychiatric Institute in the spring of 1975.

This occurred a few weeks before filming began on *The Man Who Fell To Earth*, by which time Hudson was producing the collection of garments for the Newton character, matching fedoras, smart suits,

40s-style dress shirts, flat pumps, and overcoats with wide cropped pants and unusual high-waisted slash-collared sweaters (one of which Bowie painted with broad silver paint stripes).

The clothing was also suitable for performance; for example, Bowie wore a blue Hudson suit with tan 'earth shoes' for an appearance lip-synching the single 'Golden Years' on *Soul Train* in the autumn of 1975 after filming was completed, but it is the monochromatic ensemble created by Hudson for the world-beating *Station To Station* tour the following spring which cemented the new identity of the Thin White Duke in the popular imagination.

In Hudson's wide black palazzo pants and tight-fitting waistcoat matched with white dress shirt and black flat-soled dancer's shoes, Bowie appeared center stage as a man reborn, and one who was about to enter arguably the high point of his career recording the so-called 'Berlin Trilogy.'

SHADOW
SOUNDTRACK
CHAPTER EIGHT

As soon as it was apparent that Bowie would be making the film, his fans had one big question: would he sing in it? Bowie shared a birthday (January 8) with another game-changing singer-turned-actor, Elvis Presley. Would Bowie follow the King's lead and break into song in the movie? Even if he felt more like an actor than a singer onstage, in a role so close to his unearthly, ethereal persona, might the star be compelled to unite his trades? (In terms of being an alien in the rock landscape, Bowie would later insist he'd never seen himself that way, citing the singer Roy Orbison as far more otherworldly.[1])

When *Los Angeles Times* Hollywood reporter Mary Murphy announced the casting in 1975, she also noted, 'As of now, Bowie will NOT sing in the film but will write the score and make a soundtrack album.'[2]

Some confusion as to how connected the film was to Bowie's music was understandable. Before the movie was released, *Seventeen* magazine's Edwin Miller thought that *The Man Who Fell To Earth* was inspired by Bowie's RCA LP *Space Oddity*. (It might also be worth noting that Miller also considered Nicolas Roeg's *Don't Look Now* to be 'a horror film.'[3])

Nicolas Roeg was ambivalent about his star providing a soundtrack. 'I had it in mind and not in mind,' he told Jarvis Cocker, in conversation at London's Winter Shuffle in 2013. 'I wasn't very fond of the idea. The audience would latch on to his singing performance.' Roeg felt that would be detrimental to the film.

Of course Bowie did sing in the film—in fits and starts. A scene filmed in the First Presbyterian Church in Artesia found Bowie as Thomas Newton accompanying his girlfriend Mary-Lou (herself musically renamed from the novel's Betty Jo) as the pastor invites the congregation to join in a hymn chosen especially for the visitor from England. Newton breathes in and out of 'Jerusalem,' a British standard with words by William Blake, while Mary-Lou veritably beams at him.

The small but telling moment is the only time Bowie's musical ability is evidenced in the film. Years later, as part of his bottomless descent, his character Newton will release an album called *The Visitor* (and his defensive reaction when Bryce tells him he didn't like it seems to originate straight from the gut), but not a written note from the star is heard on film. And that was a big source of conflict—and even bad blood—on the heels of an otherwise largely amiable shoot.

From the start, Bowie believed he would make a musical contribution but was clear that it would not involve singing. 'It was something we talked about a lot,' said Roeg. 'But I decided that if he sung, it would immediately take him out of character and he would become David Bowie—Rock Star.'[4] The star readily understood, and was unlikely to have argued, since he was by necessity and out of respect subservient to his director. Providing music for the film, however, was another story.

Much before filming began, Bowie had said, 'That'll be the next album, the soundtrack. I'm working on it now, doing some writing. We won't record it until the shooting's finished. I expect the film should be released around March [1976], and we want the album out ahead of that, so I should say maybe January or February.'[5] It was expected that Bowie's record company, RCA, would release the soundtrack.

Screenwriter Paul Mayersberg in particular looked forward to Bowie's contribution. 'When he finishes his score for *The Man Who Fell To Earth* it should complete for the movie a complex romantic

155

view of the world,' he wrote, in *Sight & Sound* magazine. 'His style is unique and because it is unique it is vulnerable, like the character he plays in the movie.'[6]

When filming wrapped in New Mexico early in September 1975, Bowie returned to Los Angeles, where he would stay at his Hollywood manager Michael Lippman's villa while assembling a team of musicians to work on the music. At Bowie's insistence, Roeg and producer Michael Deeley contacted arranger and producer Paul Buckmaster, a friend of Bowie's who'd done the strings for his 1969 'Space Oddity' before going on to work with Elton John. Roeg told Buckmaster, then in London, 'Bowie has asked for you. He trusts you and admires your work, and I'm sending you there [Los Angeles]. Do you want to go to Los Angeles and work with Bowie?'

Buckmaster did not hesitate. 'Of course, yeah,' he replied.[7] Bassist Herbie Flowers, who'd also worked on the 1969 classic as well as the *Diamond Dogs* album, was enlisted to join Buckmaster, fellow bass player George Murray, guitarists Earl Slick and Carlos Alomar, drummer Dennis Davis, and classically trained pianist J. Peter Robinson in sessions with a view toward a soundtrack. Other instruments slated for use stretched beyond the familiar rock'n'roll ensemble, such as the then-rare ARP Odyssey synthesizer and a Solina Strings Machine.

Alomar later insisted that the lines between the soundtrack and what would become Bowie's next album, *Station To Station*, were blurred. 'We had this strange overlap with *Station To Station* and the movie,' he told George Cole. 'It was pretty seamless.'[8] One of the album's subsequent songs, the somewhat overwrought ballad 'Word On A Wing,' resulted, Bowie told author Angus Mackinnon, from the stress he felt while making the movie. 'The passion in the song was genuine, something that I needed to produce from within myself to safeguard myself against some of the situations that I felt were happening on the film set,' he said.[9] He also—not surprisingly, given the bank of TVs Newton watched—wrote some of 'TVC15' on location.

Sessions were loose and informal. 'David and I enjoyed ourselves tremendously,' Buckmaster said. 'We were both very busy with what we were doing, but we had plenty of time to listen to records, especially the Kraftwerk stuff. ... We had plenty of time in which we would just talk, which we loved to do. We loved to converse about whatever science fiction we were reading at that time.'[10]

Bowie and Buckmaster were after a cello-heavy orchestrated sound and Buckmaster also introduced more unusual instruments such as the mbira, an African thumb piano. 'It sounds very liquid ... very bell-like,' Buckmaster told Campion. 'They sounded wonderful. I laid down tracks on a multitrack, just me and the engineer, in a sort of gentle African six-eight pulse piece, and then I overlaid two or three tracks of cello on top of that.'[11]

Significantly, the music was not strictly synced to the film. Instead, they played what they had put together against a Beta videotape of the film. 'We just recorded at Cherokee [Studios] what we'd come up with—more or less—at David's place and then ran it against the picture. Both David and I liked how it fitted,' Buckmaster said.[12]

He told Chris Campion that such primitivism wasn't by choice. 'We didn't have the technology either at David's home or at Cherokee Studios to lock what we were doing. We would have had to re-record the picture and mix music onto a second Beta tape machine, which we didn't do. So nothing was actually locked to the picture. Once it was recorded we would…hand play it, just press the Play button to see how it fitted. And a lot of it fitted well.'[13]

Looking very much like his movie character, Bowie appeared on the iconic American urban dance show *Soul Train* on November 4, 1975. It was a bold and savvy move by Bowie, who was one of the few white musicians to break the show's unofficial color barrier. In the second half of the program, he was interviewed by its baritone-voiced host, Don Cornelius—a pinnacle moment that would cement credibility for his rhythm & blues–tinged album *Young Americans*. To be a hit and to be accepted on *Soul Train* would indicate that David Bowie had arrived in the hybrid-soul genre to which he aspired. He would lip-synch 'Fame' and 'Golden Years.'

'We're very proud to have with us one who is easily one of the world's most popular and important music personalities,' Cornelius announced, urging the studio dancers to give 'a great welcome, gang, for the gifted singer, composer, producer, Mr. David Bowie.'

Cornelius then explained that the audience had questions that he would facilitate 'after I get my dumb ones out of the way.'

'Oh, I have some dumb answers,' Bowie—who'd admittedly knocked back several drinks before going on the show—replied.

After asking about the film (hardly a dumb question), Bowie told Cornelius, 'Um, the director of the film is called Nicolas Roeg, who started out as someone I didn't know, and ended up as a friend of mine. It's called *The Man Who Fell To Earth* and it's a bit like a Howard Hughes story. But he's sort of an alien. But he doesn't look like sort of an alien.'

An audience member, Ella Walker, asked Bowie if he planned on doing any soundtracks. Bowie asserted that he was doing one for the film, with his friend Paul Buckmaster. A follow-up question had to do with Bowie making a film with Elizabeth Taylor. The megastar was considering him for a role in *The Bluebird*. His reply was an emphatic 'no.'

Writer Robert Christgau, the self-tenured Dean of American Rock Critics, insisted that the very discerning audience was underwhelmed by Bowie's appearance and had much preferred Elton John, who'd been on the show in May and sang 'Philadelphia Freedom,' garnering a more enthusiastic reaction (or, indeed, any reaction whatsoever). 'He [Bowie] inspires no fancy steppings—no stepping at all,' Christgau wrote. Yet author Christopher Lehman defended the artist. 'Even if the *Soul Train* dancers didn't move to Bowie's music, they still recognized the music as legitimate R&B.'[14]

Lehman, however, felt that Bowie certainly didn't put his best foot forward by being so out of it. Plus he didn't sing live, which could have provided spontaneity, if not, given his inebriated state, courted disaster. It's likely the usually confident star was nervous in front of the hip, clued-in, and well platform-heeled audience he badly wanted to impress. However, with his jumpy, sentence-halting, skittish demeanor, the audience didn't know how to read the star. But one thing his guest shot assuredly did was evidence his excitement about doing the film's music.

Bowie and his assembled musicians began recording at Cherokee Studios, the lauded but nondescript looking twenty-four-track studio on the west side of Fairfax Avenue in Hollywood formerly owned and operated by MGM Records, whose parent film division had in fact coined the term 'soundtrack.' The languishing space was purchased and refitted in 1972; famed producer George Martin heralded it as the best recording studio in the nation. Harry Maslin was to produce, with David Hines acting as engineer. Six instrumentals were swiftly recorded, including 'Wheels,' purportedly about the film's decidedly organic-looking train (which had understandably given Roeg pause when it arrived after being cobbled together on set).

Bowie played piano on 'Wheels,' thought to have been a lovely, moving piece. It was followed by two rock-based instrumentals, plus synthesizer- and keyboard-based songs. Bowie was looking for music that was strong on melody and encouraged the collaborative atmosphere. 'It was great working with David and Paul,' Robinson told Cole. 'You'd say, Let's try this … and David or Paul would go to the piano. Some of the tracks would emerge this way.'

Alomar described Bowie's studio working method to Cole. 'David always called on the bass, rhythm guitar, and drums first, and then called a synthesizer player or a guitarist [Slick, when he came on board] as an invited guest.'

As quickly as the sessions had begun, however, work, and focus—Robinson referred to the brief period as 'the days of blurred reality'—started to lag. Bowie, whose relationship with cocaine made demands of its own, simply did not have the mental stamina or concentration a soundtrack demanded. He'd managed to come up with half a dozen songs in three months—not nothing, but not enough. 'Two thirds into it, it became obvious he didn't want to do it,' Roeg told Jarvis Cocker. 'Nothing was said. I thought, Thank God for that.'

However, producer Si Litvinoff, who'd urged Bowie's musical involvement from the offset, believing it would make the film more lucrative, was said to be happy with the goods. Roeg was too, according to Bowie biographer Paul Trynka. The fact that the music wasn't used was not because it was in any way inferior. Instead it was monetary; the result of Deeley trying 'to get David to accept a lesser deal and [being] told to take a hike,' according to Litvinoff. Litvinoff very much liked the soundtrack, going so far as to call it remarkable, and Robinson concurred. 'I really enjoyed the music and was very depressed it wasn't in the film. I think it worked really well.'[15]

Other sources disagree, saying Roeg felt that some of the electronic and synthesizer-based music was decidedly ill suited to the film he'd made. 'Roeg wanted banjo and folk music and Americana for the film,' said John Phillips, who would ultimately get the soundtrack gig. 'David really can't do that kind of thing.'[16]

Upon the rejection of his work, Bowie became extremely angry and withdrew altogether. 'I was under the impression that I'd be writing [all of] the music for the film,' Bowie told the *NME*. 'I was then told that if I would care to submit my music along with other people's.' Understandably offended, he retorted, 'Shit, you're not getting any of it.' The matter was glossed over as a conflict related to contracts; Bowie walked away, but did not forget.

'I don't think it was in a form yet,' Buckmaster concluded. 'But if we had had the opportunity to do some orchestral recording, it might have really flown with Nic.'[17]

★

In a tight spot, Roeg quickly contacted John Phillips, late of The Mamas & The Papas, about doing a replacement score for $50,000. Phillips was no film music novice—he'd worked on soundtracks for the colossal flop *Myra Breckinridge* as well as *Brewster McCloud*, a Robert Altman effort. His own musical background was diverse, embracing jazz, doo-wop, and folk, plus he had a keen interest in

Americana and roots music. He'd been a friend of Roeg's since 1970, and he had been living in London for a few years with his third wife, Geneviève Waïte.

As mentioned earlier, the waif-like Waïte was reportedly Roeg's first choice for the part of Mary-Lou (something Candy Clark vehemently denied). 'He told John he wanted me to do it,' Waïte said, after Roeg approached Phillips with the idea in the New York City nightclub Reno Sweeney, where Waïte was performing. Phillips thought better of it—he'd written an outer-space rock musical for Waïte with an eye to Broadway—and their impassioned disagreement led to blows. 'He and Nic Roeg were so drunk they had this terrible fight and knocked over tables and stuff,' Waïte said.[18] (Such outbursts followed by forgiveness were not uncommon for the director, according to Chris Campion and film editor Graeme Clifford.[19] And of course Phillips, the Wolf King of LA, was no oasis of calm either.)

After being contacted by Roeg, Phillips went along to the Los Angeles house Roeg shared with Candy Clark to watch a cut of the film on a portable television set. He was awed by what he saw but puzzled about being asked. Wasn't Bowie the logical choice?

Phillips soon realized he was being given the opportunity because Roeg wanted banjos and downhome type music and, as he not so tactfully, and perhaps pejoratively, said, 'Bowie can't do banjos.'[20] After listening to what Bowie had come up with, Phillips allowed that it was 'haunting and beautiful, with chimes, Japanese bells, and what sounded like electronic wind and waves.'[21]

Back in London having been given a ludicrously tight three-month deadline, Phillips enlisted the help of 'someone who could really play'—former Rolling Stone Mick Taylor—and set about working in Chelsea's Glebe Place, where Phillips was living, not far from Mick Jagger's Cheyne Walk home.[22] Keith Richards dropped by one day and was alarmed to find Taylor, who'd left the Stones on less than good terms in December 1974, in the house. The awkward moment was assuaged when Richards picked up a guitar and began to play along with the series of traditional country-music standards. That led to an assemblage of music set to gel with the film. 'Some of the music was very improvised,' engineer Richard Goldblatt recalled. 'The recordings were quite innovative.'[23]

By February 1976, Phillips was mixing the tracks and taking copious bathroom breaks when he said he heard clicks and noises on the tape. Goldblatt assured him the sounds were imaginary, but the situation escalated to the point the engineer walked out, only to return the next day to find out he'd been replaced.

'He was doing unbelievable amounts of coke,' Goldblatt said, and Rafe McKenna, assistant engineer, watched as Roeg made a visit to the studio for 'a serious discussion with Phillips about his behavior. Told him off basically and said stop pissing off the engineers and get it finished tonight.' The intervention was successful, and Phillips shaped up enough to deliver a diverse and compelling—at times elegant, at others, clumsy, but never commonplace or pedestrian—soundtrack. It is both memorable and nonintrusive.

In fact, the sole wrong note was Phillips's composition 'Bluegrass Breakdown,' which seemed far more Kentucky Appalachia than Southwestern pueblo. (Strangely, it might have worked provided the book had not been transposed from its original bluegrass setting.)

Also included in the soundtrack are pieces by Stomu Yamashta; humpback whale songs recorded by Frank Watlington; the Bournemouth Symphony Orchestra performing excerpts from

Gustav Holst's *Planets Suite*; plus inspired inclusions 'Make The World Go Away,' sung by Jim Reeves, and 'A Fool Such As I,' performed by Hank Snow. 'Hello Mary Lou' is an obvious, harmless choice. Phillips added his wife Waïte's mournful 'Love Is Coming Back' to great effect, and Artie Shaw's version of the Hoagy Carmichael standard 'Stardust' underscored the film's final scene. 'Stardust' is likely an allusion to Bowie's signature album *The Rise And Fall Of Ziggy Stardust And The Spiders From Mars*, but it's worth remembering that clarinetist Shaw had bought the first option for the film. Shaw's biographer, Tom Nolan, insisted that if Shaw had any chance of insinuating his work's placement into any resultant film, he surely would have taken it.[24]

Among the most affecting pieces are those by Yamashta: 'Poker Dice' and 'One Way,' from his album *Floating Music*; 'Mandela' and 'Memory Of Hiroshima,' from *Soundtrack From Man From The East*; and 'Wind Words,' from *Freedom Is Frightening*. Their appearance in the film was thanks largely to Graeme Clifford.

'In 1972 I edited Robert Altman's film *Images*, starring Susannah York,' he explained. 'John Williams wrote the music score and brought in a young Japanese percussionist, Stomu Yamashta, to supply ethereally mysterious musical sounds. I had been very impressed by the results, so Stomu's work found its way into my first assembly of *The Man Who Fell To Earth*. Later, I removed some of it in favor of a temp track taken from *Dark Side Of The Moon* by Pink Floyd.

'When it became apparent that David Bowie was not going to supply the score as intended, John Phillips was hired with a ridiculously short schedule. It was not enough time to write a decent score from scratch, [so] most of the music would have to be sourced from existing cues. John elected to watch the movie with the temp tracks Nic and I had been working on, to get a sense of where we had been going, and he chose to keep the Stomu tracks (and some humpback whale songs I had used), which was a great personal moment of satisfaction for me in amongst all the disappointments surrounding the score.'[25]

The Kyoto-born percussionist, keyboard player, and avant-fusion composer Yamashita Tsutomu phonetically simplified his name to Stomu Yamashta when he arrived in New York City at age seventeen. As a kind of teen prodigy, he'd already played on soundtracks for Japanese films before coming to the USA to study at Julliard and the Berklee School of Music. His and most of the pioneering sounds Phillips selected perfectly encapsulated *Man Who Fell*'s visual language.

Reaction to Phillips's efforts was mixed, however. Litvinoff dismissed it as 'adequate,' and some members of the audience at the film's London premiere expressed displeasure that Bowie had not provided the music. The *Hollywood Reporter*'s Charles Ryweck did not concur. 'John Phillips, the musical director, has supplied electronic music that seems to emanate from the stars,' he wrote.[26] For his part, Roeg was satisfied, if resigned, feeling that some of the music at least matched that of what they'd heard on the jukeboxes while on location in New Mexico.

One piece that Bowie had written for the film eventually made its way onto one of his subsequent albums. 'Subterraneans,' a brooding beauty on *Low*, is a survivor from the soundtrack sessions (its original inception was keyboard-driven). Buckmaster expressed surprise the song did not make it into the film. 'It's a great track, evocative and appropriate for the theme of the story, and the sax gives it a noir-ish mood,' he said in 2016. 'It most certainly would have worked very well in the film!' Another track intended for the film, 'Some Are,' didn't make it onto *Low* but appeared a bonus track on the album's 1991 re-release.

When *Low* was released, Bowie sent a copy to Roeg with a note stating, 'This is what I wanted for the film.' Roeg's reaction is not known, but when asked by *Circus* magazine in 1977 what she thought of the album, Candy Clark replied, 'I think he should have put an *S* in front of the title.'[27]

Rumors swirl about the existence of Bowie's elusive soundtrack, sometimes in the form of a bootleg album called *The Visitor* (named after Newton's final offering in the film), or as material sequestered into the musician's archives. 'There is a great mystery at the heart of *The Man Who Fell To Earth*, Nicolas Roeg's cult movie: its soundtrack,' Chris Campion, who spearheaded the eventual release of the film's score in 2016, wrote in the *Guardian*. 'There is a persistent rumor that long-lost music for the film—recorded by its star David Bowie—sits somewhere in a vault. There's only one problem: Bowie's soundtrack to *The Man Who Fell To Earth* doesn't exist.'[28]

Bowie's *Station To Station* is often said to contain soundtrack material, but guitarist Earl Slick, who played on the 1976 album, disagreed. 'That movie and the record [*Station To Station*] are completely separate, though, because he was writing some other music. I don't know if it was even used or what happened to it.'[29]

'Given that Bowie spent appreciably more time working on *Station To Station* than on any of his previous albums, there has been much speculation over the years about what else might have been recorded during those two-and-a-half months at Cherokee Studios,' Tom Seabrook wrote in *Record Collector*. That nothing has emerged is puzzling but not incomprehensible. 'The most likely explanation for this seems to be that David Bowie is just as protective of his master tapes as he is of his memories.'[30]

Writer Mike Flood Page interviewed Roeg shortly after filming for *Street Life* magazine and reported that Roeg played him a microcassette featuring music by Bowie that was intended for the film. Its style was 'simple melodic instrumental based around organ, drum, and bass.'[31]

Michael Deeley felt that what little Bowie had provided 'didn't have any original quality to it which may be just as well because the film was very original and difficult. So, maybe the familiarity of the music [by Phillips] wasn't such a bad idea.'[32]

Graeme Clifford, by then busy editing the film in Soho, did not concur. 'The music, the score to *Man Who Fell To Earth*, is my only disappointment,' he said, adding that editing has a big effect on a film score. 'Personally that was a disappointment to me, and it remains so.'

Clifford had his own idea as to what music would suit best. 'When an editor typically cuts a movie, the editor uses music of one's choosing so that it's in line with the cut, so that when the editor shows it to the director, it's got some kind of music on it.'

Clifford wove in *Dark Side Of The Moon* alongside the humpback whale sounds and Yamashta's work and told Roeg he thought they should pursue the rights to the album. 'It was perfect, it was absolutely perfect, and I said to Nic we should just go and buy the rights to this record because no one is going to do this any better. But here's the deal: I guess when Bowie was hired—I don't know this for sure and I've never asked Nic—I presume they probably made a deal for him to do the music because that would make sense. I'm sure Bowie had some kind of intention to do the music. And he did go into the studio after the film and he spent months in the studio, and nothing ever came out of it. Unfortunately Bowie didn't come up with anything, not a single piece. Nothing.

'I presume Nic was conversant with what was going on. The end result was that after at least a couple of months of being in the studio—this was concurrent with my editing, it wasn't some sort of mix-up—nothing appeared. So that was then abandoned, and in the meantime they had not gotten the rights to Pink Floyd and I didn't know any of the Pink Floyd members personally. I now do and they vaguely remember their agent talking about it. There was never any real formal offer.

'If you listen to the score, there are elements of Pink Floyd in there. It was not that the music was copied but that the emotional content of the Pink Floyd music that was carried over. I think nothing was as good as the Pink Floyd score. It was so far superior to what is now on the movie that to me there's no comparison. It was unfortunate that we didn't buy the Pink Floyd album. I put forward my case and then I just left it there. It wasn't my decision.'[33]

In 2016, a double CD of the soundtrack was released. None of Bowie's work appeared, of course, and what was initiated as Chris Campion's labor of love to see it come to light fell prey to record company greed and unsavory dealings. Campion searched and sourced the master tapes at Pinewood Studios, but then was marginalized, as was Phillips's estate, which was not consulted as inferior takes and even a work-in-progress demo were selected as well as versions of songs that weren't from the film, such as 'Jazz II,' 'Windows,' and an instrumental take of Ricky Nelson's 'Hello Mary Lou.' The jazzy, innovative music that introduced Nathan Bryce is left out altogether. Another piece Roeg mentioned in the 1992 commentary accompanying the Criterion re-release of the film was a recording by The Squadronaires featuring Christopher Townshend (father of the Who's Pete) and saxophonist Derek Wadsworth, who added it to his impressive list of credits. The song, which comes late in the film when Mary-Lou and Bryce are dining out, is absent from the 2016 soundtrack album.

Phillips, so crucial to the soundtrack, is not credited on the cover, and the liner notes are focused almost entirely on Bowie, with only a modest paragraph about the music. (For more on the soundtrack, see Extra #2.)

Writer and filmmaker Tom Ropelewski had an interesting thought. 'The big mystery to me is why isn't *Station To Station* the soundtrack? A song like "TVC15," what else is it but for a science fiction film? "Wild Is The Wind," it [the film] was probably on his mind when he recorded it. Someone on YouTube should recut the movie set to that music. It'd be the movie it should have been, more coherent, without that goofy score.'[34]

Or maybe recut it to that album and the second half of *Low*?

CUT TO THE CHASTE
CHAPTER NINE

I n late-1975 London, Graeme Clifford's remit was editing the film. As he labored away in Soho to the strains of *Dark Side Of The Moon*, Bowie was in Los Angeles recording *Station To Station*, which he would tour in support of in 1976—a detail that didn't escape the notice of one Chuck Mittlestadt, the intrepid New Mexico Hollywood Reporter still smarting from being denied access to the film's star.

'Superfreak David Bowie, who made *The Man Who Fell To Earth* in NM last summer—is finally going to let his local fans see him. He's set for an Albuquerque Civic Auditorium concert Feb. 16,' Mittlestadt wrote. 'You may recall, when he was here for the filming, he refused to meet the public and declined all interviews. Even arrived at the airport, in drag, to remain anonymous.'[1] Bowie plus airport did not compute, of course. And drag, in 1975? Mittlestadt added that the film was set for a February 11 release from Paramount Pictures.

The date sounded about right—'Typically the postproduction in those days was around six months,' said Clifford—but challenges were ahead. 'I found it very easy and interesting and compelling to cut,' Clifford said, and his particular method melded with the work. 'I just basically edit in a very organic way. I almost never look at the script and just go from what I see in the dailies. What I get in dailies from the director and in discussion with the director is what I cut. The only time you have editing challenges is if it's badly directed or you have an actor who is just hopeless and whose performance requires an enormous amount of propping up. Lots of actors' performances are improved enormously in editing.

'You've got infinite ways to cut the movie, literally infinite,' he continued, 'so if you had three editors cut any single movie, it'd be entirely different each time. The story would still be the same, but the way it was edited would be completely different.'

By the time the film was released in the USA, three editors would have had a go. But for now, momentum for the film's release was building. In October, *Variety* featured a breathless ad with the tagline, 'And now, the forthcoming film EVENT they're all talking about.'[2] *Circus* magazine's Paul Nelson covered the film with substance and skill, providing a capable and coherent summary of the plot. The piece came to the attention of Walter Tevis, now an English professor at Ohio University. He quickly wrote a letter.

> Your man Paul Nelson did a lovely job writing about my book, *The Man Who Fell To Earth*, and about David Bowie, who will star in the film. Nelson is absolutely right about Mr. Bowie's playing of my space man.
>
> Nelson is wrong in small ways. *The Man Who Fell To Earth* was not an obscure Lancer Books original that soon disappeared and nobody read. Lancer reprinted it. From a Gold Medal original that fed me and my family for a long time. And the book is in French, Italian, Japanese, Afrikaans, Portugese [sic], German and maybe Venusian. But I admit it was never famous. Here.
>
> Anyway, the movie of *The Hustler* made me paranoid because few people seemed to know it was derived from a book. Your magazine has done me the kindness of helping prevent that this time around. ... I've always known my students read magazines like

yours and growled when I saw them doing it. But I've been seduced. I read the whole copy (December 9), and discovered *Circus* to be smart, insightful, and—thank the good God who made Chaucer—**literate**. Thank you for that.[3]

On March 18, 1976, the film had its world premiere in London at the Leicester Square Theatre. Candy Clark was in attendance, as was Paul Mayersberg. Its star was on his Isolar tour, between dates of Boston and Buffalo, leaving co-star Clark to grab the limelight, which she did with aplomb, in her own words, 'signing autographs and waving like a queen and dancing at Tramp's all night. It's a big, rare event. It doesn't happen often,' she told *Women's Wear Daily's* Julie Kavanagh in a suite at the Connaught Hotel. Kavanagh, who later famously dated author Martin Amis, added that Clark looked 'remarkable, bright as a button' for a person who'd gone to bed at 8:30 that morning. She was wise to be savoring her role in the press junket, however—it wouldn't last long.

Also at the premiere was the actor James Coburn, a rugged star who might not immediately be associated with an arty, offbeat film, although he was rumored to have been considered for the role played by Rip Torn. 'Dad did spend a lot of time in London that year,' his daughter Lisa recalled. 'He was making preparations for [Sam Peckinpah's] *Cross Of Iron*. Wherever he was, he received a lot of invitations. That's how he came to be on the cover of McCartney's *Band On The Run* [1973]. He just happened to be in town.'[4]

Some members of the crowd exiting the cinema were disappointed that Bowie hadn't provided the soundtrack, but that was the least of Roeg's problems. The film—lengthy at two hours twenty-eight

173

minutes—was proving hard to follow, for critics and audiences alike. For his part, Roeg said, 'It isn't complex, really, if you let the film work for you instead of relying on previous terms of reference. People say they found it difficult to follow the plot, but the plot's there. There are only thirty-six plots in the world anyway.' He continued to explain his rationale. 'I wanted to take away the reliance on literary form. But when you take that crutch away it rather upsets people. I also thought I'd like to play with the one thing in life to which we're absolute slaves—and that's time. It has puzzled people whether twenty-five minutes or twenty-five years have passed in the film. It was the closest I could get to an extraordinary science-fiction feel more than look. Movies are curious time machines.'[5] Roeg would take great pains to see that no mention of time occurred in the film.

Variety had the first mainstream printed review, derived from the London premiere. Beginning with a pitch-like summary, 'Hawk' wrote, presciently, 'Offbeat, brilliantly directed cerebral sci-fier. Strong sell needed, however, to overcome somewhat hermetic plot and overlength and capitalize on David Bowie name and youth appeal. Cult future assured.'

The reviewer emphasized its niche appeal while focusing on the music. 'The David Bowie name should help with the youngsters, even if the popster doesn't "perform" but stays within his straight dramatic role. Lush music track also oozes teen appeal.' Hawk liked the film, finding it visually and aurally 'stunning.' Bowie was perfect for the role, he added, to the point where it might typecast him. He also cited Clark's 'winning ways' as well as 'robust' contributions from Torn and Henry, plus 'standout achievements for Richmond and Clifford. The sex scenes between Bowie and Clark, especially the introductory ones, are among pic highlights.'[6]

The intimate scenes would garner a lot of positive comment but serve as awkward subject matter for Clark as she continued to do publicity for the film. They were, for her, 'cringingly embarrassing,' she told the *Los Angeles Times*. 'I can't watch them. I had this vision of myself as a voluptuous type with a nipped-in waist and a tan ... looking really good. When I saw myself—looking like a white worm—I was so embarrassed. I was even more embarrassed seeing it on film and thinking what other people would think when they saw it.'

She wasn't the only one who thought the lovers' appearance in the sex scenes were suggestive of invertebrates. 'The bodies seem slug-like,' Bowie would comment in 1992.

Clark's father also wasn't best pleased when she broke the news to him over the phone that she'd done a nude scene. He told her he was ashamed, and she reluctantly replied, 'It was too late, it was done, and anyway I'm twenty-eight and a lot of people do them.' Her father continued to protest, so she hung up on him. 'But a couple of days later, he got over it. He even went to see the movie and he loved it. The only comment he made about the nude scenes was that poor skinny Bowie looked so pitiful,' she laughed. She was equally modest about the bathtub scene. 'Only my top half has to show,' she explained, but she still had a caveat. 'I wouldn't let anyone in until I had that water gray with soap.'⁷ Years later, Clark would attest that Bowie was equally squeamish about the sex scenes.

Fretting over her appearance, she also had an explanation for her pallor. 'I had just got over infectious hepatitis after a promotional tour of South America [in support of] *Fat City* and *American Graffiti*,' she said. 'I took a shower [and] a sore on my arm from a smallpox vaccine got infected.' As a result, her weight dropped from 120 pounds to 113. When she was getting ready to attend the

Academy Awards ceremony (and already prepping for another role), she was surprised to find herself looking very tan. 'Turns out I was turning yellow!' she exclaimed. 'I lost the other job, which really killed my moment. Susan Blakely played my character.'[8]

The film was also reviewed with considerable flourish in *Monthly Film Bulletin* by assistant editor Jonathan Rosenbaum, who felt that Roeg took Walter Tevis's prosaic novel through 'a steady succession of sideways "developments" that remain obstinately undeveloped. Basic to this approach is kaleidoscopic, cross-cutting between diverse narrative strands, which tends to make simple plots appear relatively complex and relatively complex plots seem downright intractable.'

Drawing from Mayersberg's *Sight & Sound* piece 'The Story So Far,' in which the screenwriter compared the piece with a circus, Rosenbaum took the metaphor and ran wild, finding 'the right elbow of the trapeze artist grafted on to the left ear of the clown which is then strained through the digestive tract of a lion and shot from a cannon.' Not that this was necessarily bad, Rosenbaum added, finding that Roeg's 'juggling of more diversified ingredients' kept the film imminently watchable and the audience engaged.

He was particularly transfixed by Bowie, whose 'extraterrestrial persona and performance … genuinely uncanny with his sexual ambivalence, surreal red hair, chiseled features, and underplayed reactions … offers one of the eeriest screen presences since Katharine Hepburn in *Sylvia Scarlett* (whom he oddly resembles in the last scene).' Bowie, Rosenbaum felt, held in check the 'overwrought' turns of Clark and Torn, as 'a cool, quivering reed at the center of a hurricane that is full of sound and fury, signifying nothing.'[9]

Yet it is a note struck by the previous review from *Variety* that would carry an ominous foreshadowing. 'The average filmgoer may, however, feel [the] pic somewhat overlong,' Hawk wrote, 'but pic is so intricately patterned as to make trimming difficult.'[10]

★

When British Lion's Michael Deeley showed a rough cut of the film to Paramount head Barry Diller (who'd wanted Robert Redford to play Newton), Diller wasted no time in opting out, insisting the studio had purchased a linear picture rather than what had been produced. Diller's focus at Paramount at the time was the innocuous and inane but highly successful *Laverne & Shirley* TV show, so it's likely *Man Who Fell* was far from his brief. He had a reputation for being less than pleasant: Deeley later said he had no regrets about being involved with the film, 'even when I was sitting with the dreadful Barry Diller.' That Paramount pulled out was, according to Deeley, 'a bad thing Diller did out of sheer silliness. He shouldn't have even been looking at the movie in a rough cut stage and I shouldn't perhaps have shown it to him, but I wanted to, to get him interested but I got disinterest.'

Deeley, for one, breathed a sigh of relief when Cinema 5, helmed by another outsized personality, Donald Rugoff, stepped in. 'When Paramount reneged on the contract, we were absolutely stuck because we had a bank lending us money—it wasn't a very confident bank and not confident in us. We were in a jam.'[11]

In London, Roeg was aware of the shaky situation, telling *Time Out* that the American distributor with whom they had a solid deal was getting cold feet because it was itself in financial straits. He had nothing but praise for Deeley, however, who he believed understood his vision. 'If you're too inflexible your whole sight of the characters gets smaller and smaller because you can't shift or have them change,'

Roeg said. 'The producer Michael Deeley has been marvelous in understanding that. Even the crew found it difficult to follow because there was no time to discuss what was happening. They were sort of lost and just ended up doing it. But Michael understood the picture from the beginning. A lot of producers would have wanted constant explanations.'[12]

Rugoff would not be big on understanding the picture. Still, Deeley was happy. 'I was so relieved when Rugoff took it over. I had nothing to do with the release in America. I was just glad to get the money. Seriously, it was critical to us, a privately owned, modest company. It mattered to me.'[13]

Donald Rugoff had come to prominence running a series of prestigious independent movie theaters started by his father in 1919. He created the distribution company Cinema 5 in 1963, and Rugoff Theaters was integrated into Cinema 5 in 1968. Making his name and success based on booking highbrow independent and foreign films such as Costa-Gavras's Z and Werner Herzog's *Kaspar Hauser*, as well as the groundbreaking American indie *Putney Swope*, he was a popular presence on the New York film scene and as it turned out, the college test-screening market.

On Friday April 9, 1976, Rugoff addressed a press conference also attended by Spikings and British Lion's Sidney Safir. 'It's the largest deal we've ever made on a picture,' Rugoff told the assembled. He did not elaborate, leaving Barry Spikings to explain that the deal was not Lion's usual 50/50 production services, but one in which they solely took on the four-million-dollar negative cost. In turn, Lion received 'heavier terms and a good sum of money' due to the film's 'enormous potential,' said Spikings. The film had earned a modest $65,000 in its first two weeks in Leicester Square.

The influential *Variety*'s canny assessment was based on a trade report that indicated Lion sought $750,000 upfront but felt that 'Rugoff's straight deal was probably less. Hints by Spikings that certain major distribs were hot for the pic (thereby hiking Rugoff's upfront pot) is considered less credible than Rugoff's pitch that he could capitalize on Bowie's cult following.'

Rugoff had his sights set on a New York premiere in May, and he knew that an *R* rating was essential to bring in the target fourteen-to-twenty-five age group. (As is, the film had an *X* rating). He was unperturbed by the *R* rating the film would receive in the USA, prohibiting minors under the age of seventeen from seeing it without being accompanied by an adult. 'They get in,' he insisted. 'They get in.'[14]

New York, Rugoff felt, would be a strong indicator of how the film would play in the rest of the country. Meanwhile, he had hopes that Bowie would promote the film, but these were far from firm. 'Bowie doesn't fly,' Spikings said. 'Having fallen to earth, he likes sticking to it.' Rugoff also had to admit that Bowie does not sing in the film, while Spikings quickly played up the star's cultivated alien trappings. 'We wanted somebody from another world, which Bowie certainly is,' he told the assembled.

Rugoff was having trouble with the film, however. 'I don't understand the film but the kids really do,' he said. 'It's one of the weirdest films I've ever seen.' Plus he had another card up his sleeve: that following Tuesday, he was taking the film to Dartmouth College in Hanover, New Hampshire, to preview it to the school's longstanding film society. 'Apparently he had screenings all the time at Dartmouth,' said documentarian and Columbia University professor Ira Deutchman. 'It was sort of a market research screening to get a sense of how films would play.'[15] As a bellwether, Dartmouth was 'remarkably accurate,' Rugoff said. 'The turnout is always good. The school is isolated. And we get to pay homage to Arthur Mayer, who teaches up there.'[16]

Aside from Rugoff's proffered flattery, the near-legendary Mayer would describe Rugoff thusly: 'Like many Americans, he is more than dominated by business—he is obsessed. As a result, he doesn't push employees up, he pulls them down. He wants to do everything.'[17]

'In a word, he was not a very nice person,' said Deutchman, who worked at Cinema 5 at the time. 'Filmmakers were the one group of people he was supportive of. They all knew he was crazy, but they were appreciative of the support he gave. Pretty much every movie he ever handled was an outlier of some sort that nobody in their right mind would have handled.'[18]

Dartmouth College, an Ivy League university in New England (from which, coincidentally, Buck Henry had graduated in 1952), had one of the country's oldest student-organized film societies, established in 1949 by Blair Watson and Maurice Rapf. In 1976, Arthur Loeb Mayer, whom Rugoff revered, taught there after a long and almost accidental career in film. After graduating Harvard in 1907, the native of Demopolis, Alabama, began to make it known he wanted a career in the picture business, not out of love of film but because he'd been working in an art gallery. A friend misunderstood and directed him to the movie mogul Samuel Goldfish (né Goldwyn), who put him to work auditing receipts. Soon Mayer, lovingly known as the Merchant of Menace, became a king of publicity stunts: he once taught seventy parrots to squawk 'It Ain't No Sin' at an opening of a Mae West film of the same name. He also pioneered the double feature, pairing *Frankenstein* with *Dracula*.

On campus, Rugoff waited in the large, modern, nine-hundred-seat Spaulding Auditorium, part of the college's Hopkins Center For The Arts, as students filed in to see *The Man Who Fell To Earth* on a crisp April afternoon. The auditorium was a state-of-the-art facility, with great sound and projection, and comfortable seats.

In the audience was Tom Ropelewski, a young Dartmouth student and dedicated Bowie fan. 'I'd been a member of the Dartmouth Film Society since my second day in Hanover,' he recalled, 'and I'd been writing movie reviews for current releases that came to the Nugget Theater. As far as I knew, I was going to be the first American reviewer to take a crack at *The Man Who Fell To Earth*,' he told me.[19]

The hall, Ropelewski noted, was two-thirds full—not bad for a screening of a film most of the students were unfamiliar with, although many did know Bowie. 'You would hear "Rebel Rebel" blasting out of the frat houses on the weekends,' he said. For all its Ivy League credibility, the college had a large fraternity contingent and reputation. 'It's an Ivy League School but it's a jock school and a frat-boy school and a party school,' Ropelewski explained. 'Of the Ivys it's the most party, outdoorsy. Dartmouth is where *Animal House* was based.'[20]

'I settle into my seat in Spaulding Auditorium next to my girlfriend, another huge Bowie fan,' Ropelewski later wrote. 'Don Rugoff ... says a few words of welcome and explains that we're going to see a test cut, which may be altered before the film's release.' Ropelewski and his girlfriend watched the unfolding action with the rest of the audience, wincing when Mary-Lou responds to Newton in his natural state. 'Clark's reaction was so over-the-top (there's even a close-up of her legs as she pees herself) the Dartmouth audience roars with laughter.'[21]

Those who stayed, that is. 'By the time Bernie Casey comes on ... the auditorium was half what it would have been. I really wanted it [the film] to come together but the audience was like, We're outta here. They were frat boys and if it didn't have them, they were not going to stick around even if it was a free movie. You could feel the grumbling.'[22]

Ropelewski had to abandon his high hopes for the film. 'I had wanted *The Man Who Fell To Earth* to be great. Now I was realizing it probably wasn't even good ... the audience had already made up its mind. They hated it.'[23]

The audience had been given preview cards, but many had left without completing them. 'You've got to keep in mind that most people didn't stay to fill out the cards,' Ropelewski said. 'Half the audience had already left. They just hated it! They wanted a party movie with Bowie and when they got what they got, they were not in the mood. People were, Okay, let's party. It's a science fiction movie with Bowie, he's an alien, and it did not deliver.'

Usually, Rugoff would have stayed on after the screening to do a Q&A, have dinner with students, or at least conduct a focus group or otherwise meet with them in a classroom. He'd done that before, with films like *Monty Python & The Holy Grail*, which Dartmouth received with open arms. But not this time. 'He felt it had gone south,' Ropelewski noted.[24]

Ropelewski went home to write his review, trying to focus on the positive. A few days later, he was surprised to be told that Don Rugoff had called, asking to speak with him. When he asked why, he was informed Rugoff wanted him 'to fix that film.' It transpired that Rugoff had been impressed by Ropelewski's review, and Ropelewski in return had respect for Rugoff. 'Rugoff was no bottom-line hack,' he said. 'He was a tastemaker and a trendsetter—and he trusted the Dartmouth audience.'

When Rugoff spoke with Ropelewski, the young man 'could hear the desperation.' He wanted Ropelewski to admit the film was a disaster, but he responded more neutrally, insisting that it could be improved. There were other issues. 'Rugoff seemed to be hung up on the many nude scenes ... [he] insisted that the pee-down-the-leg shot had to go.' For his part, Ropelewski suggested cutting the scene where Bernie Casey (as Mr. Peters) examines his conscience. 'Why do we need this scene? Bernie's the bad guy!'[25]

Ropelewski resisted casting Rugoff as a villain, however. 'Not a villain at all, no,' he said. 'That was not his attitude at all. It pained him to do it [cut the film] but he knew he had to. He knew the film was not working for audiences and he so wanted it to.'[26]

According to Deutchman, the Dartmouth screening 'was a complete disaster. Everybody there hated it. Rugoff used [Ropelewski's] review as evidence as to why the film should be cut.'

Rugoff called in screenwriter Robert Young, whose credits at the time included *Nothing But A Man*, and a film editor named Ed Beyer, who trimmed twenty minutes from the film. 'I do remember the editing room being down the hall from my office,' Deutchman said. 'The office was about two doors down from Rugoff's office, and he would waddle down a couple times a day to see what they were working on. It seemed like they were in there forever but they were also doing the trailers for upcoming movies.'[27]

On the proverbial cutting room floor was a sex scene between Nathan Bryce and one of his students (in which Torn's penis could be glimpsed—a particular bugbear of Rugoff's, according to Ropelewski); the reveal when Newton shows his true self to Mary-

Lou and she responds by urinating; the gunplay sexual escapades between Mary-Lou and Newton (which featured a shot of Bowie's prodigious penis, a surefire signifier of an *X* rating); and a late depiction of Bryce as Santa Claus.

Learning of the cuts, Roeg was horrified—'totally distressed and upset.'[28]

Candy Clark had been initially hopeful when Cinema 5 came along. 'Cinema 5 was like Miramax, a high-end distribution company,' she said. 'Their motto, or their logo, was that it was always a director's cut. They had real pride in that. But they took this film—the only reason I can think of is it is a two-hour, twenty-three-minute film, which is an odd number for a film. They saw dollar signs and wanted to make it a two-hour movie, so they'd have a good turnover. This is just my theory, so I don't really know.' Her theory is likely on the money.

'It was cut,' Clark added, 'by a man who cut commercials. He had a week to edit, and it's really not his fault, although he shouldn't have touched some other director's work without asking permission. He was following Don Rugoff's order, and he was paid, but his real work was editing toothpaste and soap commercials. He was taking stuff out and rearranging and trying to compress this film into two hours. He was able to do it, but it did not make a lick of sense.'

Rugoff, however, had bought the film 'with the right to cut it subject to the approval of the producers'—a move he cited as 'painful' but essential. Still, he was unhappy that Roeg was reportedly upset, so he made an unprecedented move: he sought the opinion of a psychologist, not to evaluate his own state of mind but rather to assess the film. Dr. Richard Simons, a member of the University of Colorado Medical Center's Department of Psychology, fit the

ABOVE Candy Clark, enrobed and reflective on the
set of *The Man Who Fell To Earth*.

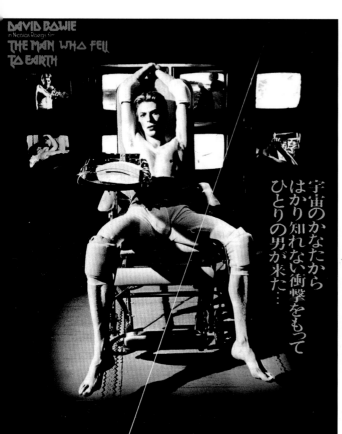

DAVID BOWIE
in Nicolas Roeg's film
THE MAN WHO FELL
TO EARTH

宇宙のかなたから
はかり知れない衝撃をもって
ひとりの男が来た…

TOP ROW A Japanese ad for *Man Who Fell*; the film's 'Jerusalem' scene.
BOTTOM ROW A print ad for Bowie's *Station To Station*; Bowie and Paul Buckmaster (*left*) parking outside Cherokee Studios; an *NME* cover from March 1976; Bowie's *Station To Station* and *Low* LPs.

TOP ROW Albuquerque's KiMo Theatre; Newton post-descent.
BOTTOM ROW Artesia's Landsun Theatre; Graeme Clifford (*left*) on the hood of his Chevy with assistant Rodney Glenn; cast member Delana Michaels; posters for the original film and 1987 remake; the 2016 Blu-ray edition.

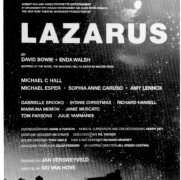

LAZARUS
by
David Bowie
and
Enda Walsh

Directed by
Ivo van Hove

NEW YORK
THEATRE
WORKSHOP

ROBERT FOX AND JONES/TINTORETTO ENTERTAINMENT
BY ARRANGEMENT WITH RUNAWAY ENTERTAINMENT AND OLIVIER ROHR PRESENTS
THE NEW YORK THEATRE WORKSHOP PRODUCTION OF

LAZARUS

BY
DAVID BOWIE · ENDA WALSH
INSPIRED BY THE NOVEL THE MAN WHO FELL TO EARTH BY WALTER TEVIS

MICHAEL C HALL

MICHAEL ESPER · SOPHIA ANNE CARUSO · AMY LENNOX

GABRIELLE BROOKS · SYDNIE CHRISTMAS · RICHARD HANSELL
MAIMUNA MEMON · JAMIE MUSCATO
TOM PARSONS · JULIE YAMMANEE

CHOREOGRAPHER ANNIE-B PARSON   MUSICAL SUPERVISOR AND ORCHESTRATIONS HENRY HEY
COSTUME DESIGNER AN D'HUYS   VIDEO DESIGNER TAL YARDEN
SOUND DESIGNER TONY GAYLE   HAIR & WIG DESIGNER RICHARD MAWBEY
ASSOCIATE PRODUCER ZELDA PERKINS   UK CASTING DIRECTOR JILL GREEN CASTING

DESIGNED BY JAN VERSWEYVELD
DIRECTED BY IVO VAN HOVE

TOP ROW Bowie in his trailer, during a break from filming. **BOTTOM ROW** John Phillips with new wife Geneviève Waïte (*left*) and ex Michelle, 1973; the 2016 soundtrack LP; the signed portrait Bowie sent to Gregg Barrios; ads for the New York and London productions of *Lazarus*; Bowie's *No Plan* EP.

ABOVE Artist Mark Wardel with a selection of his 'Silver Duke' Bowie masks.

bill. Simons had been at a conference in Baltimore with a New York psychiatrist, Dr. Wilbert Sykes, whom Rugoff knew.

Simons was a film buff, and he believed he was brought to New York to view the film 'in the context of someone who loves film and knows something about Roeg's work. I was brought in among a lot of other people for my reactions to the film. He didn't ask me to analyze it; I wouldn't even presume to do that. I'm not qualified but I do love film.

'I watched the film in a small theater,' he continued. 'I had trouble with making much headway out of the original.' Then he watched the cut version right afterward. 'It was a long afternoon. I did not really like the original version and found the cut version more comprehensible. I thought the cuts were much more understandable.'[29]

Simons didn't know what Rugoff intended to do with his input. 'I made it clear that I was not a film critic and I didn't have the background or scholarship to analyze the film. He said he wasn't interested in that. He just wanted to know if I liked it or not.'

Simons met Rugoff briefly before giving him his impressions. 'We didn't have much contact,' he said. 'I didn't have enough time with him to really comment.' He received a small fee, and his plane fare was paid for. Four decades later, Simons remained circumspect about the unusual situation. 'I was never asked to review a film again,' he said. 'I might think twice about it if it did happen again because I don't think films should be censored. The director has a right to do what he wants.'

Simons was also on the money when he concluded, 'I think Mr. Rugoff paid $800,000 for the rights, and he was afraid he was going to lose his shirt.'[30]

Deeley expressed surprise when hearing that a psychologist was brought into the scenario. 'I've never heard of the practice in my life, I promise you,' he said. 'I guess Rugoff bought this picture and then he was probably baffled about how to promote it. He's asking somebody to tell him what the public generally will respond to most favorably and how he should be selling this. It's my only guess. But I think it's pathetic because if you don't know how to sell it, why the heck are you buying it? Gosh, that makes me feel even luckier that we managed to get some money.'[31]

'I remember, when I saw the original, being completely baffled by the second half,' said Deutchman. 'But ... the cut version, the only attribute that you could say that was better was that it was shorter. Of the choices that were made as to what was left in and left out, it seemed a little misguided to me as it still didn't make any sense.

'*The Man Who Fell To Earth* was the only time he ever messed with a movie. He was known, unlike Harvey Weinstein, who part of his reputation is he's got his fingers in everything—while he may have discussed things with filmmakers ... apparently he always backed off.'[32]

Like Deutchman, *New York Times* writer Mel Gussow was in the unique position of having seen both the cut and uncut versions. He felt the first two cuts—Bryce's romp and Mary-Lou's micturating— were substantiated, but he could not defend the scrapping of the sex-and-gun scene. Rugoff felt it made the audience lose sympathy for the two characters, but Gussow believed that was exactly the intent. 'They aren't young people anymore,' he said, quoting Roeg. 'As they get older, the likelihood of extra aids to eroticism is brought in. Newton has become totally human.'

Gussow reported that Rugoff was considering inserting a prologue to the film, begging the audience's patience. Roeg biographer Joseph

Lanza wrote that Cinema 5 handed out leaflets explaining the film—something that rang a bell with Deutchman, who remembered another marketing ploy. 'The film didn't open well. [Rugoff] made up his mind that the way to sell the movie was to tell people that in order to understand it, it was necessary to see it more than once. He had hospital bracelets that said *The Man Who Fell To Earth* and everybody who came to the movie was given a hospital bracelet. As long as they continued to wear that hospital bracelet, they could come back and see the movie as often as they wanted.' It was, Deutchman said, a typical Rugoff move. 'It harkened back to the early days when he was working at his dad's movie chain and they would give away dishes if people would come to see the movies.'[33]

One person entirely out of the loop was Graeme Clifford. 'Si Litvinoff told me some cutting was going on, but nobody really knew what was being cut. I was long gone by then, and quite frankly I have never seen the cut version. Nobody would have asked me to come in and recut it, because I would have said no. Nic would have had to ask me, and of course Nic was having none of it.'

There's another reason Clifford may not have been *au courant*—he was back in New Mexico, working on *Convoy* with volatile genius Sam Peckinpah. 'Whilst I was out of town,' he surmised, 'they were hacking away at *The Man Who Fell To Earth*.'

'I got the feeling,' Deutchman concluded, 'that the whole chapter is something that the filmmakers who made the movie—not just Nic but all the others who were involved—wanted to forget!'[35]

HOW WE
LIVE HERE
CHAPTER TEN

Nineteen seventy-six was the year of the American Bicentennial, jokingly referred to in some circles as 'The Bisexual.' The nation's bicentennial was a celebration honoring the two hundredth anniversary of the Declaration of Independence (cue Elton John's 'Philadelphia Freedom,' written partly in honor of his friendship with tennis player Billie Jean King, but quickly usurped as a theme song for American patriotism). President Gerald Ford, running a campaign for re-election that he would lose to the unassuming Georgia native Jimmy Carter, said that presiding over the bicentennial was the greatest moment of his life.[1] The Ford Library's website analyzed the popularity of the yearlong event. 'It provided a much needed respite from the bleak years of the Vietnam War, the Watergate scandal, and the turbulent cultural upheavals of the previous decade.'[2] Queen Elizabeth and Prince Phillip came to the White House for a state dinner, companies created numerous merchandizing tie-ins, and there were a whole lot of fireworks.

Bowie was touring with his Isolar show, starting the performance with a screening of Luis Buñuel's eye-splitting *Un Chien Andalou* and selling a program highlighting his fascination with Kirlian photography, which was pioneered in 1939 by Semyon Kirlian, who found that items on a photographic plate became a captured image when exposed to high-voltage electric fields. Music by Kraftwerk ('Radioactivity') and Pink Floyd ('Welcome To The Machine') served as an overture before Bowie took the stage, in stark black and white and, with help from Martin Samuel, his *Man Who Fell* hair. By no means did he reflect the nation's musical zeitgeist, which was best embodied by artists such as Peter Frampton, Chicago, and the ubiquitous and quintessential California band, the Eagles.

Regardless of his more subdued appearance, Bowie was more

like an interstellar asterisk to the era. His glam era fans—initially broadsided by his Halloween Jack persona from the *Diamond Dogs* tour—were abandoning the glitter and tube tops and platform shoes in favor of double-breasted or equally tailored suits, military surplus flight suits (inspired by the one Bowie borrowed from sometime paramour Ava Cherry), and red pointed-toe Capezio dance shoes.

When Bowie played at the Los Angeles Forum, one of the guests at the after party was Steven Ford, the American president's son. By March, Bowie had abandoned plans to appear in the film *The Eagle Has Landed*, saying he'd been passed over because he asked too high a price. The part went to veteran actor Robert Duvall. Bowie told Mary Campbell of the Associated Press that his cockiness over the fee was because he'd contacted director Ingmar Bergman about a project he would partially finance involving circus performers in 1923. 'It was my suggestion that one [of the performers] is British,' he said. His assumptions about his stature with the director were optimistic and tenuous: he only knew that Bergman's cameraman had seen him in *The Man Who Fell To Earth*.[3]

Bowie was probably not overly preoccupied about the outcome of the London world premiere of *The Man Who Fell To Earth*, having been arrested in Rochester, New York, for possession of marijuana (a drug unlikely to have been his figurative tipple of choice). The charges were later dropped. Then he found himself in a further maelstrom in the UK on May 2, when, upon arrival at London's Victoria Station, he was caught mid-wave in a photograph that the *New Musical Express* quickly described as a Nazi salute. Bowie didn't help his case by suggesting that Britain might benefit from a fascist leader.

Things were not a whole lot calmer for Howard Rubin, who'd

resigned his position with the New Mexico Film Commission. The *Albuquerque Journal* took the beleaguered Rubin to task, writing, 'Where [previous film commission members] Lonesome Dave Cargo and Bruce King struggled over who owned antique pianos, moon rocks, and woodpeckers, Apodaca has his Howard Rubin, the "flamboyant hustler" from Hollywood who got a pie thrown in his face, ordered T-shirts misspelled Nueva Mexico ... wined and dined movie executives and kept beer in the refrigerator in his office.'

In response, Rubin was sanguine. 'People have painted me into a position as a Hollywood person, the Sammy Glick image, the hustler, flamboyant, but I'm not. I've proven myself to the industry.' The article allowed that Rubin had achieved one 'personal triumph,' having facilitated the filming of *The Man Who Fell To Earth* in the state.

In 1976, Britain's punk rock Summer of Hate was getting under way, but the US pop psyche had largely not yet caught on. NBC Television's *Saturday Night Live* was at its zenith, with its Not Ready For Prime Time Players including Dan Ackroyd, John Belushi, Chevy Chase, Garrett Morris, Jane Curtin, Gilda Radner, and Lorraine Newman. The late-night program, created by Lorne Michaels and broadcast live from New York, was irreverent, hip, witty, arch, young, and usually very funny.

The July 24 broadcast was no exception. It was hosted by Louise Lasser, the droll and clever redhead (once married to Woody Allen) who starred in the ironic soap opera *Mary Hartman, Mary Hartman*—itself a genre trailblazer. Lasser had recently been in a tight spot when she was arrested after causing a stir in a Beverly Hills antique shop. She'd been trying to buy a dollhouse as a birthday gift for her wardrobe person, but found herself five dollars short of its $105 price tag. Lasser refused to leave, prompting the police to arrive with outstanding traffic warrants for her. After searching her purse, they found about six dollars worth of cocaine, for which she was charged and eventually given six months' probation.

The host slot was to signal her return to the spotlight. In the opening, a freshly back-from-LA John Belushi joins the cast, wearing a white suit, Hawaiian shirt, and designer shades and boasting an attitude that is pure California snobbery combined with laid-back Los Angeles cool. (Think Woody Allen's lambasting of the city in *Annie Hall*.) Belushi radiated the kind of tanned, sunshine-and-palm-trees affect that gave the West Coast a bad name, and he played it to the hilt.

Lasser came on in vermillion flares, platform shoes, and a velour top, and promptly peppered her monologue with references to Beverly Hills. Then she pretended to freak out—one of the most convincing cons since Orson Welles's *War Of The Worlds* radio broadcast in 1938 had Americans certain they'd been invaded by little green men. Retreating to her dressing room, she refused to come out despite a series of pleas from Gilda Radner, a shark (Chevy Chase), and Dan Ackroyd, posing as her probation officer. She finally relented after being promised the cover of *Time* magazine.

Garrett Morris did a skit as Idi 'V.D.' Amin, and Curtin and Newman were two Manson girls selling human-hair potholders they'd knitted in prison. The show's centerpiece, 'Weekend Update,' found newsreader Chase referencing the Summer Olympics in Montreal and President Ford's lack of intellectual acumen. Radner posed as a petulant Olga Korbut (railing against Nadia Comaneci) before Chase closed with news of the Viking's recent landing on Mars. 'There is no life on Mars,' Chase deadpanned.

In another segment, Belushi tried to hawk his wardrobe—a check shirt and reversible vest, plus hat and shades that were the 'trademark of an underpaid actor.' He moved on to selling his record albums: Cream, the Stones, The Doors, and 'a Grand Funk Railroad LP I only listened to once.' Dan Ackroyd portrayed presidential candidate Jimmy Carter with a cheesy, outsized grin.

Among the adverts were McDonald's, now featuring breakfast items, Meow Mix, and a trailer for a movie called *Lifeguard*. Sandwiched between a corny 'Flick my Bic' lighter ad and a bevy of young women in shorts on what purported to be a New York stoop sashaying to 'Short Shorts' for a hair removal product was an even shorter trailer for *The Man Who Fell To Earth*. The emphasis was on explosions, excitement, and action; the film's stars were unidentifiable, except for the briefest of credits. There were a handful of other theatrical trailers for the film out there, likely made by Rugoff's employees. One US spot featured narration by *Star Trek*'s William Shatner, while its international cousin stressed Bowie as 'a phenomenon of our time.'

To close the show, Lasser sat cross-legged onstage and chatted candidly about her travails—a move that later prompted her manager to have the show taken off the record.

Meanwhile, shoring up the film's impending New York premiere, Candy Clark had struggles of her own. 'I was so excited because I had seen the film in England, gone to the opening there. It was really great, I was really proud of my performance and everyone's performance, and the story was easy to follow. I was supposed to go on tour of the US with the film. It'd been maybe a month since I'd seen it. I was in New York City, Cinema 5 put me up, and I was supposed to be on the road for two weeks. I asked to see the film to refresh myself: When you're on tour, you want to sell, you want to be excited about it when you're promoting.

'I was at the theater and they showed the film,' she continued. 'I almost threw up. They destroyed it. I called Nic and said, It's been hacked to bits. It caused a big ruckus. The director is in England and his whole project is falling apart. It created such turmoil.' (Roeg was probably aware of the cuts before then.)

Clark still wanted to do her bit for the film. 'I tried my best for a day or two to promote the film. The *Village Voice* had come to do an interview, and Cinema 5's PR person wouldn't leave the room because he was monitoring me. I'm supposed to be lying about this great film and telling the press about how fabulous it is, and I just could not do it.

'The PR person left the room briefly to go to the bathroom, and that's when I—I felt like I was making a prison break. I said to the guy interviewing me, I'm lying. The film has been chopped up. I hate it. Then the guy working for Cinema 5 comes back in. I was caught between a rock and a hard place. I'm just no good at lying, especially about a film I took so much pride in and I worked sooo hard to have it exact. All my ideas chopped to bits.

'I had a really restless night, I could barely sleep, and I was supposed to leave New York and start touring. It's inexcusable and not very professional, but I just packed my bags and snuck out of town.'

Clark hid out at her manager Pat McQueeney's house in Los Angeles. 'She's the one who said pack your bags and leave, because I was having a nervous breakdown. I was the only one out there. I was supposed to go cross-country and I packed and snuck out of the hotel. Then they were calling and calling, my manager was intercepting and I was hiding out, really scared.'

And then there was the inevitable insult to injury outcome: 'The film came out and it was a dud, a total dud,' she lamented.[4]

Walter Tevis was equally disappointed. 'My quarrel with Roeg was over what I felt to be an undue amount of mystification; I tried to argue him into telling a story. It's my feeling about science fiction or allegory that it's best to tell the story straight out. I thought the film was sophomoric and unnecessarily confusing.'[5]

Tevis had an ally in Richard Schickel, *Time* magazine's influential film critic. 'As it happens, I saw the film a couple weeks ago when I was in London,' Schickel wrote to Tevis. 'My impression is that there is a good story lurking underneath ... Roeg's rather pretentious cinematography ... . Meanwhile, it was kind of you to say such nice things about my movie reviewing. Coming from a writer as admirable as yourself, the compliments will be treasured.'[6]

Tevis has seen the film at its New York premiere. 'The audience was mostly David Bowie fans,' his wife, Jamie Griggs Tevis, later wrote. 'Walter gave the movie a *B*.'[7]

'I was at the premiere in New York and there were a lot of slack-jawed sixteen-year-olds,' Tevis himself recalled.[8] He likely felt marginalized, as evidenced by a letter from his future wife Eleanora Walker, then working at the literary agency which represented him.

Dear Walter: Enclosed is your Avon check for *The Man Who Fell To Earth* in the amount of $4,050.00 as we discussed. I'll try to mail it off early today so that you can deposit it in the bank in good time.

I spoke to Mr. Rugoff's assistant today again. The situation is this: there will be no critic's screenings, and there will be no formal opening in the sense of gala festivities planned, and no special publicity for the film. Therefore they will not be using you for public relations activities. Therefore they will not be paying your airfare to New York, nor will they be paying your hotel accommodations, as they would have had there been a formal premiere. They will have free passes for you to get into the cinema, and they will have posters for you.

Harrumph! Paramount, Paramount, Paramount ...

Kind regards,
Eleanora[9]

Tevis had not soured on the film's star, even though he was miffed that Bowie was on the cover of Avon's tie-in paperback re-release of the novel. 'I tried to convince Avon Books that putting him on the cover might be a mistake, because Bowie fans aren't likely to be people who read books in the first place,' Tevis said, before adding, 'He's a very fine man. I like him a lot.' Even so, he noted that Bowie's name on the cover was 'twice as big as mine, and it looks like he wrote it.'[10]

The print ads were in the papers: 'Power space time love and a visitor,' 'Explosive hypnotic mysterious mind blowing spectacular,' and the peculiar (or worryingly resonant), 'What do you do when you fall in love with someone ... and discover he's from another planet?'

The New York reviews were coming in. Richard Eder in the *Times* was impressed, stating that of the many science-fiction films set to open in the next year (one of which would be *Star Wars*), 'We shall be lucky if even one or two are as absorbing and as beautiful as *The Man Who Fell To Earth*.' In particular, Eder praised Bowie, whom he felt 'gave an extraordinary performance. The details, the chemistry of this tall pale figure with black-rimmed eyes are clearly not human. Yet he acquires a tragic, moving force.'

The early scene with the funfair drunkard belching (a burp that is bookended by Newton's in his final scene) prompted Eder to ask, 'Where is Outer Space? Right here on earth.' In addition to rating Bowie's acting, he also reserved praise for Clark as well as Henry and Torn, whom he found 'subtle and impeccable.'[11]

Frank Rich at the *New York Post* was not as convinced about Clark, whom he felt was the 'movie's oddest idea.' Clark, he said, 'was fun to watch at first' but gelled with Bowie 'as Dr. Pepper might with Bordeaux wine.'[12]

Newsweek picked up on the contemporary Howard Hughes angle, adding, 'You could call Roeg a pretentious director, but he is a gifted one and many of his pretentions pay off in beauty, tension and a mysterious, unsettling power.'[13] *Time*'s Jay Cocks dismissed Bowie as a 'master of weirdness' and felt the film 'not good enough' for Roeg.[14]

Andrew Sarris, writing in the *Village Voice*, caught the discrepancies between the novel and film, finding that the movie 'charges up Tevis's relatively chaste novel with a relentless sexual expressionism, particularly with the key earthlings.'[15] But John Simon in *New York* magazine was cattiest, correcting his mistake of attributing the film's cinematography to Roeg in an earlier review. 'After all,' he defended, 'I did not mistake *The Man Who Fell To Earth* for a good movie, which would have been a lapse.'[16]

Before the focus shifted to Hollywood, Tom Allen examined the film in the *Soho Weekly News*. He believed that fans of traditional science fiction were likely to find the film to be 'a bum trip,' and that it was also challenging because 'Roeg tends to be casual to a fault with exposition, which he obviously finds bothersome.' He cautioned that it was not 'a head film, whatever the advertising on the film may imply,' but rather 'a wry, winsome tale about the domesticating of an extraterrestrial humanoid alien.' He can't quite come to terms with Newton's family, 'a trio of queer, egg-headed, bleached, anemic, bland-featured humanoids with an eerie resemblance to Woody Allen's sperm cells in *Everything You Wanted To Know About Sex.*'

Roeg's depiction of sex was equally perplexing for the other Allen. 'For one thing, the strange ménage-a-trois, sudsy, bathtub intertwining of *Performance*, which seemed to be the sexual high point of the film, carries over to *The Man Who Fell To Earth* when Roeg seems more fascinated by Newton's vague description of a viscous form of body massage … in milky vats than with the more common rolls in the hay that are on the mind of the earthbound professor and the hotel maid.'[17]

Vincent Canby in the *New York Times* looked at the film alongside other current science fiction–related releases such as *Embryo, Food Of The Gods, A Boy And His Dog,* and *Logan's Run,* the latter of which he felt strongly leaned on set design. He concluded that *Man Who Fell* was by far the best of the bunch, relying on concerns rather than special effects and being 'anything but sentimental.'[18]

While the film did a turn at the Berlin Film Festival on June 25 (it lost out on its Golden Bear award to Robert Altman's *Buffalo Bill And The Indians*), in Beverly Hills, British Lion opened an office and announced its merger with EMI. The move left only one other major UK company, the Rank Organisation. Lion's newest employee, brought over from England, was Marion Rosenberg, who was profiled in the *Los Angeles Times* by writer Lee Grant. Asked about the difference between American and British working styles, she responded, 'We tend to have a calmer temperament, be more down to earth. Americans, on the other hand—and this sounds so pompous—are more slick.'[19]

The Man Who Fell To Earth opened quietly in Westwood at the Art Deco United Artists Cinema on July 1. Publicist John Springer stood in the lobby handing out hastily photocopied press kits and looking slightly befuddled. Springer, a veteran of Hollywood's heyday—when he represented, among others, Marilyn Monroe, Judy Garland, Elizabeth Taylor, and Richard Burton—may have felt nostalgic for an earlier time.

Writing in *New West*, Stephen Farber covered the trajectory of the film, saying that Roeg found out about the cuts after he phoned a New York cinema to check the running time. 'I had an opportunity to see Roeg's original 140-minute version (which is still playing in Europe), but since I have not yet seen the edited version I will reserve comment until next time,' he wrote, in the magazine's July 5 issue.[20] By July 19, Farber had seen the excised version, and he was not complimentary. The film was about 'society not being able to tolerate outsiders,' he wrote. 'Although David Bowie's teenage fans may take the idea about intolerance and nonconformity as profound, those ideas are less startling to the rest of us.' He was also unhappy with the aliens who looked to him like they 'stepped out of *Star Trek*,' and believed that the film's structure was 'like a mystery story; the problem is that there is no real mystery.'[21]

The film would soon open in New Mexico, and Bowie talked to a wire service in a piece picked up by the *Albuquerque Journal*. 'It's a terrifying film,' he said, 'and you're not quite sure why. There's not much blood, nothing sensational visually except the photography, which is pure eighteenth-century Romanticism.

'It's very murky, but you certainly don't think, Ah, there's a man from Mars. It's more like, Uh, oh, did I see something there? It affects you after you see the film … it hangs over you. It's not a pleasant film to watch; it doesn't have pleasant effects.'[22]

The film reviewer in the *New Mexico Independent*, Steven P. Kramer, certainly wasn't happy with the movie, as indicated by the headline, 'Bowie Lands In Tedious Mush In Sci-fi Flick Filmed In New Mexico.' 'New Mexico has long been a place for people dissatisfied with their precious abodes,' he wrote. 'Many of our own immigrants make significant contributions to life in the Land of Enchantment. Mr. Newton is colorless. … A nice setting deserves a better plot. To see the Sunport, the Downtown Plaza, White Sands, or the Jemez in the film adds to the interest of these places. It's too bad the film isn't a travelogue.'

Kramer also bemoaned the depiction of 'some dumb cops from Artesia' and the odd-looking train on Anthea. 'If that's their level of technology, one wonders how Newton made it all the way here,' he pondered. 'In short, the film is a bore, and a long one at that. This state deserves better visitors.'[23]

Eric Johnson, who'd witnessed the filming in Madrid, made the trek with his family (and the larger population of the town) to Albuquerque to see the film at the faded-glory KiMo Theater. 'It wasn't a first run theater, it ran Saturday matinees,' he said of the once great movie palace. He recalled being underwhelmed by the film but struck by shots of local passersby who seemed 'unnaturally suspicious or even threatening,' guarding their own privacy as well as any, perhaps illegal, proclivities.[24]

In a *Los Angeles Times* profile that August, Candy Clark said of the film, 'People seem to love it or hate it—there's no in between. At least that means it's having an effect on them.'[25] Clark herself continued to garner praise, not least from *Playboy*, which praised her 'spunk and spirit' while noting Bowie's 'extrasensory star power.'[26] Powerhouse critic Pauline Kael, writing in the *New Yorker*, called the film '*The Little Prince* for Young Adults' and compared its star—Bowie, not Clark—yet again to Katharine Hepburn in *Sylvia Scarlett*.[27]

Perhaps the oddest appraisal came from *McCall's* (a magazine primarily geared toward homemakers), in which Lynn Minton, writing in her column 'Movie Guide For Puzzled Parents,' found the film to be 'a strong, intriguing story. [Newton] is lonesome, unable to communicate what he thinks and feels to the people around him, and finally experiences helplessness, powerlessness and despair— all very much like the average adolescent. There's nudity and two scenes of fairly explicit sex—one tender and affectionate, one casual and raunchy—too over-stimulating surely for younger adolescents. There's also one shocking murder but it is there to make a point. As a parent, I'd be inclined to favor mature adolescents seeing this as a stimulus for the discussion of thoughts and feelings that are already present, already disturbing, but hard to get at or to get young people to talk about.'[28]

All told, by the end of the year, the film did come up with an award, the Golden Scroll (later the Saturn Award) from the Academy of Science Fiction, Fantasy, and Horror Films. The organization had been founded by Dr. Donald A. Reed, also of the Count Dracula Society, which he formed in 1962 alongside fellow members Ray Bradbury and Rock Hudson.

AFTERLIFE
CHAPTER ELEVEN

n New Year's Day, 1976, Los Angeles residents who looked up at Hollywood's Mount Lee would have found its disheveled landmark sign altered to read 'Hollyweed.' It was the playful handiwork of prankster and college student Danny Finegood, who was making a not-so-subtle comment about the state's relaxed marijuana laws, which went into effect that day. By 1977, the sign was in further disrepair—the dilapidated first *O* resembled a *U*, and the second *O* disappeared entirely. Deterioration continued to the point that by August 1978, the entire sign was taken down, leaving the hillside bare for three months until a new sign—the creation of which was spearheaded by Hugh Hefner—was erected.

Bowie was not spending much time in his bête noire, Los Angeles, during those years, but they were equally transformative for him. He'd moved to two opposing environs (pristine Vevey, Switzerland, and gritty Berlin), kicked drugs (largely, he implied, with the help of Coco Schwab), and suitably altered his life. Films, however, were still on his mind. When he attended the Paris showing of *The Man Who Fell To Earth* on June 29, 1977, at the Gaumont Theatre on the Champs-Élysées, he went on into the night with the actress Sydne Rome, with whom he'd hoped to star in on a project called *Wally* about the Austrian artist Egon Schiele.[1]

A few months earlier, in New Mexico, the movie finally made it to Artesia, where the *Daily Press* announced that 'Artesians who served as extras during the filming of scenes from the R-rated movie … may catch a glimpse of themselves this weekend when the movie comes to Artesia's Landsun Theatre.'[2] It also reported that the Artesia Hotel, where much filming had occurred, had been torn down.

Regardless of what Artesians made of the film, it had a fan—if a qualified one—in Michael Ventura of the *Los Angeles Weekly*. In a 1979 piece entitled 'We Are The Science Fiction,' Ventura wrote that the film was 'an extraordinary moment that Roeg has created,' but rued Clark's reaction to Newton as he really is. Audiences, he said, tended to have a troublesome response. 'Laugh is not the right word. They titter, almost giggle.' Still, he allowed that Clark 'plays a repetitive character without repeating herself'—a remark that drew disdain from the actor.[3]

'A repetitive character who doesn't repeat herself?' she said to me. 'That doesn't make sense. That does not make sense! A character that stays the same throughout the film—is that what he means?'[4]

Ventura felt that 'several of [the film's] moments would do nicely in a slice of life bedroom drama,' and took a philosophical if troubling view of the lovers' situation. 'If somehow any of us could see our lovers as they most deeply are, would any of us touch them?'[5]

The Man Who Fell To Earth went quiet for a while until 1981, when it was rereleased in a restored version. A full-page ad in the *Los Angeles Times* heralded, 'Before there was *Star Wars* … before there was *Close Encounters* … there was *The Man Who Fell To Earth*.'[6] A new assessment then ensued. The *Los Angeles Herald-Examiner* described Newton, rather curiously, as a 'cooled-out cast-off of the Age of Aquarius' and found the plot the reverse of the sci-fi staple 'take me to your leader.' David Ehrenstein, the reviewer, recognized that 'even the briefest of Rugoff's cuts is ruinous' and concluded that while it 'may never be a popular film … [it is] one of the most adventurous and rewarding films in recent years.'[7]

In the *Los Angeles Weekly*, Michael Ventura revisited the film, finding the uncut version more coherent. 'The cutters say they were cutting mostly for time reasons,' he wrote. 'They were cutting for skin. For Nicolas Roeg, love and skin are the same thing. …

In the uncut version … the after-image is clear: it is the expressive nakedness of lovers … the pasty nakedness of old lovers who have gone to sleaze (totally cut in the first release), the tender nakedness of people who have hope and energy, the nakedness wet with nostalgia of a man remembering a life as better than it was. Nakedness as it exists in the mind.'

Ventura was also pleased that Bryce's role was now intact. 'He's a character now instead of a gruff grace note. A necessary character, because he is the Earth's counterpart to Bowie's alien.' And he reiterated—one hesitates to say 'repeated' in case it sounds repetitive—his praise for Clark. 'Candy Clark gives one of the finest portraits in American movies of an inarticulate, lower-class girl feeling more than she can possibly hope to express with the shreds of words she calls language.'

Even though he still found the flashbacks to Anthea 'almost unwatchable,' Ventura was certain the restored film was 'even more of a cinematic love poem that the edited original release.'[8]

Stuart Payron, writing in the *Village Voice*, brought up an interesting point. Why was Oliver Farnsworth, portrayed as a straight man in the novel, turned into a homosexual character? He felt Roeg 'makes a character gay for no particular reason, just to acknowledge we exist.'[9] Indeed, Farnsworth and Trevor, his lover, are the only earthlings to die or disappear.

It would be more than a decade before the film again resurfaced, and it would have to wait for a little help from a couple of high-profile advocates and champions.

By 1980, Walter Tevis, despite his self-professed disdain for church basements, had gotten sober. He left twenty-five years of teaching ('I was beginning to repeat my jokes'[10]), moved to a small apartment in New York City, and turned out a succession of well-regarded novels. He remarried—his first wife said he felt it was 'easier to begin life with someone new'[11]—and lived contentedly with his new wife, Eleanora, until his death from lung cancer on August 8, 1984, at University Hospital—New York University Medical Center. He was buried in Richmond, Kentucky.

Tevis's passing came just eight days after his novel *The Color Of Money*, a sequel to *The Hustler*, came out. It too would be made into a movie. 'He cut it close and waited nearly too long,' author Tom Nolan wrote about Tevis's comeback, 'but he delivered the excellence … allowing the character who made his reputation in the first place to return for another shot at his own brass ring. All Tevis's protagonists, pool hustler to space man, struggle against great odds to fulfill individual potential. You see yourself in these losers/winners and you root for them. Walter Tevis wrote like a dream.'[12]

Author Jonathan Lethem has remarked that both *The Hustler* and *The Man Who Fell To Earth* are great novels that have been upstaged by film versions, and Malcolm Jones, writing for the *Daily Beast*, explored this further. Regarding the latter film, he wrote, 'However much it tries your patience, it never insults your intelligence. Time and fashion can't change it.' Though he felt that both the book and film each succeed in their own right, he credited the book with exploring Newton's alcoholism more adeptly. The novel 'tells us up front he binges on alcohol and TV to inoculate himself from the world that is too much with him but of which he can never be a part'—a fact that rendered him more sympathetic than his self-indulgent film counterpart. He praised 'the quiet, even tone of

Tevis's prose,' before concluding, 'I admire the movie but … if forced to choose, I would grab the novel more eagerly.'[13]

On April 1, 1986, a TV pilot of *The Man Who Fell To Earth* was announced. It was perfectly permissible to double take the date, but it was no joke. And the travails the television version endured almost made Roeg's problems seem trifling.

'The film version was trimmed,' said its screenwriter, Richard Kletter. 'Ours was butchered.'

'I loved my script,' he told me. 'It was more faithful to the book than the movie was.'

Indeed, the TV pilot did have an auspicious beginning, with the likes of Raul Julia expressing interest in playing the lead. That role (John Dory, aka Newton) went to Lewis Smith, and Beverly D'Angelo took over for Candy Clark as Eva Milton (né Mary-Lou). Actors with equally strong portfolios filled out the cast: Annie Potts, Bruce McGill, and a young Wil Wheaton, who played a misunderstood kid with a decidedly punk bent.

Bobby Roth, himself accomplished an accomplished director, took on the MGM Television project. Right off the bat, he and Kletter began to have problems with MGM TV head David Gerber. 'Once we started preproduction David Gerber, crank, garrulous character, tried to substitute his script,' Kletter said. 'He reshot stuff, inserted shots of people's backs, added voice-overs. Gerber would rather sabotage his own future than give in to an impudent writer.

'I got into a physical altercation with him at MGM,' Kletter continued. 'I had a bad ankle and was resting my foot on a table. Gerber came in and twisted it. I said, David, don't do that, but he did, and I put my knee in his back.'

The brouhaha was witnessed by several staff members, at least one of whom cheered Kletter on. 'I let him up and he said, Not bad for an old guy.'

But Kletter was upbeat—eventually. 'I saw Gerber in the hallways five years later. He said hello.'[14]

Director Bobby Roth, who came from an independent film background and held its attenuate sensibilities, was slightly more measured in his look back at the project. But he too had the same obstacle: Gerber. 'David Gerber was crazy,' he said. 'It was a crazy production. He was both executive producer and the head of MGM TV, which was lethal. There was no one else to appeal to; it was David's baby one way or another, and here I come from independent filmmaking and don't think I have to listen to anybody. I was a really bad choice. I'd only done movies and I got into this. I had a deal with ABC and I had to do something, so that's how I ended up with the project.

'David Gerber was a character,' Roth continued. 'I don't think he liked me much—we didn't get along. David was old school and thought he knew more than anybody. It was kind of a transition time in television—it was about to get much better, I think. It was a year after I did [an episode of] *Miami Vice. Vice* was one of the first shows that was trying to use music differently and trying to shoot more cinematically and using a different approach to casting. He kind of got caught with people like me and maybe Richard who wanted to be part of a new thing.'

As with Kletter, Roth's problems began almost immediately. 'We went to have dinner on Orsini's on Pico just prior to shooting and we were going to go over the script with [Gerber]. The pages were loose and they were literally falling under the table never to be picked up. Lynn [Loring, later to head MGM/UA TV, one of the few women to head a studio], she was David's person, Lynn was just getting through it. She was a good soul, but I don't think she had much love for him.'

Gerber was definitely a thorn in most everyone's side. 'He would do crazy things,' Roth continued, 'like I would shoot a scene, and before I got to see it—we were on film which was a day behind, it'd be a day before we'd see the dailies, and in those days you'd finish shooting and you'd go to a lab or a screening room to look at the previous day's dailies—he would already have a call sheet for me. He would see the film first, even though that was against the rules of the DGA [Directors Guild]. He would already decide what he wanted me to shoot because he didn't like the dress Beverly D'Angelo was wearing. It was pretty crazy, I'd say at least let me cut the scene to see if you want to reshoot ... I was really green, I'd done almost no television.'

Roth said he tried to take his lead from Tevis's novel rather than Roeg's film, despite having met and greatly admiring his fellow director. 'I was friends with Nic ... we hung out at a couple of film festivals before I did this project, '84, '85. He was a very talented guy and a great guy and very generous to younger filmmakers. I was pretty young at the time. I didn't really pay that much attention to the original movie. I thought we were trying to do something that went back to the book.'

Roth was forced to adopt an original twist on the alien—a move prompted by the casting of Lewis Smith as Dory/Newton. Smith, whom Roth assumed got the part on the basis of his performance in *The Adventures Of Buckaroo Banzai Across The Eighth Dimension*, was far from Roth's first choice—he favored Bruce Davison, who also read for it—so he applied a different tack. 'Lewis was such ... for lack of a better word, he was a very downhome, rural kind of guy,'

Roth said of the Tennessean actor. 'He's never going to be mistaken for David Bowie. Not that many people are, but he's not even in the same vein. The choices were limited because no one that I saw could hold a candle to him in terms of both his sensuality and his charisma. Bowie was one big, throbbing instrument.'

To deal with the disparity, Roth had a discussion with producer Lewis Chesler and suggested, 'Well, let's play everybody else is from outer space and the alien is normal.' Roth had handpicked the rest of the cast and felt that this intellectual choice would fly. 'All the other people I'd cast were friends of mine or people that I'd worked with before like Beverly. Beverly was a good friend, James Laurenson was a good friend of mine, Bruce McGill—they were all people that I knew.' Significantly, too, Roth added, 'They were all people that were capable of being eccentric.'

Roth believed that the idea to make Smith normal and the rest of the cast alien was ultimately not entirely successful. Neither, he insisted, was it intended as a knock on Smith. Instead, he was 'trying to use him to his best. Then he could just act. He didn't have to play something so different from his own persona.'

The ABC TV 'Movie of the Week' was sitting pretty with a decent script, solid actors, a creative and highly capable director, and a large budget that in 2016 would equal some twenty million dollars. But it still had one insurmountable obstacle: Gerber. 'Even in the editing, Gerber kept adding things so a guy would turn his head who was not speaking, and David would throw an expository line in. It made me crazy,' Roth sighed. 'He wouldn't even use the same actor. He was very much the television equivalent of [Roger Corman].'

The Man Who Fell To Earth aired after *Starman* (with Jeff Bridges) was theatrically released, the latter garnering considerably more attention. The August night that it was televised, Roth wasn't watching. 'My editor from features cut it, so I knew what was happening,' he explained. 'I was so horrified by stories coming from the cutting room. It had no resemblance to my cut at all. I thought I was better off not watching it.'

Still, the ratings were good; that it wasn't picked up as a series was probably a financial decision. Nonetheless, Roth said, he wouldn't have stayed on had it been selected. 'I turned my cut in and never talked to David Gerber again. I don't mean it like in a huff. There was no occasion for me to. I didn't want to do TV. In the 80s I only did *Miami Vice* and *Crime Story*, but those were for Michael Mann.

'I don't think I ever saw that version [that aired]' Roth added. 'I would probably laugh now but I took myself very seriously in those days. I would have been appalled. [Roeg's] movie had emotion, and we didn't have really any. I would direct it a lot differently now.'

One last telling clue is that *Man Who Fell* is the only time Roth didn't use his name on a show. Instead, it is credited to Robert Roth. 'I wasn't able to take a pseudonym or I would lose residuals,' he said. 'Every other thing I've done out of a hundred projects has been Bobby.'[15]

Lewis Smith, who bravely took on the Newton/Dory role, was in the unenviable position of having a director who didn't want him (and vice versa) and being cast in a role previously and entirely inhabited by David Bowie. One thing in his favor was that Smith was oblivious to the Gerber drama. That doesn't mean he was a happy camper. 'I didn't want to do the project,' he told me. 'No one wanted me. I was told that from the beginning. I said no. An alien? What in the hell is this? And the predecessor is David Bowie and Nicolas Roeg, and it's television? How am I going to do that?'

Smith arrived at his audition to find twenty network and studio executives waiting to sit in. It was like the Last Supper, he said. 'The director is this close to me—he didn't want me. My ass is on the line—the studio is going to report back to CAA [Creative Artists Agency, which represented Smith].' Smith, who said he hadn't read the script because he was certain he'd never get the part, approached the audition from another angle. 'I'm going to be a child, I'm not going to give a shit about this movie, those scenes about listening to MTV music and all this stuff.'

Naturally, he got the part. 'I got the job by not wanting it,' he laughed. He met with Roth, and their mutual dislike was palpable. 'That was the most awkward meeting of my whole career,' Smith attested. The whole production, he felt, 'got off to a bad start and it ended bad.' When it looked for a moment like the TV pilot might be picked up for a series, the network got a call from Michael Douglas, pitching his series, *Starman*. 'It was in—we were out,' said Smith. 'I woke up thinking I had a TV show, [then] I read in the *Reporter*, *Man Who Fell To Earth* replaced by *Starman*.'

The antipathy he felt for his director continued unabated, way into the future. 'This kinds of sums it up,' he said, years later. 'I'd been doing *Django* [*Unchained*] for eight months, and Quentin [Tarantino] decides to pull his ace out of his sleeve in New Orleans at two o'clock in the morning. Everyone's on the set—Leonardo's [Di Caprio] there, Sam's [Jackson] there, the full tilt. Quentin goes, So, Lewis, you did *The Man Who Fell To Earth*. He'd been waiting to say that.'

'Yeah.'
'What did you think?'

'I thought it was missing something.'

'Yeah—Nicolas Roeg.'

'The whole set just died,' Smith continued. 'No slighting Bobby: you can't take an iconic movie that Nicolas Roeg did with David Bowie and take it to television. *The Man Who Fell To Earth* shouldn't have been touched.'[16]

The *Man Who Fell* entry in *The Encyclopedia Of Science Fiction* goes to great pains to explain that the TV movie not be confused with the film, before adding, 'This soft-centered version alters the plot considerably to give a banal moral, drops all references to the alien's corruption, and imports much sentimentality.'[17]

In the TV film, a spaceship from Anthea crash-lands in the South. Dory's three companions are killed and he buries them, then heals his wounded foot with a mysterious device before lighting out for New York City. He has in his possession some supernatural healing crystals—maybe he should have considered high-tailing it to the new age mecca of Sedona, Arizona.

In New York, Dory finds Felix Hawthorne, a patent lawyer, who will manage World Enterprises. A character named Morse becomes suspicious of Dory, and Hawthorne suggests he head for New Mexico, where he can lie low. Prior to that, in a sketchy part of New York City, John has assumed the identity of a rock'n'roll star and fallen for Eva Milton, as well as developed a soft spot for her problematic son, Billy. When John reveals his true identity and form to Eva, she doesn't balk; rather, she is both accepting and love-struck.

As the threat to John becomes more grave, he decides that taking Eva and Billy to New Mexico is a good idea, thinking too that the more rustic environment could be a balm for troubled Billy. But when Billy finds out that John intends to return to Anthea to recover his real son, he feels betrayed enough to spill the beans about John to Vernon Gage. Gage intervenes and blows up Dory's project—and himself in the process. Felix helps John escape to return to his son—and some three hundred other surviving Antheans—but not before John tells Billy that he will return one day.

The pilot was scheduled to air as the ABC Sunday Night 'Movie of the Week' on August 23, 1987. A network press release described the plot as 'Sole survivor of a crashed spacecraft struggles to return to his dying planet to save loved ones.' The film went up against such stellar fare as *Circus Of The Stars*, *Staying Alive* (which starred Sylvester Stallone), and *Married … With Children*. It pulled in a respectable 14.5 audience share for the week, trailing *Alf* and inching out *Amen*.

The *Hollywood Reporter* called it 'a package tour-revisitation' of the film. Its reviewer liked Smith but understandably found him wanting in comparison to his predecessor. 'Though lithesome wonder and open-hearted goodwill animate Smith's performance, he lacks the dark, swirling undertow Bowie brought to the role.' The reviewer, Miles Beller, also felt this version needed Roeg's masterfulness, and instead was merely 'a crisply shot nursery tale, a sanitized story missing Roeg's touch of danger and defiance.'[18]

Variety pretty much concurred, writing that the whole affair 'lands flat,' but singled out for praise 'a non-touch love scene' between Smith and D'Angelo that was 'highly effective.' The writer also rated Smith's performance, which projected 'a warmth and agreeable humor that makes his space alien sympathetic despite the inconsistencies of his role.'[19]

No less a critic than Tom Milne reviewed the movie for *Monthly Film Bulletin*.

> Given the visionary scope of the Roeg–Mayersberg version of Walter Tevis's novel, a tele-movie remake only ten years later might not seem the most promising of ideas. The film is in fact a maddening mixture of good and bad, the good tending to predominate thanks to some excellent dialogue and a uniformly impressive cast.
>
> Surprisingly alert for a tele-movie to the importance of design ... the production makes equally effective use of locations ... including a chase through a crowded market (which, to judge by the reactions of startled passers-by, must have been shot with hidden camera).

Milne offered high praise for Roth. 'The real strength of the film is Bobby Roth's sympathetic handling of his cast,' he wrote. 'However, Roth is badly let down by his script. Tampering with Tevis to bring his novel more into popular line, it finally drives itself into a corner with its silly melodramatics about juvenile delinquency and surrogate fathers.'[20]

Or, as Randy A. Riddle, writing as coolcatdaddy, put it years later, 'It's a bit liked *Touched By An Angel* with an alien and bad 80s clothes and hairstyles. There's even an annoying punk kid sidekick. ... Of course, the aliens learn about human (American) culture by watching transmissions of MTV.'[21]

The TV pilot did have at least one thing in common with the

film: its special makeup effects came courtesy of Burman Studios.

★

By the early 1990s, Candy Clark was living in New Jersey. She had something weighing on her mind. 'From 1976, when the film first came out, till '92, it bothered me. It bothered me! New management came in [to Cinema 5, of which Donald Rugoff, who died in 1989, had previously lost control] and I always had it in the back of my mind to make this right, fix it somehow. I called and asked to speak to the publicity department.

'I spoke to a really nice man … I had to do my sales pitch: Hi, my name is Candy Clark and I was in one of your movies called *The Man Who Fell To Earth*. I get asked constantly about this film. People want to see it but they want to see the full version. I will do whatever it takes, go on radio, travel with it, do whatever it takes to sell the film. You don't really have to spend any money, you just have to use your same old poster, put a banner across it that says "uncut version" and people will line up to see this film.

'He said, That's a great idea! So a few weeks later I checked in, and he said, Well, you know what, our negative is all cut up. We don't have anything to print with.'

Unfazed, Clark told him she knew just where to find the full negative. 'It's with British Lion,' she said, 'here's the phone number. The guy did exactly what I said to do. I was the only one who called and pitched, so it probably would be nowhereville. It would be dead. I had to wait for my moment.'[22]

Clark was tireless and heroic, but she wasn't the only one pushing for the release of the restored film. David Bowie contacted Michael Nash at the Criterion Collection to discuss a laserdisc release for the film. He also guaranteed his and Roeg's participation in the film's commentary—a highly lucrative special feature. Nash quickly took up Bowie's suggestion. Criterion, founded in 1984 under parent company Voyager, had forged a reputation as the film buff's home-video distribution company. Its first laserdisc reissue was *Citizen Kane*.

Michael Kurcfeld was a laserdisc producer at the company in Los Angeles, where it was originally based. He described the atmosphere as 'a lair of tech-enamored bohemians. Company style was 70s laid-back mixed with intense intellectual ferment.'[23]

The subsequent release received mixed reviews. Howard Klein in the *Los Angeles Reader* believed the uncut version to be a 'futile attempt to make the Roegefied storm more comprehensible.'[24] Writing in *Entertainment Weekly*, Steve Daly was bothered by the commentary. 'If it were an ordinary no-frills laserdisc it'd be easy to ignore the most pretentious allusions … prattling on about "the luggage of otherness" (Bowie) and how "sooner or later all things are connected" (Roeg), they quickly bring an already symbol-heavy tone poem crashing to the ground.'[25] *Time*, however, was smitten by the plot's very complexity: 'Figuring out *The Man* would be like unraveling a dream.'[26]

In 1998, Fox Lorber Home Video issued 'a pale, off-color edition' of the film followed by an Anchor Bay release in 2002.[27] 'We really went all out with this DVD,' senior vice president of acquisitions Jay Douglas boasted, explaining that special features included a new twenty-four-minute featurette about the film.[28]

Glenn Abel in the *Hollywood Reporter* commented that the film captured Bowie 'just at the height of his beauty,' but added that he felt Candy Clark looked like a soccer mom.[29] Interestingly, many reviewers made note of Bowie's beauty—an attribute not often associated with a male actor, with one possible exception being Montgomery Clift.

(Monty may have had the edge on the acting chops, but both men shared a sharp and sculpted visage and ethereal presence.)

In 2005, Criterion put out a DVD with several special features and additional commentary added to Roeg and Bowie's 1992 assessments. In October of that same year, *Variety* reported that Warner/Cherry Road Films (who'd made *Donnie Darko*) had bought the rights to *The Man Who Fell To Earth* with a view to remaking it.[30] Writer Oren Moverman (who would write *I'm Not There* and *Love & Mercy*] was set to adapt the book until Bowie (who'd suffered a heart attack while onstage in Prague on June 23, 2004), quickly retrieved the rights, purchasing them in 2005. With a view toward posterity, he would hold the rights close for a decade.

The year 2011 marked the thirty-fifth anniversary of the film. In Los Angeles, it ran at the Nu-Art theater where, on Saturday nights, it was followed by a midnight showing of *The Rocky Horror Picture Show* with a 'Live Shadow Cast.'[31] This was a matter of some excitement and pride for Graeme Clifford, who edited both movies.

Re-examining the film, the *Los Angeles Weekly* objected to the 'preposterous moment when Bowie slo-mo slaps a tray of chocolate chip cookies from Clark's hands.'[32] Anthony Lane in the *New Yorker* focused on the film's more somber elements. 'Time has done nothing to reduce the cool, confounding strangeness,' he wrote. 'The tristesse of the very last scene is as piercing as ever. Where Steven Spielberg sends his aliens home, Roeg, not just a puzzle setter but a pessimist, abandons the flame-haired Newton to his fate.'[33]

There are numerous nods and references to the film, but of particular interest is one from Nick Cave. Cave, the Australian-born singer-songwriter, actor, and writer is one of the few people in possession of both a highly recognizable persona and a long polymath career that can rival Bowie's. The main difference is Cave's consistent image—the young man in his first band, The Boys Next Door, is pretty much the Cave that prevailed. British filmmakers Iain Forsyth and Jane Pollard's 2014 documentary *20,000 Days On Earth* features an homage to *Man Who Fell* as Cave stands in a similarly funky bathroom as the one in the film and gazes into the mirror, pulling on his eyelids and examining his widely opened mouth.

'There is a nod to *TMWFTE* in the bathroom scene in *20,000 Days On Earth*,' Forsyth and Pollard explained. 'We wanted the simplest visual way of communicating the layered oddity of being Nick Cave and instantly looked to the mirror scene. It gave us a language to activate ideas of self awareness, vulnerability, and an alien detachment between who we construct ourselves to be, and who we actually are in the flesh, We were also determined to make a film that belongs to the cinematic traditions—not, say, the diluted strain of "music docs." Weaving in a cinematic influence which has influenced us felt like one way we could achieve that intention.'

Despite turning in a spot-on recreation, Cave didn't assiduously study the scene. 'We composed and framed the shot we wanted, then he just did his thing!' the filmmakers said. Forsyth and Pollard revisited the pivotal moment in 2016 for a Sky Arts TV series called *Neil Gaiman's Likely Stories*. 'In one of the four stories the lead character [played by George MacKay] is taken over by a new version of himself. Again we found the coded reference of that classic scene to be a great loaded way to add articulation to the character's relationship to himself.'[34]

Roeg once posited the point of his film-as-allegory. 'If you forget the fantastical side of the story,' he said, 'you can draw a parallel to a man emigrating to America.'[35] In 1976, a group of high-school kids did something very like that, building on the emotions of being perceived as outsiders in their own land.

The year *The Man Who Fell To Earth* was first released, future playwright Gregg Barrios found himself teaching high school in a small, rural, south Texas town called Crystal City. During one class period he played Bowie's *Station To Station* for his students. To his surprise, they liked it so much they decided to create a Bowie-inspired 'Chicano Sci-Fi space opera.' *Stranger In A Strange Land* (well, this was high school, after all) would feature a character stranded on Mars but longing to return to earth. The CIA, FBI, and unscrupulous politicians intervene before he ultimately prevails.

Their play took on another level of meaning when one of the students was detained at the USA–Mexico border after visiting the neighboring country's Piedras Negras in the state of Coalhuila. 'We're looking for aliens,' the border patrol told his family,' before the cheeky student retorted, I didn't know they had landed.' Crystal City itself had once been the site of a Japanese internment camp during World War II and indeed, Artesia, New Mexico, where so much of *Man Who Fell* was filmed housed a controversial detention center for immigrants that closed in 2014.

This new element fueled the play, which also featured mime, dance, multimedia, and eighteen Bowie songs. Roles had to be double cast: many of the students were from migrant families and might be called away at any moment to labor in the fields. Students sourced their costumes from a local secondhand shop and the army & navy store. 'They decorated their jeans with patch-ons and embroidery courtesy of the homemaking ed. teacher,' Barrios said.

The film version of *The Man Who Fell To Earth* had yet to make its way to south Texas, but the local library owned a copy of the novel. 'Our libretto follows the storyline of the alien coming to earth after an encounter with the Bowie-inspired Ziggy Stardust and the Grand Control man. It has that speculative type of noir that Tevis was so good at melding,' Barrios explained.

The small play was a success, garnering press from bigger Texan cities such as Laredo and San Antonio. Barrios's students were far from amateurish—they once received acting lessons from Isela Vega, best known for her role in Sam Peckinpah's cult classic film *Bring Me The Head Of Alfredo Garcia*.

In 1980, when Bowie was appearing on Broadway in *The Elephant Man*, Barrios decided to send him the play's libretto and playbill. In return, he received a note from Bowie as well as several signed photos reading 'Many thanks, Bowie.'

Years later, in 2015, Barrios's curiosity was piqued when he learned about a play called *Lazarus*, noting that it had several elements in common with his students' admittedly modest piece. 'It isn't beyond the realm of possibility that we may have influenced the unbelievably talented genius just as he greatly inspired us in a small Texas town years ago,' Barrios said.[36]

The connection seemed fragile, tender, and of course, tenuous, but it was entirely heartfelt. Before *Lazarus* would appear, however, a proposed work of collaboration between Bowie and a Pulitzer Prize–winning author featuring handful of ghostwritten songs, a rather pedestrian but extremely well-known poem—oh, and some Mexican mariachi music—was in the works.

★

In May 2005, the author Michael Cunningham, who'd been award the Pulitzer for his 1998 novel *The Hours*, was on a train departing from New York City when he got a phone call purportedly from David Bowie. 'Whoever you are,' he told the caller, 'this is a really cruel joke.' Cunningham was certain one of his friends who knew of the author's fondness for Bowie and his work was pranking him. But what he could not deny was the highly recognizable voice on the other end of the line. Bowie.

Cunningham somehow maintained a calm demeanor as the star told him he was interested in working with him on a project, and would he be able to discuss it over lunch the following week? After signing off, it dawned on Cunningham and his younger self: 'That teenager with the inept dye-job, the one prone to singing "Space Oddity" in the frozen food section of the supermarket, had not vanished after all,' he later wrote. He had, he realized, 'only been hibernating.'[37]

Meeting with Bowie and Coco Schwab in a West Village Japanese eatery, Cunningham and Bowie began to explore the idea of a musical about an alien stranded on earth. The author had seen *The Man Who Fell To Earth* shortly after its release and liked it, allowing, 'Frankly I may have been too stoned at the time to trust my own reaction. (I was pretty young and it was exactly the kind of movie my friends and I went to, stoned).'

No matter. A strong familiarity or even affinity with the film wouldn't be required. The project Bowie had in mind was not a revisit or even a follow-up. 'Hybrid' might even be too strong a word for it. The skeletal plot Bowie sketched out would be set in the future, after Bob Dylan had died and a treasure trove of his unrecorded songs had been uncovered. Bowie would compose these songs. And it would be a musical, and there would most certainly be an alien. Over lunch, Bowie pondered the poetry of Emma Lazarus, whose poem 'The New Colossus' is written at the foot of the Statue of Liberty. He wanted to incorporate the theme of a widely exposed but literarily neglected poet in their musical.

Cunningham was intrigued. One thing was certain: it wouldn't be necessary to read Tevis's novel or re-watch Roeg's film.

'If anything,' Cunningham recalled, 'it seemed best not to be influenced by another story about the aforementioned alien [Newton]. It might have been different if David had revered the movie, if he wanted our movie to be an homage or a riff or something like that. We weren't in any way using the content of the movie, beyond the notion of an alien on earth, which is so clearly in the public domain. We weren't basing our musical on *The Man Who Fell To Earth*; in fact David only mentioned the movie once, when he said he wasn't happy with his own performance.'[38]

When they parted that day on the Village sidewalk, Coco Schwab admonished Cunningham, 'I know I don't have to tell you to keep this project a secret.'[39]

'I told my friends,' Cunningham admitted. 'I didn't see any reason not to.' And for a time neither Bowie nor Schwab were any the wiser. 'I did get in trouble with David, however, for mentioning it in an interview on another subject entirely,' he said, 'during an interview I did over the phone with an Israeli literary journal.' (Cunningham spoke about the musical in response to the requisite question, 'What are you working on now?')

'I know Coco did admonish us after our first meeting not to talk about the project, but I thought she meant the content, not the fact that we were working together,' Cunningham said. 'David and

I made up after I'd blabbed to the publication in Israel, and I never made that error again. It was, in fact, taken up all over the Internet. It seems I'd naively underestimated the degree of interest in every single thing David thought or did.'

In subsequent conversations, Bowie expressed a desire to incorporate mariachi music. This latest addition initially threw Cunningham, but still he managed to weave it and the other disparate elements into a rough book. While the mariachi idea may seem to have come out of left field, Bowie did have an appreciation of Mexico (despite performing there just once), where the violin, accordion, trumpet, and guitar-based music originated. In 1997, he gave his only concert in Mexico City, and beforehand he took time to take in the local art and culture. Photographer Fernando Reyes took photos of the star in near darkness as he visited the Pyramid of the Sun in Teotihuacan. 'Here, these photographs show him looking human—not as a rock star or a movie star but as a human being experiencing the cultural landscape of Mexico,' Reyes said.[40]

So, mariachi was in. What was still giving Cunningham pause were the Dylan songs. He was a fan of the now-Nobel laureate, but working that musical aspect into the play was proving tricky. Fortunately there was a reprieve in the wings. 'I was so focused on trying to figure out what David did want, what I wanted and how the two might conceivably be conjoined,' he said. 'I did try, if not to talk David out of it, at least move him away from the one about him writing faux Bob Dylan songs, along with the notion that in the musical, this cache of previously unknown Dylan songs had just been discovered.'

How, one might wonder, did he pull that off?

'I simply didn't bring it up again after our initial meeting, and

David didn't bring it up again either,' Cunningham said. Although the plot posed many challenges, Cunningham was in it for the long run. 'I never thought of dropping out,' he said, 'not for one second.' Plus there was a gigantic ace in the hole: the music Bowie composed for the play. What he came up with, Cunningham attested, was superb.

Their working relationship contained a healthy dose of humor, which transferred—or tried to—into the piece. 'I can't speak for how effective the humor was but, yes, the various elements (alien, mariachis, etc.) seemed to demand a certain humor with (this probably goes without saying) a certain gravitas underneath,' Cunningham said. 'It's possible to wonder if my sense of humor just didn't jibe with David's. David was hardly humorless but his sense of humor was more wry and ironic than mine.'

They wrote mostly at night, with Bowie being entirely punctual—'more so than I was,' said Cunningham. Broadway was not in their sights, nor was any particular venue. 'Broadway seems unlikely,' he said. 'What we were coming up with seemed awfully arcane and strange for Broadway.'[41]

But the project was moving along, with Bowie's sustaining and beautiful original score, which Cunningham described as 'lush and complex and heartbreaking … possessed of a soul and depth and … a rinsing whisper of melancholy.' About halfway through their time working together, however, Bowie's heart problems resurfaced, and that brought to a halt what Cunningham lovingly referred to as 'David's and my crackpot project.'[42]

Rather than being completely devastated by the musical's demise, the author instead felt the phantom weight left by something his writing partner had felt so strongly about, and then as good as forgot.

One day, when Bowie was visiting his apartment, Cunningham caught Bowie admiring his collection of tiny white, seashell-sized plastic baby doll shoes. 'I just happened upon them in flea markets, thought they were odd and cool, and sooner or later, I had, like, a dozen of them,' Cunningham explained of the pair-less Mary Jane–style shoes. After their collaboration had ended, he sent the shoes to Bowie. 'I gave them all to David … and haven't acquired another miniature shoe since then. I wonder what's become of them.'[43]

On a Saturday in May, Cunningham and Bowie had been working in a silent, separate portion of Bowie's meticulously white studio when Cunningham noticed a series of boxes reaching up to the pristine rafters. He wondered what they contained. 'They're archiving my costumes,' Bowie dismissed. Cunningham would later discover the items were headed for London's Victoria & Albert Museum and the exhibit that would become, in 2013, David Bowie Is.

Cunningham was floored by his writing partner's offhandedness and understatement. 'He was innocent of all pretensions,' he wrote. 'I still have no idea where the rock star came from, how that sweet slip of a man could summon him up.'[44]

David Bowie Is was certainly no mere slip of an exhibit. Staged in London from March 23 to August 11, 2013, it was a large, loud, dark, controlling, and at turns, overwhelming installation. Among the platform boots, glittering costumes, tape machines, and album covers were a handful of items from The Man Who Fell To Earth. One was the black suit designed by Ola Hudson, worn over a white Viyella shirt with a pointed collar suggestive of the W in World Enterprises; the British publicity poster for the film, which is vaguely reminiscent of a Pink Floyd LP cover, but with Bowie as Newton appearing in its snow dome–like center, his black-covered script held together by two gold brads; and a green-and-black cloth badge with the World Enterprises logo.

In the exhibit's companion book, *David Bowie Is The Subject* author Phillip Hoare is quoted as saying, '*The Man Who Fell To Earth* works because he's playing David Bowie. That part was written for him before he arrived. There's this sense of things going on around him as this creature falls to earth. ... This person is completely ahead of his era, and is leading the era, and is an avatar that is untouchable.'[45]

Michael Cunningham wrote an imaginary ending to his and Bowie's 2005 project.

> Imagine a wildly ambitious work of musical theater in which all the elements have somehow fallen into place and meshed into a theatrical experience stranger and more beautiful, darker and funnier, more moving, more transcendent, than anyone, including its creators, had any reason to expect. Don't worry if it doesn't make sense. It should merely be what's beautiful to you, what's most moving and true. It should be what you're hoping for, every time a curtain rises.[46]

For many, that wasn't the case with Bowie's penultimate project. For some, however, no doubt it was. But, regardless of one's take on it, *Lazarus* would have to do.

LAZARUS
WALKS
CHAPTER TWELVE

Bowie did not suffer from a lack of projects to revisit. That he identified strongly enough with Thomas Newton to revive him and propel him thirty years forward spoke volumes. Visiting London in 2013, Bowie had tea with theatrical producer Robert Fox and expressed his desire to project Tevis's ageless alien into a gin-soaked and junk food–addled (the Twinkies for which he had a predilection boasted a shelf life to rival the alien's) future on the stage.

Bowie had subtly alluded to the idea years earlier, in 2005 (the same year he began working with Cunningham), when he'd given Fox a copy of Tevis's novel as a parting gift. His inscription, laden with protective parentheses, read:

> 'I'm not a human being at all.' (Thomas Jerome Newton) (SSShhh!! (David Bowie))

When they met again, eight years later, Bowie asked Fox to suggest some writers with whom he might collaborate, and Fox immediately mentioned Irish playwright Enda Walsh, whose *Once* had been an off-Broadway success. After consideration, Bowie emailed Fox to say, 'Enda is the man for the job.' At the time he got the news, Walsh was in New Mexico.

Fox was also instrumental in connecting award-winning Belgian director Ivo van Hove and designer Jan Versweyveld with the project. Like Cunningham, van Hove would think he was the target of a prank when offered the chance to work with Bowie. 'I thought sincerely someone was making a joke,' he said. 'So I let it sit in my email for a few days.'[1] He had used some Bowie songs to great effect in Tony Kushner's play *Angels In America* at the Brooklyn Academy of Music in 2014. Versweyveld was the production designer, contributing 'a vista filled with grief, humor, and loneliness,' according to the *New Yorker*'s Hilton Als.[2]

Walsh met with Bowie in his New York City home on Lafayette Street and was given a four-page précis containing four characters: Newton, a girl ghost, the murderous Valentine, and a woman emotionally connected with the nineteenth-century writer Emma Lazarus.

Lazarus (1849–87) was born into a prosperous New York City family. Her reading of George Eliot's *Daniel Deronda* prompted her to explore her Jewish identity, which her subsequent works reflected. She wrote a novel, several collections of poetry, and a political pamphlet before being asked to contribute a poem for the base of the Statue of Liberty as a fundraiser—a request she initially declined. After reconsidering, she wrote a sonnet, 'The New Colossus,' which was engraved onto the base of the statue in 1903. The poem's visibility and higher than high profile all but eclipsed her career.

A man now without a career, Newton instead had an objective: building a rocket to take him home. His troubled mind, among other obstacles, severely hampers his progress. He also pines for his lost love, Mary Lou (here not hyphenated).

'Yeah, but what happens?' Coco Schwab is reported to have asked Walsh and Bowie.

As with his collaboration with Michael Cunningham, the songs were the irreproachable stars. Many were from his back catalogue, but there were four new ones: 'Lazarus,' 'No Plan,' 'Killing A Little Time,' and 'When I Met You,' in this story of, as Bowie put it, 'this man who can't leave and can't die.'[3] Walsh felt Newton was driven by 'the wish to find rest in a world where he's alien.'[4]

The work-in-progress was noted by August Brown in the *Quick*

Takes section of the *Los Angeles Times* on January 4, 2015, headlined 'Bowie Brings Pen To *Lazarus*.' By April 2, an off-Broadway theater in New York's East Village, the New York Theatre Workshop, announced it would be putting on the play as part of its 2015–16 season. Previews would begin on November 18, with the run initially slated for December 13 through January 17 (later adjusted to December 7–January 20). James Nicola, the theater's artistic director, was soon faced with the fastest-selling production in the theater's thirty-six years. Tickets were second only to Broadway's smash *Hamilton* in terms of their scarcity.

By June, *Variety* announced that Michael C. Hall would play the part of Newton. Hall had starred in cable television's *Dexter* as a charismatic serial killer and had earned his theatrical stripes playing the lead role of a rock star in a Broadway musical, *Hedwig & The Angry Inch*. 'He's magic in a lot of ways,' Hall would say of Bowie.[5] The lyric 'the monster fed/the body bled' was, according to Hall, the only time he received direction from Bowie.

'Deliver them as if all the world deserves this crap lyric—just spit it out like that,' Bowie told him.

'It was probably the only acting note he gave me,' Hall recalled, 'but it was brilliant.'[6]

According to Nicola, during production meetings Bowie was 'conscious of how his legend and celebrity could intimidate or disturb the creative process. He was there when he needed to be ... he was always reachable.'[7]

In the summer of 2014, Bowie was informed he had cancer, a diagnosis he shared with very few people. By fall, he broke the news to van Hove and some of the creative personnel via Skype— illness precluded him being there in person. 'I was blown away,' van

Hove said. 'I don't think I uttered two words because it was entirely unexpected. But did it influence the work? No.'[8] Van Hove had always sensed the urgency of the project, and was now even more driven to complete it in time so Bowie could see it through.

There was a brief interlude of remission before Bowie's cancer was back, and his vulnerability, fear, and anxiety was evident. Nonetheless, he attended *Lazarus* rehearsals when he was able. During one run-through, Cristin Milioti (who played Elly, Newton's assistant, in the New York production) sang 'Changes,' completely unaware he was in attendance. 'I actually didn't know he was in the room because I didn't have my glasses on,' she said. 'He sort of crept in while I was singing it.'[9]

'You could see a heartbroken man in his eyes, if you knew it,' van Hove said.

Meanwhile, press-free previews occurred, followed by *Lazarus's* premiere on December 7, 2015. With what must have taken monumental effort, Bowie dressed to his customary nines and attended with his wife, Iman. Also in the audience was Michael Cunningham, who'd come across a poster for the play while walking past the theater. He'd emailed Bowie to say he'd like to attend the opening. After seeing the performance, he admitted he found any likeness to their collaborative effort very scant. Instead, he said, the play 'resembled David's and my musical only in that it centered on an alien.'

The new music was equally dissimilar, said Cunningham. 'The few new ones [songs] were nothing like the riffs he'd come up with for himself and me.' Cunningham knew from his own experience where the title had originated, but he found no reference to Emma Lazarus in the book.

At the play's conclusion Bowie was able to take the stage and smiled beamingly during his bows and accolades. Attending the after-party, however, was beyond his reach. In the lobby Cunningham waited for him and they sat together and had a brief conversation after Bowie exited from backstage. 'I told him I was glad our idea hadn't just vanished,' Cunningham said.[10] Bowie nodded and squeezed his former collaborator's hand in affirmation.

The reviews came in, many of which were troubled and confused, and a few were completely negative. There was much about *Lazarus*—not least of which was the music—that was redemptive and soaring. The sticking points were the plot, or lack thereof; the subsequent over-reaching by the performers; and the decidedly pedestrian dialogue.

David Cote in *Time Out New York* had the holidays on his mind when he wrote his review, despite it being the warmest festive season on record in the city. *Lazarus*, he said, put him in mind of 'one of those old-timey TV Christmas specials, in which an isolated celebrity receives visits from other stars, trades banter and duets on beloved carols.' For snow, he substituted the static on the many onstage monitors, also the means of communication for a cameo by Alan Cumming as Valentine (who would be replaced by an onstage actor for the London run). Cote singled out what came in the intervals between songs—plot and dialogue—for failing to foster empathy or even understanding. 'If I got any of that wrong,' he said of his plot summary, 'complain to the creators, who don't make *Lazarus* easy to follow.' He cited Elly and her boyfriend Zach's exchange about her dyeing her hair blue (in efforts to evoke Mary Lou) as symptomatic of the 'vague banal badinage, none of it very convincing, despite the actors' fine work.'[11]

Kory Grow in *Rolling Stone* was far more kind, finding that since the play appeared to be 'more an homage to Tevis than to Bowie, the story stands on its own and that's why it's good.'[12] But then he also felt *Lazarus* came off like a public service announcement about alcoholism without making it clear if addiction was the source of Newton's problems. *Slate*'s Chris O'Leary clocked Bowie's love of the cutup writing technique employed by William S. Burroughs as an influence and recalled Bowie's early play *Ernie Johnson* (1968), which was about a suicide party.

If it was truer to Tevis than Mayersberg, that could explain why Eleanora Walker Tevis, the author's widow, loved the work, taking it in three times during its New York engagement. (In 2017, Eleanora passed away aged eighty in Bellevue Mental Hospital after a failed suicide bid—jumping from a three-story building and severing her feet in the process—in late 2016.)

The deepest and most comprehensive review appeared not surprisingly in the *New Yorker*, where Hilton Als described this version of Newton as 'a kind of post-Sondheim protagonist … built, it seems, to feel nothing or to neutralize everything that might cause feeling—or interest us. … Newton is spiritually dead, a Lazarus who cannot rise to life, let alone the kind of life the stage demands.' None of the characters 'have an inner life: Bowie and Walsh and van Hove didn't imagine one for them.'[13]

Lazarus was a labyrinthine dead end with a talented cast who belted out often-delicate songs to their detriment. *Lazarus* musically is to *Hunky Dory* like a youthful Judy Garland singing 'You Made Me Love You' is to her crooning 'The Man That Got Away' at the London Palladium in 1964. Michael C. Hall is extremely talented and capable but with too strong a physicality to pull off the alien's weightlessness. He oddly pines for Mary Lou after falling out of love with her in the novel and film. However, the emphasis on blue is touching; the shade recalling the light at the lake in the film's scene that so strongly references Jay Gatsby's love for Daisy Buchanan. Another problem is that the play is long: it's as if the almost immobile cutout of the rocket ship resembles the plane icon on a seatback sky map during an interminable transatlantic flight.

Bowie may have titled the play after the poet, but as an inventive wordsmith he could have thought of a laser and us—the words are divided thusly in the show's typeface—or as a laser and the US, and finally, as a student of old Hollywood, a veiled reference to super-agent Irving 'Swifty' Lazar, who certainly was a major proponent of the fame game. No doubt his own mortality weighed on him: with that in mind, who wouldn't put stock in Lazarus, the man Jesus Christ resurrected from the dead? As a work of art, *Lazarus* is, without a doubt, in the Romantic and New Romantic senses of the word, *sublime.*

On January 8, 2016, David Bowie quietly turned sixty-nine. He was buoyed by the many well wishes and emails from friends and fans, as well as the apparent public if not critical triumph of his play and acclaim for his new album, *Blackstar*, which featured the track 'Lazarus.'

Then suddenly, on January 10, after falling to earth and catching a life he'd rendered extraordinary, David Bowie died.

He left behind a bereft legion—not to mention a group of dedicated actors with eight remaining days in the play's run. Their method of coping was to immediately head for the studio to record the play's soundtrack. 'There was no better way to get through that day,' Milioti said. 'We held hands and curled up in the couch in the recording studio. I think all of just cried, all day.' The following night's performance was no easier. 'There was this sense of every audience member sitting on the edge of their seats and asking for an explanation,' Milioti said.[14]

With a heavy pall hovering over the remainder of the year, 2016 nonetheless saw quite a bit of *The Man Who Fell To Earth*. On January 15, the *New York Times* suggested the play would be moving to Broadway. It didn't, but it would transition to London later that year, not long after the film celebrated its fortieth anniversary with a Blu-Ray release featuring fresh commentary; several big-screen engagements in London, New York, Los Angeles, San Francisco, and other cities; a limited-edition book; and, at long last, the CD release of the film's soundtrack.

Lazarus's run at London's Kings Cross Theatre included a celebrity-studded premiere and equal amounts of ecstatic and puzzled reviews. Milioti did not travel with the show; instead, her part was filled by Amy Lennox, who spoke to the *Scottish Sun* about the musical. 'There's no jazz hands going on. It feels like an art installation and a play with some killer songs.'[15]

But perhaps Tom Ropelewski, who'd advised Donald Rugoff on the film's cuts all those years before, gave *Lazarus* and its film precursor one of the best appraisals. 'Looking at the film forty years later, I still find it infuriating and often mesmerizing,' he wrote. 'There was something worth saving, wasn't there?' As for the play, he added, 'I have yet to read a critic who has been able to make sense of the plot—which somehow seems about right.'[16]

The film proved beyond all shadow that Bowie, a multifaceted superstar, was a movie star. 'No wonder the movies discovered him,' Mick LaSalle wrote in the *San Francisco Chronicle*. 'He was beautiful as few men are beautiful. Like Fred Astaire, he had an elegance of movement that made it a pleasure just to watch him walk down the street. And like Astaire, it was always rather surprising when you saw him stand next to someone else, to realize he was a person of average height. The illusion of elongated chic was a function of his thinness, proportions, and consummate grace.'

LaSalle saw *The Man Who Fell To Earth* as a metaphor for fame. 'First you're weird, then you're rich, and then everybody's out to get you, and you end up broken, sad, and addicted to alcohol. … One of the ways it worked as a film is that it explained Bowie to the public.'[17]

Nile Southern concluded, 'The themes of *The Man Who Fell To Earth* are timeless and terrific and dystopian and revealing about modern society and its commercialism and lack of humanity. It's an enduring masterpiece.'[18]

David James, whose breadth of work ranges from the early 70s through various twenty-first-century *Star Wars* franchise additions, still rates *The Man Who Fell To Earth* very highly. 'It's a great memory,' he said. 'I don't think I was ever really sure what it was about, not sure if I [am] now, but it was in the days when crews were much smaller and film was not all about moneymaking. Everybody who was on that film was dedicated to that film and they gave their all to it. There were no lines.'[19]

When her then-husband departed in mid-1975 to make the film, Angela Bowie had mixed emotions, one of which was apprehension. 'I was concerned that he would find himself surrounded by predators who would commit perhaps too much to the camera lens and there would be no mystery left,' she said.[20] Best intentions notwithstanding, she needn't have worried. As it turned out, there was enough mystery to resonate into the far stars and back.

A NOTE ON
THE TYPE
POSTSCRIPT

The Man Who Fell To Earth was, of course, filmed in New Mexico, until that time primarily the setting for movie and television shoot-'em-ups. The first and only all-British crew ever to work together in the United States arrived in the unrestricted, wide-open right-to-work state with mostly no clue as to either its extraterrestrial connections or its breathtaking scenery. That, simply put, was synchronicity. David Bowie, in his first starring film role, embodied Thomas Jerome Newton and complemented the landscape, his hair a mercurial jolt of red rock against a flayed yellow sunset. Candy Clark, fresh from her star-making supporting part in *American Graffiti*, gave an endearingly natural performance. Anthony Richmond's cinematography still induces awes, and Roeg's empathetic direction alternately warms and chills. Walter Tevis, an American original of an author, unwittingly gifted Bowie with the cloak of a persona he could wear and then shed, and finally swaddle himself with, shroud-like, as he gracefully bowed out. When I began this project in 2015, I could not have fathomed that, and indeed the larger part of me remains inconsolable.

I saw *The Man Who Fell To Earth* in its preview in Westwood, California, by talking my way into the screening—probably by saying I worked for the *Santa Ana Register* newspaper in Orange County. I believed I was properly attired for the film: I wore a khaki ex-army flight suit purchased from the Children's Hospital Thrift Store, again in Santa Ana, which I'd copied from the David Bowie in-store standup that I'd persuaded the local Licorice Pizza or possibly Wherehouse Record Store to give me. I had the movie's poster up on my bedroom wall—RCA, then in the Capitol Records Building on Vine Street in Hollywood told me just to come on by and pick it up. Regardless of the hour-long drive, that was a particularly convenient location—not necessarily for its iconic appearance but because the Capezio shoe store across the street stocked the pointy flats Bowie wore (naturally, I followed in those footsteps). My hair was orange courtesy of messy Egyptian henna. It had bits of straw in it, but then so did my hair. Its blonde front was all Sun-in hair lightener, complemented by the Southern California real thing. Eventually, it broke off.

I was too enthralled with Bowie to be able to form an intelligent opinion of the film. Having seen it at least two dozen times since (eighteen of which were in 1976 alone), I am still of two minds: my Bowie self and that other person. *The Man Who Fell To Earth* looks stunning: I know I wouldn't like it half as much if it had a backdrop of somewhere other than New Mexico. The acting hits the right notes; the screenplay is exemplary. It's long, though—by the time Newton and Mary-Lou are playing table tennis, I don't know whether to rally or forfeit.

Newton watches a bank of TV sets: onscreen at times are *Love In The Afternoon*, *Billy Budd*, an Elvis movie called *Tickle Me*, wildlife footage, *The End Of The Line*, and, later, *The Third Man*. Newton might be taking in what he watches but he is not enjoying what he sees. Instead he is hedging his bets like a compulsive gambler hoping to catch a glimpse of his home. He is not looking for entertainment, he is looking for solace.

Certain parts of the film don't fit nearly as well as the jigsaw-puzzle-patterned shirt Newton wears, but it hardly matters. Once he bows his head in the final scene, down-at-heels Westlake Park's boats moored tight to the docks against any mayhem or vandalism just offscreen, my heart sinks like the waning, no longer blinding, sun. Beneath the stagnant waters of this particularly polluted manmade lake, Icarus tries to wave.

EXTRA #1
SCENE AND SEEN AGAIN

What follows is a scene-by-prominent-scene guide to locations. Any errors—including precise times—are mine. When I became exasperated by where a scene was filmed, I was tempted to blame New Mexico, certain that the state is an avowed shape-shifter. The truth of course is slightly more prosaic, and I had first-rate assistance from local film historian Jon Bowman. He immediately clarified matters.

'I notice a kind of mixing-up happening,' he said. 'For instance, when the movie goes to Fenton Lake, there might be 80 percent shot there, with other small snippets from the Rio Grande, Los Alamos, or elsewhere in the Jemez Mountains. Same down in Artesia. Most is there but there are short snippets from Santa Fe and the Belen area buried within the shots.'

Bowman also noted that shooting occurred along the Rio Grande north of Espanola via helicopter, 'and it looks like the same day they were shooting some helicopter stuff in the Jemez Mountains.'

Now, back to earth. Just about.

00:01 Stock shot of rocket.

01:12 A voluminous cloud hovers in the distance, the size and breadth of a giant circus's big-top tent. It captivated both Tony Richmond and some of his local crew who were more inured to such sky-theatrics. They still pulled over to take pictures of the aerial spectacle outside of Belen.

01:14 Newton's capsule splashes down into Fenton Lake, 455 Fenton Lake Road, Jemez Springs. The thirty-seven-acre lake sits surrounded by Ponderosa pine trees at an altitude of 7,650 feet in the Jemez Mountains near Los Alamos. 'It is not very big,' allowed Park Manager Manny Sanchez. 'It is anywhere from 75 yards to 200 yards wide and 300 to 400 yards long.'[1] Part of Fenton Lake State Park, the stocked lake is a favorite of seasoned fishermen like Rip Torn (Nathan Bryce) and, even once, David Bowie (Thomas Newton). The lake and its environs will factor in several locations throughout the film, and its connection to same causes it to be mentioned in *New Mexico Campgrounds: The Statewide Guide* under the seemingly unlikely heading 'Hiking, Canoeing, And David Bowie.'[2]

01:15 Hoodie in place, Newton gingerly walks downhill, viewed only by a mysterious watcher, in Madrid. Madrid is located in the Ortiz Mountains and part of what's known as the Turquoise Trail, a section of Highway 14 that skirts the Sandia Crest peaks. Pronounced MAD-rid, it was part of the coalmining boom in the 1880s and then boasted a population larger than that of Albuquerque's. After a bust and some wilderness years, Madrid re-emerged as an artist's colony with a balancing dose of biker element. The huge, ruined Breaker House—the decaying structure visible aside Newton—was demolished down for safety reasons in the 1980s.

01:34 Newton proceeds across the bridge into Haneyville. The bridge is in fact in Los Lunas and goes across the Rio Grande at Main Street NE. The fetching wooden structure was the first automobile crossing over the river in the state. The funfair, with its drunk leering from a children's ride and a clown-shaped bouncy feature, plus the antiques shop in front of which Newton lounges on a wooden bench are all in Los Lunas. Trini's Bar, visible in the frame, is long closed. That Bo Diddley lived there for a time in the 1970s was one of the town's claims to fame before Facebook's data center bulldozed into the dusty town in the late 2010s.

10:04 Businessman Newton descends a spiral staircase, briefcase in hand, at the home of Oliver Farnsworth (Buck Henry). This is the interior of a house in Santa Fe or Albuquerque.

13:46 There is a stock shot of New York City, followed by driver Arthur (Tony Mascia) and Newton in the limo, with Albuquerque standing in for the metropolis.

16:15 Professor Bryce's college campus is the New Mexico Military Institute in Roswell. The military prep school opened in 1891 and is on the National Register of Historic Places. Hotelier Conrad Hilton, Sci Fi writer G. Harry Stine, and actor Owen Wilson are all alumni.

20:21 Newton dines and watches Kabuki theater in a Japanese restaurant in Los Angeles.

20:51 World Enterprises HQ is in Albuquerque, likely Central Avenue. There is a shot of the Sandia Mountains, which border the city.

23:32 Newton is in his limo, being driven around downtown Albuquerque, first in the vicinity of the Plaza Hotel and then around the Sunshine Building between Central and Gold Avenues downtown.

25:30 The Hotel Artesia was in Artesia, New Mexico. The elevator in which Newton passes out, his hair mirroring the veneer of the paneling, was inside the now-demolished hotel. Local actor and former New Mexico Screen Actors Guild president Richard Breeding portrayed the hotel's receptionist. When Mary-Lou drags Newton to Room 505, he's actually lying on a skateboard with a bicycle seat and vertical pole affixed to it. Ill in the room, he vomits an egg-white solution. When Newton gazes out the window and says, 'They're so strange here, the trains,' the previous shot is of a train pulling into the Santa Fe Train Depot.

38:40 Bryce flies into Albuquerque's Sunport Airport. His office is in Albuquerque.

44:32 Newton and Mary-Lou attend services at the First Presbyterian Church, 402 W. Grand, Artesia.

46:51 White Sands National Monument is Newton's home planet, Anthea. The first atomic bomb tests occurred just north of the monument at Jornada de Muerto in the White Sands Proving Ground during World War II.

46:56 The train at the level crossing, with Newton and Mary-Lou waiting in the limo, is in Belen. Clark's monologue about riding trains during her childhood was one of the few ad-libbed portions of the film, and was greatly admired by Bowie.

48:27 Newton and Mary-Lou pass a series of cabins in Madrid. The cabins were brought by train from Kansas in the late nineteenth century for the miners and their families. Their red or green roofs were painted that way because of Madrid's reputation for over-the-top Christmas lights and decorations. The shacks were in various states of disrepair during filming and later restored to house, not miners but artisans.

49:51 The time-slip moment where Newton sees the frontier family was in the Valles Caldera, a 13.7-mile wide circular depression created by a volcanic eruption over a million years ago. Some visible scientific apparatus are related to Los Alamos National Laboratory in the Jemez Mountains just outside the city limits.

50:00 Newton and Mary-Lou arrive at the home he has built in Fenton Lake. Newton's Japanese style house is a set and its southwestern-inspired interiors, a home in Santa Fe.

54:05 An aerial view of the Rio Grande just north of Espanola, heading toward Taos.

56:00 Bryce's home is a requisitioned park ranger's house at the lake.

56:11 The intimate interlude between Mary-Lou and Newton was shot in a Santa Fe home.

1.08:16 The large drive-thru silo structure was a cement works near Algodones north of Albuquerque.

1.08:31 The spacecraft, with its lining made from craft service cups, was filmed in a small studio in Santa Fe. The white lights winking through were made by an enveloping white silk sheet covering the structure.

1.11:50 Farnsworth and Mr. Peters (Bernie Casey) walk through Albuquerque's Civic Plaza, Tijeras NW, and 3rd Street.

1.20:16 The reveal scene—with Bowie not present for some of it—was an amalgam of the Santa Fe home (Mary-Lou curls up in its kitchen under scrutiny of a fish eye lens) and a motel bathroom, possibly Artesia.

1.26:00 The milky alien sex scenes were filmed at a drained swimming pool in Los Angeles. The aliens' nude outfits were made of very thin Lycra.

1.33:26 Bryce visits Newton in his shack with its sidekick windmill on Belen's East Mesa off a dirt roadway, 'probably today's paved Manzano Expressway,' according to belenmainstreet.com The makeshift solar still was Rip Torn's idea. As another intriguing cloud formation appears, it makes for cinematographer Richmond's favorite scene: 'When Rip Torn goes to see Newton who is in that little shack and he asks him where he's from. Newton says, Somewhere down there.'[3] The gas station forecourt is in Belen, and a bank sign is visible.

1.37:31 Alamogordo is where Captain James Lovell wades through the adoring crowd as Newton is rushed to what he believes will be his mission home.

1.34:22 Peters and his wife (Claudia Jennings) cavort poolside in an Albuquerque home.

1.36:04 The abandoned Sunshine Building, between Central and Second and Gold Street SW, Albuquerque, was Newton's multi-decorated prison. The 1924 six-story building was the city's first 'skyscraper' and housed a huge movie palace that was later used as a music venue. Waiter Albert Nelson from the Hilton delivered Newton's drinks on a cart.

1.39:00 Bryce and Mary-Lou dine in the back of Butterfields Restaurant, which was tucked away on the south side of Sunset Boulevard (#8426). It was situated on a portion of early Hollywood film star John Barrymore's estate, in what would have been the guesthouse frequented by Errol Flynn. 'It was a great restaurant,' David James lamented.

2.10:00 Newton, suddenly freed through a surprisingly unlocked door, emerges into the lobby of Albuquerque's Plaza Hotel, now the Hotel Andaluz.

2.10:30 Mary-Lou and Bryce buy holiday liquor at the former Gil Turner's Liquor Store on corner of Sunset and Doheny in the jumped-up heart of the Sunset Strip. Gil Turner opened the iconic establishment in 1953, and it obviously but still impressively featured in artist Ed Ruscha's 1966 work 'Every Building On The Sunset Strip.' Sometimes cited as the most famous liquor store in the world, its habitués included members of The Doors who'd come by at breaks during their residency at the Whisky A Go-Go (the storied club didn't yet have a liquor license). Legions of music fans ranging from flower children to glitter rockers to punks to metal hair-band devotees passed through its angled doorway and came out with surreptitious items placed brown paper bags. It survives as Terner's Liquor and likely does a fair amount of deliveries to denizens in the Hollywood Hills and its canyons. There is a relocated Gil Turner's a few doors down on Sunset, but if its optic walls could speak, they wouldn't have nearly as much to say.

2.14:00 Bryce finds Newton's album, *The*

Visitor, in the iconic Tower Records on the Sunset Strip. The store, opened in 1971 at the northwest corner of Sunset and Horn, was the place to be seen shopping for records. It was featured in Colin Hanks's 2015 documentary *All Things Must Pass*, having closed—apart from occasional special event—in 2006.

2.15:13 Bryce locates Newton at a lakeside wooden snack bar in Westlake/MacArthur Park near downtown Los Angeles. The extremely attractive but at times sketchy park opened in the 1880s, making it an absolute relic by city standards, and its reputation was somewhat shady (other than the kind provided by its trees) as early as the Raymond Chandler/Philip Marlowe 1940s noir mystery era. The troubled snack stand—the alcohol Newton imbibed would not have been sold—burned down in 2014.

EXTRA #2
ORIGINAL SOUNDTRACK 2016

It took monumental effort to bring about the release of the score to *The Man Who Fell To Earth*. There were some disappointments to be sure—among them, the failure to include John Phillips's perky, pornish 'Devil On The Loose,' which accompanies the scene of Nathan Bryce striding across campus. 'Devil' was a relic from Phillips's band The Jazz Crusaders and repurposed for *Space*, a musical he'd written for then wife Geneviève Waïte. Also missing are Frank Worthington's 'Songs Of The Humpback Whale'; Frank Glazer's 'Enfantillages Pittoresques'; Hank Snow's version of 'A Fool Such As I'; Jim Reeves's classic rendition of 'Make The World Go Away'; Roy Orbison's 'Blue Bayou'; Bing Crosby singing Cole Porter's 'True Love'; and Artie Shaw's version of Hoagy Carmichael's evergreen 'Stardust.'

Despite these shortcomings, one thing remains certain: When Chris Campion concluded that it's impossible to imagine *The Man Who Fell To Earth* without Phillips's soundtrack, there is no argument. As a result, the music he created and curated, especially the quintessential contributions by Stomu Yamashta, is as indispensable as the film's star.

DISC ONE

1. 'Poker Dice' Stomu Yamashta
A haunting, suitably otherworldly track that turns surprisingly jazzy.
2. 'Blueberry Hill' Louis Armstrong
Fats Domino's signature tune, as recorded in 1949 by New Orleans jazz stalwart Armstrong.
3. 'Jazz II' John Phillips

4. 'Venus: Bringer Of Peace' Bournemouth Symphony Orchestra
5. 'Boys From The South' John Phillips
A little too hoedown-ish to approach classic country, but with a suave vocal.
6. '33 1/3' Stomu Yamashta
Wind chimes led to emphatic drums and excitable tambourine.

7. 'Rhumba Boogie' John Phillips
A novelty country song.
8. 'Try To Remember' The Kingston Trio
A classic showtune from 1960's otherwise forgettable The Fantasticks.
9. 'Mandala' Stomu Yamashta

10. 'America' John Phillips
11. 'Wind Words' Stomu Yamashta
Dreamlike, lovely, and difficult to disassociate from the film's tender love scene.
12. 'Jazz' John Phillips

DISC TWO

1. 'One Way' Stomu Yamashta
2. 'Space Capsule' John Phillips
An elegant, hopeful, and appropriately rising piece.
3. 'Bluegrass Breakdown' John Phillips
A jaunty piece that punctuates one of the film's few clumsy lines, likely played for laughs, as Bryce asks Newton, 'Are you crazy?'
4. 'Desert Shack' John Phillips
Apt and interesting, effectively absorbs the language of the landscape.
5. 'Memory Of Hiroshima' Stomu Yamashta
6. 'Window' John Phillips
7. 'Alberto' John Phillips
A fun sax solo accompanies the movement of this beloved bartender.
8. 'Mars: The Bringer Of War' Bournemouth Symphony Orchestra

9. 'Liar Liar' John Phillips
Not in the film, a strange song that's almost reminiscent of very early Bowie.
10. 'Hello Mary Lou' John Phillips
An instrumental version of what's in the film, with a rollicking guitar solo from Mick Taylor.
11. 'Silent Night' Robert Farnon
12. 'Love Is Coming Back' Geneviève Waïte
An unforgettable singer who never really took off in the way, say, Bernadette Peters or Maria Muldaur did.
13. 'The Man Who Fell To Earth' John Phillips
The most bizarre inclusion on the soundtrack is an obvious demo and likely even a first take of a ballad. It's baffling as to why it made the cut. It's certainly not going to give 'The Man Who Shot Liberty Valance' a run for its money.

EXTRA #3

THE FINAL FOUR

David Bowie wrote four songs for *Lazarus*, partly at the suggestion of Ivo van Hove: the title song, 'No Plan,' 'Killing A Little Time,' and 'When I Met You.' Each is exemplary in its way and a credit to his catalogue. And that's saying a lot. They also go a long way toward expressing musically what the fevered and frenetic play often oversteps: the agony of a life on hold. The songs feel medicated and lucid; dispassionate and angry, helpless yet defiant. The artist's body had gone turncoat as he sought to disrobe from its entanglement. It had to have been a Herculean—no, in deference to Bowie's personal iconography—Arthurian effort, and it soared.

Recorded in New York's Magic Shop and Human Worldwide Studios and augmented by performances from saxophonist Donny McCaslin, guitarist Ben Monder, bassist Tim Lefebvre, drummer Mark Guiliana, and keyboard player Jason Lindner, the songs appeared on the original cast recording of the play; on *Blackstar*, in the case of 'Lazarus'; and of course in the play itself, albeit in abbreviated form. Time lengths below refer to Bowie's versions on the musical's soundtrack and on the *No Plan* EP.

'LAZARUS' (6:24)

This Joy Division–esque lament broodingly addresses Thomas Newton's mindset thirty years on and gives a glimpse of an alien's strikingly human idea of heaven. It 'helps establish the hero's anguish as he seeks the transcendence of death while being unable to die literally,' as Bruce Hardy in the *Hollywood Reporter* put it. Michael C. Hall (Newton) and the Teenage Girls open the play with this song. Hall also gave moving renditions on *The Late Show With Steven Colbert* on December 18, 2015, and onstage at the Arts Club in London the following October.

'NO PLAN' (3:40)

A painkiller in limbo, with McCaslin's sax like a droning respirator hovering over New York's Second Avenue, 'No Plan' is suitably adrift. Its lyrics, however, concern 'the continual satisfactions of a marriage that has lasted longer than anyone predicted,' according to Alfred Soto in *Spin*. Soto places the piece as more Bowie biography than Newton perspective: 'Not for him rage against the dying of the light, a mode to which artists understandably succumb—he appreciated the texture and tint of the light while he still had eyes to see.' Sophia Anne Caruso's version in the play shifts between rather bombastic and relatively subdued.

'KILLING A LITTLE TIME' (3:46)

A raging song that nonetheless wavers between anger and languidness with a dissonance that disturbs. *Spin*'s Soto found Bowie's vocals deliciously ridiculous, adding, 'When a key shift happens during the "I'm falling, man/I'm fading, man," you'll stop smiling.' The piece's abrupt end has a similar effect.

'WHEN I MET YOU' (4:09)

A sliver of classic pop Bowie, this song is initially joyous, original, and manic before spiraling away into repetitiveness. 'My general sense was that it harked back to older Bowie,' sax player Danny McCaslin told *Mojo*'s Paul Trynka. 'Tim Lefebvre might have said *Lodger*. [Bowie] had a beautiful way of describing things: "Put a couple passages in the corner … throw a small pen-light beam on the rest, like a PI scouting a motel room." He's never saying something like, Can I have a bass drum on two or four? He would do that a lot, say these poetic things that were also invitations for you to think.' *Spin*'s Soto was not so sure about the song, finding it 'kicks up a lot of dust for naught.' In the play it is a duet between Newton and Teenage Girl 1.

ENDNOTES

PREFACE

1 Mark Wardel, email to author, March 31, 2017

CHAPTER ONE

1 Don Swaim interviews Walter Tevis, CBS Radio, January 6, 1984; included on *The Man Who Fell To Earth* (Criterion Collection DVD, 2005)

2 'He's Writing A Second Novel,' *Louisville Courier Journal*, June 17, 1960

3 Michelle L. Brandt, 'Mommy, Where Do Children's Hospitals Come From?' *Stanford Medicine Magazine*, Spring 2006

4 Griggs Tevis, *My Life With The Hustler* (GreatUnpublished)

5 Andrew Weiner, 'Tevis Now On The Wagon Rides On To Success,' *Toronto Globe & Mail*, April 11, 1981

6 Herbert Mitgang, *New York Times*, August 11, 1984

7 Griggs Tevis, *op. cit.*

8 Swaim, *op. cit*

9 Fred Walther, *Wanderon* (XLibris Corp, 2008)

10 'He's Writing A Second Novel,' *Louisville Courier Journal*, June 17, 1960

11 Criterion DVD commentary, 2005

12 *ibid*

13 Weiner, *op. cit.*

14 Shirley Williams, 'Toasting The Best Of Times,' *Louisville Courier-Journal*, January 27, 1980

15 Griggs Tevis, *op. cit.*

16 Williams, *op. cit.*

17 Griggs Tevis, *op. cit.*

18 William S. Murphy, 'Pocket Reader: Bumper Reprint Crop,' *Los Angeles Times*, April 28, 1963

19 Griggs Tevis, *op. cit.*

20 Weiner, *op. cit.*

21 Danny Peary, *Cult Movies 2* (Dell, 1983)

22 Weiner, *op. cit.*

23 Tom Nolan, *Three Chords For Beauty's Sake: The Artie Shaw Story* (Norton, 2010)

24 *Circleville Herald*, June 8, 1966

25 Nolan, *op. cit.*

26 A.H. Weiler, *New York Times*, March 27, 1971

27 Mary Murphy, *Los Angeles Times*, July 30, 1971

28 *Contemporary Authors Online: MLA 7th Edition* (Gale, 2002)

29 Dick Wheelwright, *The Man Who Fell To Earth (Steppingstone)*, Tevis ms., Manuscripts Department, Lilly Library, Indiana University, Bloomington, Indiana

30 Howard Rubin, author interview, Santa Fe, New Mexico, August 17, 2016

31 Si Litvinoff, email to author, July 18, 2016

32 Nicolas Roeg, Criterion DVD commentary, 1992

33 Criterion DVD commentary, 2005

34 *ibid*

35 Paul Mayersberg, 'The Story So Far … The Man Who Fell To Earth,' *Sight & Sound*, Autumn 1975

36 *ibid*

37 Roeg to Cocker, *Winter Shuffle*, December 2013 (via YouTube)

38 Mayersberg, screenplay

39 *ibid*

40 Graeme Clifford, author interview, July 9, 2016

41 Mayersberg, *op. cit.*

42 *ibid*
43 Script comments are from the Walter Tevis Collection, Lilly Library, Indiana University, Bloomington, Indiana. Used by permission of Eleanora Tevis.

44 Weiner, *op. cit.*
45 Scott Eyman, 'Walter Tevis Is Hustling Again,' *Sunday Plain Dealer Magazine*, May 27, 1978

CHAPTER TWO

1 Candy Clark, author interview, April 1, 2015
2 *ibid*
3 John Phillips with Jim Jerome, *Papa John: An Autobiography* (Doubleday, 1986)
4 Clark, author interview
5 Ian Penman, 'Wham Bam Teatime,' *London Review Of Books*, January 5, 2017
6 Wendy Leigh, *Bowie: The Biography* (Gallery, 2014)
7 Nicolas Roeg, *The World Is Ever Changing* (Faber, 2013)
8 Litvinoff, author interview
9 Clark, author interview
10 Criterion DVD commentary, 1992
11 Bruce Meyer, 'Bowie Invades Filmland,' *Albuquerque Journal*, August 5, 1976
12 Paulo Hewitt, liner notes to *The Man Who Fell To Earth: Original Soundtrack* (Universal Music, 2016)
13 Tony Richmond, author interview, Burbank, California, July 26, 2016
14 Lisa Robinson, *There Goes Gravity: A Life In Rock And Roll* (Riverhead Books 2015)
15 May Routh, author interview, Studio City, California, August 3, 2016
16 Angela Bowie, email to author, March 20, 2017
17 Rob Hughes, 'The Inside Story Of The Man Who Fell To Earth,' *Uncut*, April 2, 2015; Criterion DVD commentary, 1992
18 Sadie Plant, *Writing On Drugs* (Farrar Straus & Giroux, 1999)
19 *ibid*
20 *ibid*
21 Routh, *op. cit.*
22 Shirley Halperin, 'Michael E And Nick Lippman Expound On Their Homegrown Management Firm,' *Billboard*, July 23, 2016
23 *ibid*
24 Leigh, *op. cit.*

CHAPTER THREE

1 www.nmartmuseum.org
2 Tom Sharpe, 'Howard Rubin: The Unconventional Bureaucrat,' *Santa Fe New Mexican*, July 25, 1975
3 Rubin, author interview
4 Fred Buckles, 'More Movies Planned in NM,' *Roswell Daily Record*, July 3, 1975
5 *ibid*
6 Howard Bryan, 'Pie-In-The-Sky Talk Marred By Pie In The Face,' *Albuquerque Tribune*, March 13, 1975
7 Sharpe, *op. cit.*
8 Buckles, *op. cit.*
9 'British Film Set For NM,' *Albuquerque Journal*, April 29, 1975
10 Routh, author interview
11 hopeandglitter.com, March 12, 2013
12 Routh, author interview
13 Brian Eatwell, Criterion DVD commentary, 2005
14 Julie Kavanagh, 'Nicolas Roeg's Time Machine,' *'Women's Wear Daily*, April 2, 1976
15 Max Evans, 'One Hundred Years Of Filmmaking In New Mexico,' *New Mexico Magazine*, 1998
16 'British Film Set For NM,' *Albuquerque Journal*, April 29, 1975
17 Litvinoff, author interview

18 'British Film Set For NM,' *Albuquerque Journal*, April 29, 1975
19 Mary Murphy, *Los Angeles Times*, May 3, 1975
20 Timothy Ferriss, 'David Bowie In America; The Iceman, Having Calculated, Cometh,' *Rolling Stone*, November 9, 1972
21 *Box Office*, June 9, 1975
22 Geoff MacCormack, *Station To Station: Travels With Bowie 1973–1976* (Genesis Publications, 2007)
23 Angela Bowie, email to author
24 *ibid*
25 Rubin, author interview
26 Routh, author interview
27 'Movie Filming Set For Artesia,' *Artesia Daily Press*, April 24, 1975
28 'Film Set In Eddy,' *Roswell Daily Record*, April 25, 1975
29 Kay Woolton, 'Southwest Charm Returns To Old Hilton,' *Albuquerque Tribune*, September 3, 1974
30 Clark, author interview
31 Criterion DVD commentary, 2005
32 Routh, author interview
33 Alan Swain, author interview, August 23, 2016
34 *ibid*
35 Jean Jordan, 'Movies Filming In New Mexico Include Bowie's Boy Who Fell To Earth,' *New Mexico Independent*, June 13, 1975
36 'You Cannot Talk With David Bowie,' *News Bulletin*, June 5, 1975
37 Martin Samuel, author interview, February 15, 2016
38 Tony Richmond, email to author, July 26, 2016
39 Samuel, author interview
40 Kavanagh, *op. cit.*
41 *News Bulletin*, *op. cit.*
42 Tevis ms., *op. cit.*
43 'Bowie Stars In Film Being Shot In LL,' *Valencia County News*, June 5, 1975
44 Routh, author interview
45 Chris Duffy and Louis Cann, *Duffy/ Bowie: 5 Sessions* (ACC Editions, 2014)
46 George Perry, author interview, London, November 9, 2016
47 Eric Johnson, author interview, April 5, 2017
48 *Valencia County News*, *op. cit.*
49 Swain, author interview
50 Griggs Tevis, *op. cit.*
51 Walter Tevis, letter to *Circus*, December 30, 1975
52 Griggs Tevis, *op. cit.*
53 Richmond, author interview
54 *Hollywood Reporter*, June 10, 1975
55 Clarke Taylor, 'A Maverick For All Media: Rip Torn, The Texas Tornado,' *Los Angeles Times*, November 28, 1976
56 Rubin, *author interview*
57 W.K. Stratton, email to author, February 6, 2017
58 Nile Southern, author interview, February 2, 2017
59 Taylor, *op. cit.*
60 *Variety*, June 18, 1975
61 Michael Deeley, author interview, November 23, 2015
62 Litvinoff, author interview
63 Rubin, author interview
64 Southern, author interview
65 *ibid*
66 Swain, author interview
67 Routh, author interview
68 David James, author interview, March 13, 2017; Criterion DVD commentary, 2005
69 James, author interview
70 Max Evans, *100 Years Of Filmmaking In New Mexico* (New Mexico Magazine, 1998)
71 Routh, author interview
72 Linda de Vetta Richmond, author interview, London, November 4, 2016
73 James, author interview
74 'Extra Men Requested For Film,' *Artesia Daily Press*, June 17, 1975
75 Clark, author interview
76 Evans, *op. cit.*

77 Clark, author interview
78 Chuck Mittlestadt, 'New Mexico Hollywood Reporter,' Observer, July 2, 1975
79 MacComack, op. cit.

CHAPTER FOUR
1 Perry, author interview
2 Duffy, op. cit.
3 Clifford, author interview
4 Perry, author interview
5 De Vetta, author interview
6 ibid
7 Tom Burman, author interview, July 8, 2016
8 Clifford, author interview
9 Nicolas Roeg, author interview, London, November 5, 2016
10 Kevin Weber, author interview, October 6, 2016
11 Swain, author interview
12 Richmond, author interview
13 Howard Bryan, 'Rock Star David Bowie Kept Under Wraps In Albq,' Albuquerque Tribune, June 14, 1975
14 Routh, author interview
15 'Ten Young Women Seek Albq Title,' Albuquerque Tribune, June 26, 1975
16 Swain, author interview
17 Delana Michaels, author interview, January 5, 2017
18 Clark, author interview
19 Rex Reed, Valentines And Vitriol (Delacorte Press, 1977)
20 Lesley Polling-Kempes, The Harvey Girls: Women Who Opened The West (Da Capo, 1994)
21 James, author interview
22 Duffy and Cann, op. cit.
23 'Shootout Spurs Tight Security At Bowie Film Site,' Hollywood Reporter, July 9, 1975
24 Steve Shroyer and John Lifflander, 'Spaced Out in the Desert,' Creem, December 1975
25 'Production Systems In,' Hollywood Reporter, July 8, 1975
26 Routh, author interview
27 Perry, author interview
28 Angela Bowie, email to author
29 Angela Bowie, email to author
30 Angela Bowie, email to author
31 Duffy, op. cit.
32 Swain, author interview
33 Perry, author interview
34 James, author interview
35 De Vetta, author interview
36 Deeley, author interview
37 Richmond, author interview
38 Routh, author interview
39 Clifford, author interview
40 Deeley, author interview
41 Swain, author interview
42 ibid
43 Rubin, author interview
44 Manny Sanchez, author interview, July 6, 2016
45 Rubin, author interview
46 Joyce Haber, 'Bowie: Apollo 1 Of The Space Rock Era,' Los Angeles Times, July 24, 1975
47 Variety, August 1, 1975
48 Clark op. cit.
49 'Howard Rubin Resigns Post As State Movie Panel Chief,' Albuquerque Tribune, March 18, 1976
50 Dave Pirie and Chris Petit, 'After The Fall,' Time Out, March 12–16, 1976
51 Scott McCoy, 'Domino Sounding Better Than Ever,' Albuquerque Journal, August 6, 1975
52 MacCormack, op. cit.

CHAPTER FIVE

1 Joseph Cosandaey, *100 Years Of Filmmaking In New Mexico* (New Mexico Magazine, 1998)
2 Samuel, author interview
3 Litvinoff, author interview
4 Swain, author interview
5 David Bowie, Criterion DVD commentary, 1992
6 Routh, author interview
7 Richmond, author interview
8 Perry, author interview
9 Rubin, author interview
10 Duffy, *op. cit.*
11 Tom Burman, author interview, July 8, 2016
12 Weber, author interview
13 Esther Padilla, 'Student Acts In Movie,' *Albuquerque Journal*, August 2, 1975
14 Robert Greenfield, *Bear: The Life And Times Of Augustus Owsley Stanley III* (Thomas Dunne Books, 2016)
15 Samuel, author interview
16 De Vetta, author interview
17 Routh, author interview
18 Weber, author interview
19 Roeg, *The World Is Ever Changing*
20 Routh, author interview
21 De Vetta, author interview
22 Jimmy Kay Dale, *Alamogordo Daily News*, August 17, 1975
23 Southern, author interview
24 Swain, author interview
25 Richmond, author interview
26 Routh, author interview
27 *ibid*

CHAPTER SIX

1 Pirie and Petit, *op. cit.*
2 Criterion DVD commentary, 2005
3 MacCormack, *op. cit.*
4 Ed Kelleher, *David Bowie: A Biography In Words And Pictures* (Sire/Chappell & Co, 1977)
5 Vivian Claire, *David Bowie* (Flash Books 1977)
6 Reed, *op. cit.*
7 *ibid*
8 Joseph Lanza, *Fragile Geometry* (Paj Publications, 1989)
9 Pirie and Petit, *op. cit.*
10 Roger Corman and Jim Jerome, *How I Made 100 Movies In Hollywood And Never Lost A Dime* (Da Capo Press 1998)
11 Tom Weaver, *Double Feature Creature Attack* (McFarland Classics, 2003)
12 Gene D. Phillips, *The Life And Films Of David Lean* (University Press of Kentucky, 2006)
13 *ibid*
14 Diana Lisignoli, *Magill's Cinema Annual 1983* (Salem Press, 1983)
15 Perry, author interview
16 Routh, author interview
17 Justin H. Smith, *Withnail And Us* (Tauris, 2010)
18 Scott Salwoke, *Nicolas Roeg: Film By Film* (McFarland and co., 1993)
19 Shroyer and Lifflander, *op. cit.*
20 Maggie Abbott, email to author, December 5, 2016
21 Simon Reynolds, *Shock And Awe: Glam Rock And Its Legacy* (Faber, 2016)
22 Tom Seabrook, *Bowie In Berlin* (Jawbone Press, 2008)
23 Roeg, *op. cit.*
24 Haber, *op. cit.*
25 Kavanagh, *op. cit.*
26 Smith, *op. cit.*
27 Hughes, *op. cit.*
28 Perry,, author interview
29 Tom Milne, *Sight & Sound*, Summer 1976
30 Rubin, author interview
31 Burman, author interview
32 Roeg, *op. cit.*
33 John Preston, 'The Director Who Fell To Earth,' *Daily Telegraph*, July 19, 2013

34 Swain, author interview
35 Roger Griffin, bowiegoldenyears.com
36 Swain, author interview
37 De Vetta, author interview
38 Clifford, author interview
39 Criterion DVD commentary, 2005
40 'David Bowie: In His own Words,' *Sunday Express*, January 17, 2016
41 Reed, *op. cit.*
42 Mel Gussow,'Roeg: The Man Behind The Man Who Fell To Earth,' *New York Times*, August 22, 1976
43 Kavanagh, *op. cit.*
44 Lee Hill, *Great Directors: Nicolas Roeg* (Sensesofcinema.com, May 2002)

45 Roeg, author interview
46 John Lifflander and Stephan Shroyer, *Interview*, March 3, 1976
47 Joyce Haber, 'A Sinatra Biopic By David Bowie?' *Los Angeles Times*, July 24, 1975
48 Haber, 'Bowie: Apollo 1 Of The Space Rock Era'
49 Chris Campion, interview with Paul Buckmaster, July 16, 2005
50 Mary Murphy, 'Fanne Leaps Again,' *Los Angeles Times*, August 23, 1975
51 *Films & Filming*, October 1975
52 Southern, author interview

CHAPTER SEVEN
1 Andy Webster,'The Man Who Fell Into Movie Acting,' *New York Times*, August 2, 2013; David Bowie, Criterion DVD commentary, 1992
2 Haber,' Bowie: Apollo 1 Of The Space Rock Era'
3 Angela Bowie, email to author
4 Harvey Kubernik and Scott Calamar, *Canyon Of Dreams* (Sterling, 2009)

5 'All Together,' *Los Angeles Times*, July 22, 1973
6 hopeandglitter.com, March 12, 2013
7 Routh, author interview
8 Clark, author interview
9 Routh, author interview
10 *ibid*
11 'On Fashion,' *Los Angeles Times*, April 20, 1976

CHAPTER EIGHT
1 David Bowie, Criterion DVD commentary, 2005
2 Mary Murphy, *Los Angeles Times*, May 5, 1975
3 Edwin Miller, *Seventeen*, November 1975
4 Kavanagh, *op. cit.*
5 Shroyer and Lifflander, *op. cit*
6 Mayersberg, *op. cit.*
7 Campion, *op. cit.*
8 George Cole, 'A Long Time Lost In Space,' *Record Collector*, January 2017
9 Angus Mackinnon, 'The Future Isn't What It Used To Be,' *NME*, September 13, 1980
10 Campion, *op. cit.*
11 *ibid*
12 Cole, *op. cit.*
13 Campion, *op. cit.*

14 Christopher P. Lehman, *A Critical History Of Soul Train On Television* (McFarland, 2008)
15 Cole, *op. cit.*
16 Phillips with Jerome, *op. cit.*
17 Campion, *op. cit.*
18 Campion, *op. cit.*
19 Chris Campion, telephone conversation with author, April 3, 2015
20 Phillips with Jerome, *op. cit.*
21 *ibid*
22 Campion, *op. cit.*
23 *ibid*
24 Tom Nolan, email to author, April 1,2015
25 Clifford, email to author, July 10, 2017
26 Charles Ryweck, 'The Man Who Fell To Earth,' *Hollywood Reporter*, June 23, 1976

27 Drew Abrams,'Candy Clark Grows Up,' *Circus*, August 4, 1977
28 Chris Campion, 'Bowie And The Missing Soundtrack: The Amazing Story Behind The Man Who Fell To Earth,' *Guardian*, September 8, 2016
29 Getintothis.com, March 2016

30 Tom Seabrook, 'White Shirt Black Noise,' *Record Collector*, January 2011
31 Griffin, bowiegoldenyears.com
32 Deeley, author interview
33 Clifford, author interview
34 Tom Ropelewski, author interview, February 6, 2017

CHAPTER NINE

1 Mittlestadt, *op. cit.*
2 *Variety*, October 22, 1975
3 Tevis, letter to *Circus*, December 30, 1975
4 Lisa Coburn, email to author, December 28, 1976
5 Kavanagh, *op. cit.*
6 'The Man Who Fell To Earth,' *Variety*, March 24, 1976
7 Sue Rhodes Calhoun, 'The Woman Who Fell To The Earth In Hollywood,' *Los Angeles Times*, August 29, 1976
8 Clark, author interview
9 'The Man Who Fell To Earth,' *Monthly Film Bulletin*, April 1976
10 Hawk, *op. cit.*
11 Deeley, author interview
12 Pirie and Petit, *op. cit.*
13 Deeley, author interview
14 Aljean Harmets,'Hustling Lipstick, Chopping Classics, Rating Previews,' *New York Times*, May 9, 1976
15 Ira Deutchman, author interview, December 29, 2016
16 'Rugoff's Fast Deal On Sci-Fi Pic,' *Variety*, April 14, 1976

17 Stuart Byron, 'Don Rugoff, Ballyhoo With A Harvard Education,' *Film Comment*, June 2013
18 Deutchman, author interview
19 Tom Ropelewski, 'Reel Oddity,' *Dartmouth Alumni Magazine*, August 2016
20 Tom Ropelewski, author interview, February 6, 2017
21 Ropelewski, 'Reel Oddity'
22 Ropelewski, author interview
23 Ropelewski, 'Reel Oddity'
24 Ropelewski, author interview
25 Ropelewski, 'Reel Oddity'
26 Ropelewski, author interview
27 Deutchman, author interview
28 Gussow, *op. cit.*
29 Gussow, *op. cit.*
30 Dr. Richard C. Simons, author interview, July 22, 2016
31 Deeley, author interview
32 Deutchman, author interview
33 *ibid*
34 Clifford, author interview
35 Deutchman, author interview

CHAPTER TEN

1 geraldrfordfoundation.org
2 fordlibrarymuseum.gov
3 Mary Campbell, 'Bowie Likes The "Safety" Of A Tightrope,' *AP Newsfeatures/Albuquerque Journal*, May 17, 1976
4 Clark, author interview
5 Eyman, *op. cit.*
6 Richard Schickel to Walter Tevis, May 21, 1976, Tevis ms., Lilly Library

7 Griggs Tevis, *op. cit.*
8 Williams, *op. cit.*
9 Eleanora Walker, letter to Tevis, May 21, 1976 (Tevis ms., Lily Library)
10 Williams, *op. cit.*
11 Richard Eder, 'Man Who Fell To Earth Is Beautiful Science Fiction,' *New York Times*, June 6, 1976
12 Frank Rich, 'Roeg's Plunge Into Tedium,' *New York Post*, May 29, 1976

13 Jack Kroll, 'Howard Hughes From Another Planet,' *Newsweek*, June 14, 1976

14 Jay Cocks, 'Heavenly Body,' *Time*, June 14, 1976

15 Andrew Sarris,'A Science Fiction Film Falls To Earth,' *Village Voice*, June 14, 1976

16 John Simon, *New York*, July 20, 1976

17 Tom Allen, 'Roeg's Glide Into Science Fiction,' *Soho Weekly News*, June 3, 1976

18 Vincent Canby, 'How Sci-Fi Films Support The Status Quo,' *New York Times*, July 18, 1976

19 Lee Grant, 'Movie Call Sheet,' *Los Angeles Times*, June 19, 1976

20 Stephen Farber, *New West*, July 5, 1976

21 Farber, 'Exiles And The Kingdom,' *New West*, July 19, 1976

22 Bruce Meyer, *op. cit.*

23 Kramer, Steven P, 'Bowie Lands In Tedious Mush,' *New Mexico Independent*, August 20, 1976

24 Johnson *op. cit.*

25 Calhoun, *op. cit.*

26 *Playboy*, September 1976

27 Pauline Kael, *The New Yorker*, November 8, 1976

28 Lynn Minton, *McCall's*, September 1976

CHAPTER ELEVEN

1 Seabrook, *op. cit.*

2 *Artesia Daily Press*, April 28, 1977

3 Michael Ventura, 'We Are The Science Fiction,' *Los Angeles Weekly*, July 13–19, 1979

4 Clark, author interview

5 Ventura, *op. cit.*

6 *Los Angeles Times*, March 6, 1981

7 David Ehrenstein, 'The Man Who Fell To Earth Whole,' *Los Angeles Herald Examiner*, March 10, 1981

8 Ventura, 'The Man Who Fell To Earth: Expressive Nakedness Restored,' *Los Angeles Weekly*, March 13–19, 1981

9 Stuart Payron, *Village Voice*, October 21, 1981

10 Williams, *op. cit.*

11 Griggs Tevis, *op. cit.*

12 Tom Nolan, 'Homage To Fast Freddie's Father,' *Los Angeles Times Book Review*, March 29, 1987

13 Malcolm Jones, 'Man Who Fell To Earth Is A Classic Twice Over,' *Daily Beast*, February 14, 2014

14 Richard Kletter, author interview, July 13, 2016

15 Bobby Roth, author interview, January 13, 2017

16 Lewis Smith, author interview, January 16, 2017

17 'PN,' *Encyclopedia Of Science Fiction*, February 25, 2016

18 Miles Beller, 'The Man Who Fell To Earth,' *Hollywood Reporter*, August 21, 1987

19 'The Man Who Fell To Earth,' *Variety*, September 2, 1987

20 Tom Milne, 'The Man Who Fell To Earth,' *Monthly Film Bulletin*, April 1987

21 coolcatdaddy.wordpress.com, July 8, 2010

22 Clark, author interview

23 Mark and Deborah Parker, *The DVD And The Study Of Film* (Springer, 2011)

24 Howard Klein, *Los Angeles Reader*, April 19, 1993

25 Steve Daly, *Entertainment Weekly*, March 26, 1993

26 'Sci-Fi Enigma,' *Time*, March 22, 1993

27 Kenneth Sweeney, *American Cinematographer*, January 2006

28 Brett Sporich, 'Anchor Bay Tills Bowie's Earth,' *Hollywood Reporter*, July 25, 2002

29 Glenn Abel, *Hollywood Reporter*, March 17, 2003

30 Pamela McClintock,'WIP Brings Alien Pic To Earth,' *Variety*, October 28, 2005

31 *Los Angeles Times* advert, July 7, 2011
32 Nick Pinkerton, *Los Angeles Weekly*, July 8, 2011
33 Anthony Lane, *The New Yorker*, June 27, 2011
34 Iain Forsyth and Jane Pollard, email to author, December 8, 2016
35 Gussow, *op. cit.*
36 Gregg Barrios, 'Bowie In Aztlan,' *Texas Monthly*, June 26, 2016
37 Michael Cunningham, 'Stage Oddity: David Bowie's Secret Final Project,' *GQ*, February 2017

38 Cunningham, email to author, January 14, 2017
39 Cunningham, *op. cit.*
40 Brenda Rees, 'Bowie Through A Lens,' *Arroyo Magazine*, February 17, 2017
41 Cunningham, email to author
42 Cunningham, *op. cit.*
43 Cunningham, email to author
44 Cunningham, *op. cit.*
45 Victoria Broackes and Geoff Marsh, *David Bowie Is The Subject*, (V+A, 2013)
46 Cunningham, *op. cit.*

CHAPTER TWELVE

1 Bruce Handy, 'David Bowie's Final, Imaginative, Awesome Year,' *Hollywood Reporter*, January 6, 2017
2 Hilton Als, 'Static,' *The New Yorker*, December 21 and 28, 2015
3 *Lazarus* program, Kings Cross, London, 2016
4 Paul Trynka, 'Lazarus: A Trilogy Of Memories,' trynka.net, January 7, 2017
5 Trynka, 'Lazarus: The Joy Of A Mash-Up,' trynka.net, January 8, 2017
6 Trynka, 'Lazarus 3: Beyond The Bounds Of Earth,' trynka.net, January 10, 2017
7 David Ng, 'Bowie's Touch Lifted "Lazarus,"' *Los Angeles Times*, January 11, 2017
8 Handy, *op. cit.*
9 *ibid*

10 Cunningham, *op. cit.*
11 David Cote, 'Lazarus,' *Time Out New York*, December 7, 2015
12 Kory Grow, 'Lazarus Is Surrealistic Tour De Force,' *Rolling Stone*, December 7, 2015
13 Hilton Als, *op. cit.*
14 Handy, *op. cit.*
15 John Dingwall, 'Tribute To A Star,' *Scottish Sun*, January 8, 2017
16 Ropelewski, *op. cit.*
17 Mick LaSalle, 'Man And Music Made For The Movies,' *San Francisco Chronicle*, January 12, 2016
18 Southern, author interview
19 James, author interview
20 Angela Bowie, email to author

EXTRA #1

1 Manny Sanchez, author interview
2 Christina Frain, *New Mexico Campgrounds: The Statewide Guide*

(Westcliffe Publishers, 2004)
3 Tony Richmond, email to author, July 26, 2016

INDEX

ACKNOWLEDGMENTS

I was sitting in Santa Fe, New Mexico's Santa Fe Bite, being entertained by Johnny D. Boggs, Thomas Clagett, and David Edgerley Gates, each man as good a writer as they are raconteur. Warren Oates, whom I'd written about previously, was proving a tough act to follow, and Johnny suggested I write a biography-of-a-movie book. For days I mentally scrolled through films, screening them in my drive-in movie theater of a head. A couple that leapt to mind, *Night Of The Hunter* and *Some Like It Hot*, were already well served; others, such as *Carnival Of Souls*, could prove interesting if somewhat obscure. Then there was a personal favorite, *Car Wash*. Well, maybe next time.

It wasn't until I was running with a friend who mentioned her birthday was January 8, which I knew was also David Bowie's, that I hit upon *The Man Who Fell To Earth*. Of course! I'd seen it more than any other film, loved Bowie and Nicolas Roeg, and was aware that Walter Tevis was a fine writer with a character arc of a life. Why not? (Of course, January 8 is also the birthday of Elvis Presley, so you might just as easily be reading about the making of *Kissin' Cousins*.)

I'm grateful to *all* of my interviewees, especially those (May Routh, Linda De Vetta, and Harriet and Nicolas Roeg) who welcomed me into their homes, as well as others who contributed tirelessly and generously: Si Litvinoff, Martin Samuel, Alan Swain, Delana Michaels. Howard Rubin in New Mexico and George Perry in London treated me to lunch and enchanting conversation.

Albuquerque at times can be unsettling on street level. When I was waiting for a bus and a mother admonished her child not to play in a certain spot 'because there were needles,' I don't think she was referring to the kind that fall from pine trees. With that in mind, I can't imagine what Lisa Kendrick, Genealogy Center Librarian at the Albuquerque Public Library, thought when I walked in straight off a sixteen-hour train trip on the Southwest Chief, unintentional Robert Smith hair, eyes looking like they did in my goth days (this time no kohl was necessary), my luggage trailing me, and a zebra-print blanket spilling out of my carrier bag. But she didn't miss a beat when I announced I was writing a book and she graciously guided me to city directories and newspaper archives, before providing a referral to the equally superb Eileen O'Connell in Special Collections. This segues into a litany of librarians and staff to which I am indebted: Stefanie Dennis Hunker, Browne Popular Culture Library, Bowling Green University; Laura Calderone, Southwest Collection, New Mexico State Library; William Stolz, Kentucky History Librarian, Kenton County Public Library, and Michael Pierce of the Pasadena Public Library, who ran up and down stairs to find a particular copy of *Billboard* magazine.

Nancy Dunn, museum manager at the Artesia Historical Museum and Cultural Center, was unflagging in her support, as well as extremely helpful. Plus she never lost patience with my appetite for minutiae. Melinda Bonewell, affiliated with Visit Madrid and charmingly housed in its Mineshaft Tavern, also came through.

How anyone writes a film or TV book without Ned Comstock, film historian at USC's Cinematic Arts Library, I do not know. Sometimes I check those books' acknowledgments, and if he's mentioned, I read the book. (Turns out I read a lot.) The delightful, ageless, and astoundingly great Katy Haber—or should I say Katy Haber MBE—is equally essential.

Then there was June, working behind the counter in the wildly busy Kings Cross branch of Barclays Bank, who never gave up on finding a way to print a document I needed for entry into the British Library. In my life I have never seen anyone with that much tenacity. She should be head of the Bank of England.

Heartfelt thanks also to Eddi Fiegel, who suggested I send the book's proposal to Tom Seabrook at Jawbone Press (Tom and Jawbone's Nigel Osborne are an author's dream team), and to Camille Adair and Jim Norwick, who inspired and entertained me (and put me up/put up with me). I would have been entirely lost without film historian Jon Bowman. Thanks also to Susan Andres, the Criterion Collection's Susan Arosteguy, Sharon H.C., Steve Connell, Chris Campion, Toni M. Fitzpatrick, Henry Lopez-Real, Paul Gorman, Barney Hoskyns, Eric Johnson, Mike Malloy, Charles McNulty, Robert Nott,

Paul Seydor, Nile Southern, Chuck Stephens, Albuquerque's charming and non-ironically vintage Monterey Non-Smokers Motel, Lecie Williams and Paul Gailunas, Derek Ridgers, Donna Sugimoto, Penny and Chuck, Susan Schulman, Eleanora Tevis, Paul Trynka, Tony W., Chris Wallace, Mark Wardel, Kevin Weber, David Weight, and Joanna Woodworth, who both prompted the idea and then patiently listened to its travails and triumphs over a variety of weekend miles and landscapes.

Some time ago I walked into Book Soup on the Sunset Strip as David Bowie walked out. I felt the jolt of a shoplifter as we passed through the security gates. My initial instinct was to grab a copy of my first book, in which Bowie figured prominently, and run after him as he walked west, but I didn't. It's unlikely he would have included it in his list of *100 Favorite Books*, but he did mention works by my mentors, Hubert 'Cubby' Selby, Jr. and John Rechy. I like to flatter myself by thinking some of their grit and glamour rubbed off on me as I wrote, all the while remaining in deepest debt to the Starman upstairs.

PHOTO CREDITS

The photographs used in this book come from the following sources. If you feel there has been a mistaken attribution, please contact the publisher. *Author photograph* Sharon Cockroft; *97, top* William P. Gottlieb Collection, Library of Congress; *bottom left* courtesy of the estate of Walter Tevis; *98, top* Duffy/Getty Images; *bottom* Greman Studio, Library of Congress; *99, left* Frank Edwards/Fotos International/Getty Images; *right* Artesia Daily Press; *100, top* Thomas Timlen; *bottom* Jack Delano/Library of Congress; *101* National Park Service (x3); *102, top* Steve Schapiro/Corbis via Getty Images; *bottom* Kevin Weber (x3); *103, top* Steve Schapiro/Corbis via Getty Images; *bottom* Kevin Weber (x3); *104, top* Steve Schapiro/Corbis via Getty Images; *185* Michael Putland/Getty Images; *186, top* Andrew Smyth; *bottom right* Brad Elterman/FilmMagic; *187, top* Michael Ochs Archive/Getty Images; *188, top* Carol M. Highsmith Archive, Library of Congress; *bottom left* John Margolies Roadside America photograph archive (1972–2008), Library of Congress; *bottom right* Melinda Rees; *189, top* Michael Ochs Archive/Getty Images; *bottom left* Delana Michaels; *190, top* Steve Schapiro/Corbis via Getty Images; *bottom left* Ron Galella/WireImage; *bottom right* Gregg Barrios; *191, top* Steve Schapiro/Corbis via Getty Images; *192* Mark Wardel.

ALSO AVAILABLE IN PRINT AND EBOOK EDITIONS FROM JAWBONE PRESS